FISHING CALIFORNIA
Freshwater

A Travel Guide to Proven Spots & Proven Methods

by

David Colby

SABERTOOTH
Publishing
Company

Mission Viejo / California

First Printing—1994
Printed in the United States of America

Cover Art by Tom Waters

Publisher's Cataloging in Publication Data
Colby, David P.
FISHING CALIFORNIA—Freshwater: A Travel Guide to Proven Spots & Proven Methods
Includes Index.
ISBN 0-9628688-3-3: $14.95 Softcover

Contents

How To Use This Guide 4

Fishing Opportunities Map 5

RV and Trailer Rental Centers 6

Northern California Calendar 7

Southern California Calendar 16

THE BASICS 22

Key to Alphabetic Sport Fish Listings 24

LARGEMOUTH BASS (Also Smallmouth, Spotted): 25

STRIPED BASS 62

WHITE BASS 74

CATFISH:

    CHANNEL CATFISH, BLUE CATFISH, WHITE CATFISH 76

    FLATHEAD CATFISH 79

CORVINA 82

CRAPPIE 85

SACRAMENTO PERCH 88

SALMON 89

KOKANEE SALMON (Sockeye) 97

SHAD 102

STEELHEAD 108

STURGEON 120

TROUT: GENERAL 123

    BROOK TROUT 124

    BROWN TROUT 126

    CUTTHROAT TROUT 129

    GOLDEN TROUT 131

    MAKINAW TROUT (Lake Trout) 134

    RAINBOW TROUT 137

Glossary 170

Appendix A: Sources of Current Fishing Information 175

Appendix B: Knots 176

How To Use This Guide

This guide is organized to make it easy for you to plan and enjoy successful California fishing trips. The book's goal is to minimize your frustration and maximize your fish catching fun. To make it easy we have included several graphic and tabular indexes such as the following two illustrations. They give the roving angler some general guidance on where and when to go fishing.

The Guide to Fishing Opportunities map shows the varieties of fish found in different parts of California. You might ask, "I'm going to the California northwest this summer with the kids. I wonder what kind of fishing they do up there?" Or you might think, "I've always wanted to fish for golden trout. Where can I find them?" A quick glance at the fishing opportunities map answers these "where" questions.

The RV & Trailer Rentals map assists the camper. Call ahead to reserve your RV near your vacation destination. Then use the convenience, comfort and economy of your own car to reach the RV rental city.

The next sections are the Fishing Calendars for northern California and southern California. These calendars list the best fishing for each month of the year. These pages answer "when" questions like, "I'm planning on taking a vacation in March in southern California. What are the hot fishing prospects then?"

So you know where and when you're going and the fish you are targeting, now what? Turn to the main section of the book which is organized alphabetically by fish name. Say you want to fish for salmon in the Klamath River. The "Salmon" section lists all the information you need to catch fish. It gives you specifics on Where, When, Structure, Bait/Lures, Rigs, Techniques, Current Info Sources, Best Guides, The Law, etc. You're now ready to go. You have the right rig and tackle and you know the best techniques. But where are you going to stay?

Each map, in this case the Klamath River, indicates national forest, state and county campgrounds or lodging nearest the fishing.

Ok, so now you know where you will be staying. Can you go now? Of course, but don't forget to take this guide. It has a detailed map that can get you from your doorstep right to the fishing hole.

Have a great trip!

Fishing Opportunities Map

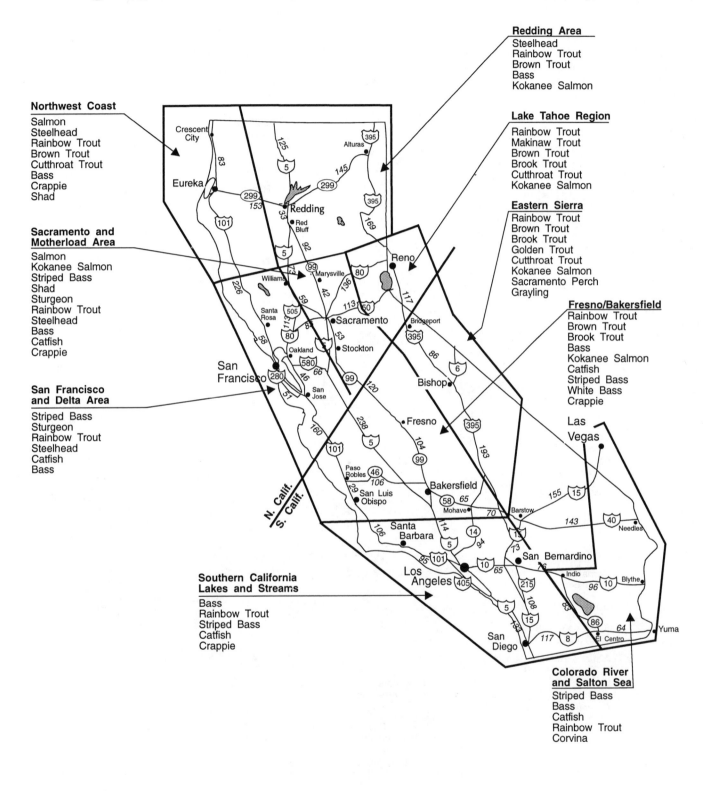

Redding Area
Steelhead
Rainbow Trout
Brown Trout
Bass
Kokanee Salmon

Lake Tahoe Region
Rainbow Trout
Makinaw Trout
Brown Trout
Brook Trout
Cutthroat Trout
Kokanee Salmon

Eastern Sierra
Rainbow Trout
Brown Trout
Brook Trout
Golden Trout
Cutthroat Trout
Kokanee Salmon
Sacramento Perch
Grayling

Fresno/Bakersfield
Rainbow Trout
Brown Trout
Brook Trout
Bass
Kokanee Salmon
Catfish
Striped Bass
White Bass
Crappie

Northwest Coast
Salmon
Steelhead
Rainbow Trout
Brown Trout
Cutthroat Trout
Bass
Crappie
Shad

**Sacramento and
Motherload Area**
Salmon
Kokanee Salmon
Striped Bass
Shad
Sturgeon
Rainbow Trout
Steelhead
Bass
Catfish
Crappie

**San Francisco
and Delta Area**
Striped Bass
Sturgeon
Rainbow Trout
Steelhead
Catfish
Bass

**Southern California
Lakes and Streams**
Bass
Rainbow Trout
Striped Bass
Catfish
Crappie

**Colorado River
and Salton Sea**
Striped Bass
Bass
Catfish
Rainbow Trout
Corvina

RV and Trailer Rental Centers

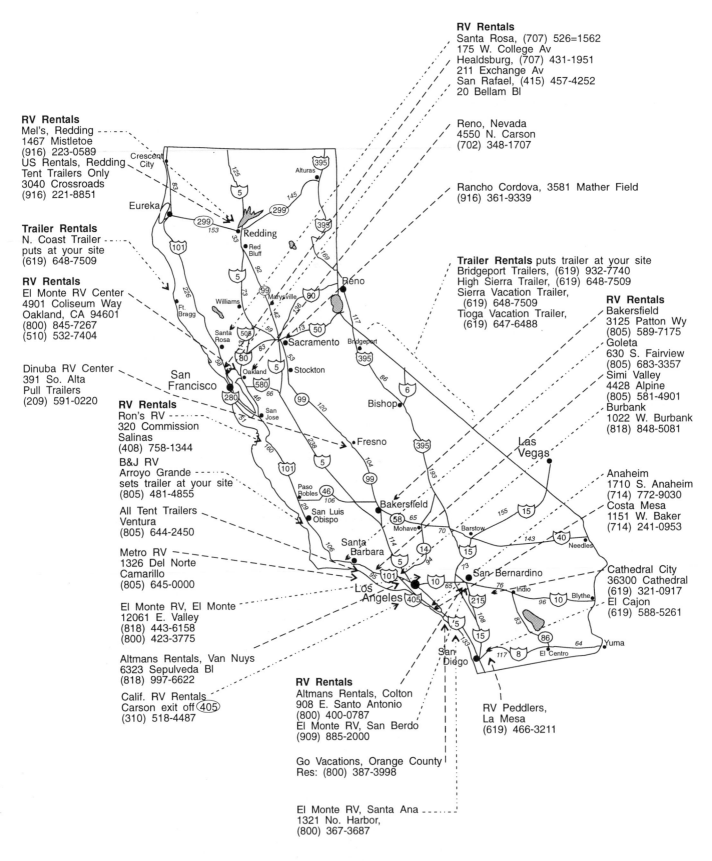

RV Rentals
Santa Rosa, (707) 526=1562
175 W. College Av
Healdsburg, (707) 431-1951
211 Exchange Av
San Rafael, (415) 457-4252
20 Bellam Bl

Reno, Nevada
4550 N. Carson
(702) 348-1707

Rancho Cordova, 3581 Mather Field
(916) 361-9339

RV Rentals
Mel's, Redding
1467 Mistletoe
(916) 223-0589
US Rentals, Redding
Tent Trailers Only
3040 Crossroads
(916) 221-8851

Trailer Rentals
N. Coast Trailer
puts at your site
(619) 648-7509

RV Rentals
El Monte RV Center
4901 Coliseum Way
Oakland, CA 94601
(800) 845-7267
(510) 532-7404

Dinuba RV Center
391 So. Alta
Pull Trailers
(209) 591-0220

RV Rentals
Ron's RV
320 Commission
Salinas
(408) 758-1344

B&J RV
Arroyo Grande
sets trailer at your site
(805) 481-4855

All Tent Trailers
Ventura
(805) 644-2450

Metro RV
1326 Del Norte
Camarillo
(805) 645-0000

El Monte RV, El Monte
12061 E. Valley
(818) 443-6158
(800) 423-3775

Altmans Rentals, Van Nuys
6323 Sepulveda Bl
(818) 997-6622

Calif. RV Rentals
Carson exit off 405
(310) 518-4487

Trailer Rentals puts trailer at your site
Bridgeport Trailers, (619) 932-7740
High Sierra Trailer, (619) 648-7509
Sierra Vacation Trailer,
(619) 648-7509
Tioga Vacation Trailer,
(619) 647-6488

RV Rentals
Bakersfield
3125 Patton Wy
(805) 589-7175
Goleta
630 S. Fairview
(805) 683-3357
Simi Valley
4428 Alpine
(805) 581-4901
Burbank
1022 W. Burbank
(818) 848-5081

Anaheim
1710 S. Anaheim
(714) 772-9030
Costa Mesa
1151 W. Baker
(714) 241-0953

Cathedral City
36300 Cathedral
(619) 321-0917
El Cajon
(619) 588-5261

RV Rentals
Altmans Rentals, Colton
908 E. Santo Antonio
(800) 400-0787
El Monte RV, San Berdo
(909) 885-2000

Go Vacations, Orange County
Res: (800) 387-3998

El Monte RV, Santa Ana
1321 No. Harbor,
(800) 367-3687

RV Peddlers,
La Mesa
(619) 466-3211

Northern California Calendar

Although the following fish runs are fairly consistent, you should check current information sources close to your fishing date.

JANUARY

Northwest Coast

- Flyfish or drift the northwest rivers for bright, fresh run **steelhead** to 27 pounds. (pg. 108)
- The Smith River has the biggest **steelhead** in the state. The really big ones move into the river this month. (pg. 108)
- **Steelhead** fishing peaks on the Eel River as waters clear between the storms. (pg. 108)
- Adult **steelhead** move in good numbers into the Klamath and Trinity Rivers. (pg. 108)
- If you can catch the Mattole River between the rains, you'll have a good shot at a **steelhead**. (pg. 108)

Redding Area

- Drop a line near the Carr Powerhouse at Whiskeytown Lake for good winter **trout** fishing. (pg. 137, 148)
- You can get some quality dry fly **trout** and **steelhead** action now on the upper Trinity River and Lewiston Lake. (pg. 137, 148, 108)

San Francisco and Delta Area

- San Francisco area lakes are boiling with planted **trout.** Look for clearing waters. (pg. 137, 155, 156)
- Putah Creek offers quality **trout** flyfishing just minutes from San Francisco. (pg. 137, 54)
- Winter storm runoffs turn on the bite for **sturgeon** in the delta and Suisan Bay. (pg. 120)
- Persistence and finesse can nab big **stripers** in the delta backwaters. Drift minnows or shad. (pg. 62)

Sacramento and Motherlode Area

- The **catfish** action can be tops this month at Lake Berryessa. (pg. 76)
- **Spotted bass** get big at Collins Lake and they're in their spawning frenzy now. (pg. 25, 157)
- For winter **trout** action, Lake McSwain is the place to be. (pg. 137, 166)
- The **steelhead** action peaks in the Sacramento River and on the Feather River near Oroville. (pg. 108)
- **Sturgeon** will arrive at Knights Landing and Colusa on Sacramento River. Get out there and welcome them. (pg. 120)
- Sacramento river **channel catfish** are tugging on lines from Freeport to Colusa. (pg. 76)

Lake Tahoe Region

- Take a trip to Pyramid Lake, Nev. where anglers are pulling in **cutthroat trout** to 14 pounds! (pg. 129)
- **Mackinaw trout** fishing is good at Lake Tahoe but it gets mighty cold. (pg. 134)
- Topaz lake holds some hefty **cutthroat** and **rainbows** and it's open this month. (pg. 129, 137, 160)

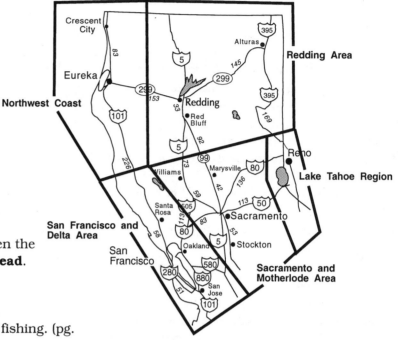

FEBRUARY

Northwest Coast

- The winter run of big **steelhead** to 27 pounds is happening now in northwest rivers. (pg. 108)
- Book a guide for Smith River **steelhead** and scattered late **salmon**. (pg. 108, 89)
- The best Eel River **steelhead** runs are this month. You should call ahead for river conditions. (pg. 108)
- The Mattole River **steelhead** are here. (pg. 108)

Redding Area

- The **steelhead** fishing is still good on the Trinity River. Get out there now or you'll have to wait until next year. (pg. 108)
- Drop a line near the Carr Powerhouse, Whiskeytown Lake for good winter **trout** fishing. (pg. 137, 148)
- Silver and King **Salmon** are hungry and waiting for you at Lake Almanor. (pg. 89)
- **Trouting** turns on for anglers plying the Sacramento river north of Red Bluff, from Redding to Anderson. (pg. 137,150)

San Francisco and Delta Area

- February is the best month for **sturgeon** action in Suisan Bay and the delta. (pg. 120) See *FISHING CALIFORNIA - SALTWATER* for hot action in San Francisco Bay.
- The long awaited ocean **salmon** season opens for San Francisco area anglers. (pg. 89)
- Scrappy **crappie** are schooling to spawn and are biting with a vengence at Clear Lake, Berryessa and Uvas reservoirs. (pg. 85)

Sacramento and Motherlode Area

- Collins Lake **brown trout** grow big and fat. They come out of the winter doldrums this month and start bending rods and breaking lines. (pg. 126)
- Go now to catch a boat load of **catfish** in the run off coves at Lake Berryessa. (pg. 76)
- **Spotted bass** get big at Collins Lake and they're in spawning frenzy now. (pg. 25, 157)
- **Trout** action turns on at Camanche, Pardee and Amador if the waters clear from the winter storms. (pg. 137, 159)
- Lake McSwain **trout** fishing is tops this month. (pg. 137, 159)
- Nows the best time to match wits with **steelhead** lurking in the Sacramento River and on the Feather River near Oroville. (pg. 108)
- Be ready for **sturgeon** to show at Knights Landing and Colusa on Sacramento River. (pg. 120)
- Sacramento river **channel catfish** are filling stringers from Freeport to Colusa. (pg. 76)
- Take your ultra-light rig to Black Butte lake for some ultra-fun catching spring **crappie**. (pg. 85)

Lake Tahoe Region

- The **Cutthroat trout** are biting at Walker and Pyramid Lakes, Nevada. And they grow big, to 14 pounds! (pg. 129)
- Take some of your casino winnings and book a guide for **mackinaw trout** on Lake Tahoe or Donner Lake. (pg. 134)
- Topaz lake holds some hefty cutthroat and rainbow **trout** and it's open this month. (pg. 129,137,160)

MARCH

Northwest Coast

- The **steelhead** season winds down the early this month. Go now or you'll have to wait until next year. (pg. 108)

Redding Area

- **Bass** fishing is good on Lake Shasta and Trinity Lake. The smallmouth spawn first followed by the largemouth. (pg. 25, 52, 149)
- **Trout** action heats up when mayfly hatches bloom later this month at famed Lewiston Lake. (pg. 137,149)
- Sacramento River **rainbow trout** near Redding are turned on by the heavy caddis hatch that starts this month. Flyfishing is the way to go during this hatch. (pg. 137,148)
- Just for fun, take your light tackle gear and some cut nightcrawlers to Copco or Iron Gate lakes for non-stop **yellow perch** action. The fillets are small but delicious. (pg. 148)

San Francisco and Delta Area

- Get in on the **striped bass** spring run in the Sacramento Delta. This and the fall run are the best times of the year. (pg. 62)
- The San Luis Reservoir can be the prime spot for **striped bass** this month. Be prepared for fish to over 50 pounds! (pg. 62)

- **Largemouth Bass** fishing turns on later in month as the fish start their move to the shallows to spawn. (pg. 25)
- Pack your light tackle for lots of fun catching **crappie** at Berryessa, Uvas and Clear lakes. (pg. 85)
- Regional lakes are stocked heavily and **trout** fishing action gets hot as waters clear later this month. (pg. 137, 155, 159)
- **Catfish** action is usually good in the delta sloughs after winter storms, especially Old and Middle Rivers, Miner Slough, Steamboat and Cache Slough. (pg. 76)

Sacramento and Motherlode Area

- Motherload **trout**ing will peak as waters clear about mid-month. (pg. 137, 159)
- As their waters clear Oroville, Collins, Rollins and Folsom lakes are loading up stringers with **rainbow trout**. (pg. 137, 157)
- Get some light tackle fun catching **crappie** at Berryessa, Black Butte and Clear lakes. (pg. 85)

Lake Tahoe Region

- **Cutthroat trout** to 14 lbs. beckon shoreline anglers at Walker and Pyramid lakes in Nevada. (pg. 129)
- The **makinaws** are still biting and it's still chilly at Lake Tahoe. (pg. 134)
- Topaz lake holds some hefty cutthroat and rainbow **trout** and it's open this month. (pg. 129, 137, 160)
- Fly fish the Nevada Truckee River trophy **trout** area—open all year! (pg. 158)

APRIL

Northwest Coast

- Stream **trout** fishing opens the last Saturday in April. See DFG special regs. (pg. 137)
- If the water is clear the **trout** fishing is good at Ruth Lake. (pg. 137)
- Freshwater Lagoon, Stone Lagoon and Big Lagoons are regularly stocked with **trout**. Freshwater Lagoon has some hefty **cutthroats**. (pg. 129)

Redding Area

- Sacramento River **trout** near Redding are still gorging themselves on the caddis hatch. (pg. 137, 150)
- Attention **trout** flyfishermen! The spring callibaetis mayfly hatch is on at Lewiston Lake. (pg. 137, 149)
- **Bass** fishing is good on Lake Shasta and Trinity Lake. The smallmouth spawn first followed by the largemouth. (pg. 25, 52, 149)
- Stream **trout** season opens the last Saturday of this month. Lakes open in the Fall River Valley. See special DFG regs. (pg. 137, 151)
- You can have a ball on Lake Almanor catching scrappy **smallmouth bass**. (pg. 25, 152)

San Francisco and Delta Area

- Stream **trout** fishing opens the last Saturday in April in counties north of San Francisco and south of San Francisco in Alameda, Contra Costa and Santa Clara counties. (pg. 137, 155, 156)
- Take your ultra-light rig to Berryessa, Uvas or Clear lakes for some ultra-fun catching spring **crappie**. (pg. 85)
- The **black bass** fishing really turns on as the fish stage for spawning in shallow waters of 15 feet or less. This is the easiest time of year to catch bass, especially big bass. (pg. 25)
- Get in on the Sacramento delta spring spawning run for **striped bass** to 50+ lbs. (pg. 62)
- The San Luis Reservoir can be the prime spot for **striped bass** this month. Be prepared for fish to over 50 pounds! (pg. 62)
- April is a premier month for stocked **trout** fishing at lower elevation and urban lakes. (pg. 137, 146)

Sacramento and Motherload Area

- Take your ultra-light rig to Black Butte lake for some ultra-fun catching spring **crappie**. (pg. 85)
- **Black bass** fishing turns on as fish stage for spawn in shallower waters of 15 feet or less. This is the easiest time of year to catch bass, especially big bass. (pg. 25)
- Look for **striped bass** in Sacramento River-between Grimes and Colusa. (pg. 62)
- April is one of the best months for stocked **trout** fishing at lower elevation and urban lakes. (pg. 137)

Lake Tahoe Region

- The big **cutthroat trout** of Pyramid and Walker lakes are moving to the shallows and the shoreline bite is on! (pg. 129)
- The good winter **makinaw** bite can still be had at Tahoe. Book a charter boat now! (pg. 134)
- Fly fish the Nevada Truckee River trophy **trout** area—open all year! (pg. 158)

MAY

Northwest Coast

- Try Dead Lake, just south of Lake Earl, for some surprisingly large **largemouth bass**. (pg. 25)
- Freshwater, Stone and Big Lagoons are regularly stocked with **trout**. Freshwater Lagoon has some hefty **cutthroats**. (pg. 137)

Redding Area

- Spring **trout** action is good almost everywhere. For special places see pg. 146.
- **Bass** fishing is good on Lake Shasta and Trinity Lake. The smallmouth spawn first followed by the largemouth. (pg. 25, 52, 149)
- You're surrounded by blue-ribbon **trout** streams. The upper Sacramento, McCloud, Pit, Hat and Fall rivers are loaded with fish. (pg. 137, 148, 151)
- Later this month, higher elevation (4,000 to 6000') lakes like Almanor, Frenchman, Davis will be ice free and the **trout** are hungry. (pg. 137, 152)
- You can have a ball on Lake Almanor catching scrappy **smallmouth bass**. (pg. 25, 152)
- The bite peaks for wild **rainbow trout** on the Sacramento River south of Redding. (pg. 137, 150)
- **Trout** fishing is great at Lewiston Reservoir and Trinity River below Lewiston dam. A strong mayfly hatch has started. (pg. 137, 149)
- Famous Eagle Lake opens the end of May. Lahontan **trout** grow fat and feisty there. (pg. 137, 153)

San Francisco and Delta Area

- Intense **striped bass** angling action can still be had by savvy anglers at San Luis Reservoir. (pg. 62)
- The spring **striped bass** run in the Sacramento Delta will end early this month. (pg. 62)
- **Black bass** fishing turns on as fish stage for spawn in shallower waters of 15 feet or less. This is the easiest time of year to catch bass. Calero Reservoir holds some hefty largemouths. (pg. 25, 156)
- **Trout** action is still great at San Francisco area lakes and Lake Berryessa. (pg. 137, 155, 54)

Sacramento and Motherlode Area

- Spring **trout** action is good almost everywhere. For special places see pg. 146.
- This is your last chance to get in on the hot spring **crappie** bite at Black Butte lake. (pg. 85)
- The **striped bass** have invaded the Sacramento River between Grimes and Colusa. See page 62 for where to find them.
- Get some early season, light tackle fun catching **shad**, "fresh-water tarpon" in and around Sacramento. (pg. 102)
- Look for light tackle and fly fishing action as **shad** invade the Feather and Yuba Rivers the end of this month. (pg. 102)
- Get great **largemouth bass** spawn action from motherlode and Sacramento area lakes. (pg. 25, 55, 56)

Lake Tahoe Region

- The higher elevation (4,000 to 6000') lakes like Donner, Stampede and Prosser are now ice free and the **trout** are hungry. (pg. 137, 158)
- This is the best month for catching giant **cutthroat trout** at Pyramid Lake, Nevada. (pg. 129)
- Look for Carson River **trout** action to start hopping the end of May. (pg. 137, 160)
- Eastern Sierra **trout** turn on with the warmer weather later this month. (pg. 137, 146)

JUNE

Northwest Coast

- Freshwater, Stone and Big Lagoons are regularly stocked with **trout**. Freshwater Lagoon has some hefty **cutthroats**. (pg. 137)

- The **shad** run will peak in the Klamath River this month. Bring light tackle spinning or fly tackle and have a ball! (pg. 102)

Redding Area

- Eagle Lake is open! Go **trout** fishing now! (pg. 137, 153)
- Spring **trout** action is good almost everywhere early this month. For special places see pg. 146.
- Those fat Sacramento River rainbow **trout** are still biting aggressively early this month. (pg. 137, 150)
- The **smallmouth bass** at Lake Almanor will still be active the early part of this month. (pg. 25. 152)
- Davis and Frenchman lakes and the nearby Feather River are still prime spots for **trout** limits early this month. (pg. 137, 154)

San Francisco and Delta Area

- Deeper lakes like Berryessa and San Pablo will yield holdover **trout** to deep trollers. (pg. 137, 155, 54)
- There's some hefty **catfish** waiting for you in Uvas, Parkway, and Clear Lake. (pg. 137, 155)
- The **trout** are biting all summer long at Lake Merced. Or troll deep at San Pablo Reservoir. (pg. 62)

Sacramento and Motherlode Area

- Early this month the **striped bass** are still hitting on the Sacramento River between Grimes and Colusa. (pg. 62)
- **Striper** top water action will start later this month at New Hogan. A loud splash on a top water lure can set your heart to thumping. (pg. 62)
- The **shad** action will peak on Sacramento between Red Bluff and Los Molinos providing great fly gear action. (pg. 102)

Lake Tahoe Region

- Early June still sees some good action for hugh **cutthroat trout** at Nevada's Pyramid Lake. (pg. 129)
- Carson River **trout** action should be hopping. It's a great flyfishing stream. (pg. 137, 160)

JULY

- Except for lakes above 6000 feet, **trout** fisherman will have to start fishing deeper this month. The action is still good with plenty of stockers left over. (pg. 137, 146)

Northwest Coast

- I'd go ocean fishing this month. See *FISHING CALIFORNIA - SALTWATER*. Or head east to the Redding area for world class trout action.

Redding Area

- You're surrounded by blue-ribbon **trout** streams. The upper Sacramento, McCloud, Pit, Hat and Fall rivers are loaded with fish. (pg. 137, 148, 151)
- Trinity Wilderness lakes will yield many pan-sized **trout** to anglers willing to hike in. (pg. 137, 149)

San Francisco and Delta Area

- The channel **catfish** are still on their hot summer bite. Especially big cats are caught at Uvas, Parkway and Clear Lake. (pg. 76)
- Lake Merced, near San Francisco Park, is stocked with **trout** all year! (pg. 137, 155)
- Lake Mendocino has a good top-water **striper** bite starting this month if you know what you're doing. Book a guide and get in on the fun. (pg. 62)
- Fish for **trout** on the east fork of the Russian River (just above Lake Mendocino). It's stocked all summer long! (pg. 137, 66)

Sacramento and Motherlode Area

- New Hogan **striped bass** are busting shad at the surface! Bring your light tackle and have some fun. (pg. 62)
- The warm weather brings the big **catfish** out at Amador, Clear, Folsom, and other local lakes. (pg. 76)

Lake Tahoe Region

- Flyfish for wild **trout** in the Truckee River above (east) of Truckee city. (pg. 137, 158)
- The high country is open. Mountain lakes yield many pan-sized tasty **trout**. (pg. 137, 146)
- Carson River **trout** action should be hopping. It's a great flyfishing stream. (pg. 137, 160)

AUGUST

Northwest Coast
- The salmon run is on! Big, bright **king salmon** are moving into the Klamath River mouth. (pg. 89)
- Trinity Wilderness lakes will yield many pan-sized **trout** to anglers willing to hike in. (pg. 137, 149)

Redding Area
- The salmon run is on! Big, bright **king salmon** are arriving south of Red Bluff. (pg. 89)
- Trinity Lake **kokanee salmon** will start congregating out from Coffee Creek. (pg. 97)

San Francisco and Delta Area
- Top-water action for **striped bass** continues at Lake Mendocino. (pg. 62, 66)
- Fish for **trout** on the east fork of the Russian River (just above Lake Mendocino). It's stocked all summer long (pg. 137, 66) or tangle with feisty **smallmouth bass** on the river from Healdsburg to Monte Rio with guide Bill Adelman (415) 232-9991.
- The channel **catfish** are still on their hot summer bite. Especially big cats are caught at Uvas, Parkway and Clear Lake. (pg. 76)
- Lake Merced, near San Francisco Park, is stocked with **trout** all year! (pg. 137, 155)

Sacramento and Motherlode Area
- New Hogan **striped bass** are busting shad! Bring your light tackle and have some fun. (pg. 62)
- The weather and the fishing is hot for **smallmouth bass** on the Feather River between Live Oak and Verona. Book a trip with Guide John Morrison (916) 677-3912.
- The **catfish** are biting at Amador, Clear, Folsom, and other nearby lakes. (pg. 76)

Lake Tahoe Region
- Flyfish for wild **trout** in the Truckee River east of Truckee city. (pg. 137, 158)
- The **kokanee salmon** will start to concentrate for their spawn. Fishing success will greatly improve at Tahoe, Donner, Stampede, Pardee and Whiskeytown. (pg. 97)
- Fish the high country **trout** lakes in Desolation Wilderness or flyfish the Rubicon River. (pg. 137, 136)
- The elusive big Tahoe **makinaws** are spawning late this month and will hit trolled plugs. (pg. 134)

SEPTEMBER

Northwest Coast
- The salmon run is on! Big, bright **king salmon** are moving into the Klamath River mouth. Salmon fishing is hot upstream at Pecwan Bar and the Trinity River mouth. (pg. 89)
- The **steelhead** move into the Klamath and Trinity Rivers. Flyfishing for "half-pounders" can be fantastic! (pg. 108)

Redding Area
- The fall **salmon** run heats up on the Trinity River. (pg. 89)
- The Sacramento River fall **salmon** run will peak this month south of Red Bluff. I hope you reserved a guide early. (pg. 89)
- Later this month a heavy mayfly hatch will set the **trout** afire at Lewiston Lake and Trinity River below Lewiston dam. (pg. 137, 149)
- The fall season will bring a renewed **crappie** bite at Black Butte lake. (pg. 85)
- Trinity Lake will turnover late this month bringing some good top-water **trout** action. (pg. 137, 149)
- **Steelhead** show in the Trinity beginning with some great "half-pounder" action. (pg. 108)
- Lake Almanor should come alive again with the cooling waters late this month. Hefty **lahontan trout** will set caution to the wind as they fatten up for winter. (pg. 137, 152)

San Francisco and Delta Area
- **Crappie** will start on a fall feeding binge getting ready for winter. Get in on the action at Berryessa, Uvas or Clear Lake starting later this month. (pg. 85)
- The channel **catfish** are still on their hot summer bite. Especially big cats are caught at Uvas, Parkway and Clear Lake. (pg. 76)
- Lake Merced, near San Francisco Park, is stocked with **trout** all year! (pg. 137, 155)
- Top-water action for **striped bass** continues at Lake Mendocino. (pg. 62)
- Look for San Antonio Reservoir to kick out some good **striped bass** fishing this month. (pg. 62)

Sacramento and Motherlode Area

- Look for clearing water and good **salmon** fishing on the Feather River. Try the Thermolito Afterbay outlet, upstream from Gridley bridge, at Shanghai Bend, Star Bend or the mouth at Verona. Book a guide trip with Jim Zanocco (916) 673-5716. (pg. 89)
- The fall season will bring a renewed **crappie** bite at Black Butte lake. (pg. 85)
- **Striped bass** top water boiling continues at New Hogan. (pg. 62)
- Stream **trout** fishing can be excellent this month for anglers plying the north fork of the Stanislaus River. (pg. 137, 159)
- Local **salmon** fishing peaks later this month in the American River. (pg. 89)

Lake Tahoe Region

- This is the best month to jig for **kokanee salmon** as they concentrate near their spawning streams at Tahoe, Donner, Stampede and Whiskeytown. (pg. 97)
- Flyfish for wild **trout** in the Truckee River above (east) of Truckee city. (pg. 137, 158)
- Go to the high country **trout** lakes in Desolation Wilderness or flyfish the Rubicon River. (pg. 137, 136)
- There's a special season at Heenan Lake. This lake's loaded with hugh breeder **cutthroats**! (pg. 129)
- The elusive big Tahoe **makinaws** are spawning early this month and will hit trolled plugs. (pg. 134)

OCTOBER

- Lake turnovers starting this month will bring hungry **trout** to the surface and spark a caddis hatch which can drive the trout bonkers. (pg. 137, 147)

Northwest Coast

- The north coast **salmon** river runs are on! (pg. 89)
- Klamath River **salmon** action continues. Salmon fishing is hot upstream at Pecwan Bar and the Trinity River mouth. (pg. 89)
- The **steelhead** move into the Klamath and Trinity Rivers. There are hundreds of "half-pounders" and some adults. (pg. 108)
- The **salmon** action will peak mid-month on the upper Trinity near Douglas City. (pg. 89)
- The first big rain opens the river doors for **salmon** waiting to enter the Smith and Eel. (pg. 89)

Redding Area

- The Trinity River **salmon** will peak this month. (pg. 89)
- **Steelhead** have joined the salmon in the Trinity River. (pg. 108)
- The **salmon** run is still strong on the Sacramento. (pg. 89)
- On the Sacramento River above Red Bluff, wild **rainbow trout** are eating every thing in sight before winter comes. (pg. 137, 150)
- Rainbow and brown **trout** and **salmon** fishing gets even better this month at Lake Almanor. (pg. 137, 126, 152, 89)
- Eagle Lake trouting will peak as hefty **lahontan trout** will set caution to the wind as they fatten up for winter. (pg. 137, 153)

San Francisco and Delta Area

- **Crappie** continue their fall feeding binge at Berryessa, Uvas and Clear Lake. (pg. 85)
- Get in on the **striped bass** "world series bite" in the Sacramento Delta. The fall and spring runs are the best times of the year. (pg. 62) Enter the Rio Vista Striper Derby and win a boat! Call The Trap. (pg. 68)
- San Antonio Reservoir can kick out some nice **striped bass** for the in-the-know angler. (pg. 62)
- Top-water **trout** action turns on as the water turns-over at Berryessa. (pg. 137, 54)
- There's more top water action for **striped bass** at Lake Mendocino. (pg. 62)
- The channel **catfish** are still on their hot summer bite. Especially big cats are caught at Uvas, Parkway and Clear Lake. (pg. 76)
- **Trout** plants begin again later this month. Try San Pablo for some great action. (pg. 137, 155)

Sacramento and Motherlode Area

- Local **salmon** fishing peaks this month on the American River. (pg. 89)
- **Largemouth bass** are searching for something to strike in the delta, especially in Middle River, Franks Tract, Old River, and Big Break. (pg. 25)

- **Smallmouth bass** action is steady for delta anglers on Miner, Elk, and Steamboat sloughs. (pg. 68)
- **Salmon** and **steelhead** action can be rewarding now on the Feather and Yuba rivers. (pg. 89, 108)
- **Trout** action picks up as water turns-over at Berryessa and motherload lakes. (pg. 137, 54, 159)
- Lake McSwain **trout** usually good this month. (pg. 137, 159)
- Wet your line at Folsom or Oroville for some good **smallmouth bass** action. (pg. 25, 55, 157)
- New Hogan **striped bass** stage their last top water bite the first half of this month. (pg. 62)

Lake Tahoe Region
- Go to the high country early this month for **trout** lakes in Desolation Wilderness or flyfish the Rubicon River. The October caddis hatch will ignite the bite. (pg. 137, 136)
- Walker Lake and Pyramid Lakes cool this month and start providing good **cutthroat** action. (pg. 129)
- Heenan Lake is only open for a very short time. It's full of trophy-sized **cutthroat trout**. (pg. 129)

NOVEMBER

Northwest Coast
- **Stream trout** season closes mid-month. See special DFG regs. (pg. 137)
- Half-pounders and some adult **steelhead** move into the Klamath and Trinity Rivers. (pg. 108)
- **Salmon** will enter the Smith and Eel river mouths after the first big rain. (pg. 89)
- Lake Shasta will turnover late this month bringing hungry **brown trout** and **rainbow trout** to the surface. (pg. 124, 137, 52)

Redding Area
- Stream **trout** season closes mid-month. Lakes close in the Fall River Valley. See DFG regs. (pg. 137)
- There's still good **salmon** fishing on the Trinity River. It'll slow considerably by mid-month. (pg. 89)
- The **steelhead** are in the Trinity now! (pg. 108)
- The **salmon** run peaks on the Sacramento River. (pg. 89)
- The wild **rainbow trout** are hitting drifted lures on the Sacramento above Red Bluff. (pg. 137, 150)
- Rainbow and brown **trout** and **salmon** catching gets good this month at Lake Almanor. (pg. 137, 126, 89)
- Eagle Lake trouting peaks as hefty **Lahontan trout** throw caution to the wind as they fatten up for winter. (pg. 137, 153)

San Francisco and Delta Area
- **Stream trout** season closes mid-month. See special DFG regs. (pg. 137)
- Top-water action for **striped bass** is still good but winding down at Lake Mendocino. (pg. 62)
- Go early this month and you'll still find a hot **crappie** bite at Clear Lake, Berryessa, or Uvas. (pg. 85)
- **Trout** action can get red hot when the water turns-over at Berryessa. (pg. 137, 54)
- The Sacramento Delta **striped bass** run is winding down. This fall run and the spring run are the best times of the year. (pg. 62)
- San Antonio Reservoir can kick out some nice **striped bass** for the in-the-know angler. (pg. 62)

Sacramento and Motherlode Area
- Get out early this month and you'll still find a hot **crappie** bite at Black Butte. (pg. 85)
- **Striped bass** bait fishing is still good in the Delta, but the fall run is coming to an end. (pg. 62)
- Top water **trout** action could explode as water turns-over at motherlode lakes. (pg. 137, 159)
- **Smallmouth bass** action is good at Folsom and Oroville. (pg. 25, 55, 157)
- Look to Lake McSwain for consistent **trout** catches. (pg. 137, 159)
- The last of the **salmon** run is happening in the American, Yuba and Feather rivers. There's some **steelhead** out there too. (pg. 89, 108)
- The Sacramento Delta **striped bass** run is winding down. This fall run and the spring run are the best times of the year. (pg. 62)
- There's a good fall bite for **largemouth bass** in the Delta, especially in Middle River, Franks Tract, Old River, and Big Break. (pg. 25)
- Great fighting **smallmouth bass** are hitting lures in Miner, Elk, and Steamboat sloughs. (pg. 68)

Lake Tahoe Region
- Walker Lake and Pyramid Lakes cool providing good **cutthroat** action. (pg. 129)
- The Tahoe **makinaw** bite will pick up late this month. You may even get pleasant weather. (pg. 134)
- Fly fish the Nevada Truckee River trophy **trout** area—open all year! (pg. 158)

DECEMBER
Northwest Coast
- Flyfish or drift the northwest rivers for bright, fresh run **steelhead** to 27 pounds. (pg. 108)
- Fish the Smith River for **steelhead** and some scattered late **salmon**. (pg. 108, 89)
- The Eel River **steelhead** action gets serious later this month. (pg. 108)
- The **steelhead** are moving into the Klamath and Trinity Rivers. There are hundreds of "half-pounders" and a growing population of adults. (pg. 108)

Redding Area
- The bigger **steelhead** are now in the Trinity River. (pg. 108)
- Due to last month's turnover at Lake Shasta and Trinity, **brown trout** and **rainbow trout** will still be actively feeding at the surface the first part of this month. (pg. 126, 137, 52, 149)
- Drop a line near the Carr Powerhouse at Whiskeytown Lake for some good winter **trout** fishing. (pg. 137, 149)
- Silver and king **salmon** are hungry and waiting for you at Lake Almanor. (pg. 89, 152)
- The first half of this month can still be good for Eagle Lake **trout**. (pg. 137, 153)
- **Trouting** turns on for anglers plying the Sacramento River north of Red Bluff, from Redding to Anderson. (pg. 137, 150)

San Francisco and Delta Area
- Persistence and finesse can nab big **stripers** in the delta backwaters. Drift minnows or shad. (pg. 62)
- The **catfish** action can be lively this month at Lake Berryessa. (pg. 76)
- Early this month is your last chance for **striped bass** angling adventure at Lake Mendocino. (pg. 62)

Sacramento and Motherlode Area
- Collins Lake **brown trout** grow big and fat. They come out of the winter doldrums this month and start bending rods and breaking lines. (pg. 126)
- **Spotted bass** get big at Collins Lake and they're in spawning frenzy now. (pg. 25, 157)
- Nows the best time to match wits with **steelhead** lurking in the Sacramento River and on the Feather River near Oroville. (pg. 108)
- Be ready for **sturgeon** to show at Knights Landing and Colusa on Sacramento River. (pg. 120)
- Sacramento River **channel catfish** are on the prowl and ready to bite from Freeport to Colusa. (pg. 76)
- For winter **trout** action, Lake McSwain is the place to be. (pg. 137, 159)

Lake Tahoe Region
- Enjoy the scenic beauty while angling for **mackinaw trout** at Lake Tahoe or Donner Lake. (pg. 134)
- Walker Lake and Pyramid Lakes cool providing good **cutthroat trout** action. (pg. 129)
- Fly fish the Nevada Truckee River trophy **trout** area—open all year! (pg. 158)

Southern California Calendar

Although the following fish runs are fairly consistent, you should check current information sources close to your fishing date.

JANUARY

Fresno/Bakersfield Region

- Freshwater fishing is slow and cold. Book a Baja longrange trip. The weather is warm and the fishing is world class! See FISHING CALIFORNIA - SALTWATER.
- **Trout** fishing is good at Pine Flat when waters clear between winter storms. (pg. 137, 166)

Eastern Sierra

- **Cutthroat trout** action picks up with cooling waters at Walker Lake. (pg. 129)
- Fly fish the Nevada East Walker River trophy **trout** area— open all year! (pg. 161)

So. Calif. Lakes & Streams

- The trophy **largemouth bass** season heats up this month at L.A. and San Diego Lakes. (pg. 25) Call now to get in on the Lake Barrett lottery! (pg. 60)
- This month and next are the best times to try for a world record **spotted bass** at La Perris. (pg. 25)
- Every year about now someone catches a giant stringer of **catfish** from a San Diego lake. Check pg. 76 to see why!
- Good **trout** fishing continues but may be interrupted if winter storms muddy lakes and streams. (pg. 137, 146)
- **Striped bass** can turn on with the trout plants this month. Really big fish prowl the waters of Pyramid, Silverwood and Skinner lakes. (pg. 62)

Colorado River & Salton Sea

- Freshwater fishing is slow and cold. Book a trip to Cabo. The weather is warm and the striped marlin fishing is outstanding! See FISHING CALIFORNIA - SALTWATER.
- **Trout** fishing can be good at Willow Beach and Laughlin when the weather clears. (pg. 137, 72)

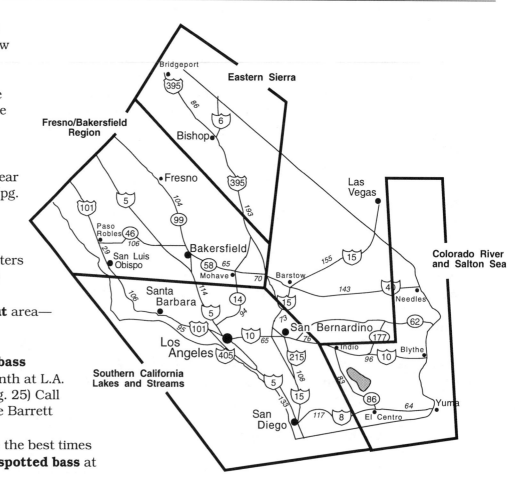

FEBRUARY

Fresno/Bakersfield Region

- Lake Isabella should dole out some fast-paced **crappie** action starting late this month. (pg. 85)
- **Trout** fishing is good at Pine Flat especially when waters clear between winter storms. (pg. 137, 166)

Eastern Sierra

- Walker Lake cools providing steadily improving **cutthroat** action for fish to 14 pounds. (pg. 129)
- Fly fish the Nevada East Walker River trophy **trout** area—open all year! (pg. 161)

So. Calif. Lakes & Streams

- This is prime time for big **largemouth bass** at the world famous L.A. & San Diego Lakes. (pg. 25) Call now to get in on the Lake Barrett lottery! (pg. 60)

- **Striped bass** action can turn on this month. Really big fish prowl the waters of Pyramid, Silverwood and Skinner lakes. (pg. 62)
- Every year around this time someone catches a giant stringer of **catfish** from a San Diego lake. Check pg. 76 to see why!
- Later this month, schools of ravenous **crappie** will move into the shallows. Fill your stringer at Silverwood, Irvine, Henshaw, El Capitan, Wohlford, or Lake Hodges. (pg. 85)
- The rainiest month of the year may squelch the **trout** action with muddied waters. If it stays dry, go fishing! (pg. 137, 146)

Colorado River & Salton Sea
- **Trout** fishing can be good at Willow Beach and Laughlin when the weather clears. (pg. 137, 72)

MARCH

Fresno/Bakersfield Region
- Lake Isabella **crappie** action continues this month. (pg. 85)

Eastern Sierra
- Fish the early **trout** opener, the first weekend of March, south of Independence. Independence, Symmes, Shepard, George, Lone Pine, Tuttle and Cottonwood creeks are heavily planted. (pg.146)
- **Cutthroat trout** to 14 lbs. beckon shoreline anglers at Walker and Pyramid lakes in Nevada. (pg. 120)
- Fly fish the Nevada East Walker River trophy **trout** area—open all year! (pg. 161)

So. Calif. Lakes & Streams
- The Lake Nacimiento **white bass** spawning frenzy starts later this month. (pg. 74)
- **Striped bass** can turn on with the trout plants this month. Really big fish prowl the waters of Pyramid, Silverwood and Skinner lakes. (pg. 62)
- **Largemouth Bass** fishing turns on later in month as the fish start their move to the shallows to spawn. Even whopper bass can be caught with shallow water techniques! (pg. 25)
- The **crappie** bite is on at Silverwood, Irvine, Henshaw, El Capitan, Wohlford and Lake Hodges. (pg. 85)
- Good **rainbow trout** fishing continues but may be interrupted if winter storms muddy lakes and streams. (pg. 137, 146)

Colorado River & Salton Sea
- **Trout** fishing can be good at Willow Beach and Laughlin when the weather clears. (pg. 137, 72)

APRIL

Fresno/Bakersfield Region
- The Lake Isabella **trout** derby draws crowds this month. **Crappie** are biting too. (pg. 58, 85, 166)

Eastern Sierra
- The **trout** season opens the last Saturday of April. (pg. 137, 146)
- Fish the early **trout** opener south of Independence. Independence, Symmes, Shepard, George, Lone Pine, Tuttle and Cottonwood creeks are heavily planted. (pg.146)
- Big **brown trout** are very hungry and unusually careless during bad weather, early season days. Get out there and bag yourself a trophy! (pg. 126)
- The big **cutthroat** of Pyramid and Walker lakes have moved to the shallows, the bite is on! (pg. 129)
- Fly fish the Nevada East Walker River trophy **trout** area—open all year! (pg. 161)

So. Calif. Lakes & Streams
- The Lake Nacimiento **white bass** spawning frenzy is going full blast. Bring 2 stringers! (pg. 74)
- Spawning **crappie** are hitting everything that moves at Silverwood, Irvine, Henshaw, El Capitan, Wohlford and Hodges. (pg. 85)
- **Largemouth bass** fishing turns on as fish stage for spawning in shallower waters of 15 feet or less. This is the easiest time of year to catch bass, especially big bass. (pg. 25)

- The DFG plants continue, the lake water is still cool, and it's warm enough to work on your tan. Go **trout** fishing. (pg. 137, 146)
- The striper action continues at Pyramid Lake and Silverwood Lake. Really big **striped bass** usually go on a tear at Lake Silverwood sometime from late April to mid-May. (pg. 62)

Colorado River & Salton Sea
- The Salton Sea still has **corvina**. They're biting this month. And it's not yet blazing hot. (pg. 82)

MAY
Fresno/Bakersfield Region
- Flyfisherman should go fishing for wild **trout** on the Kings River above Cedar Grove. (pg. 137, 166)
- Probe the shallow brush and load up with a stringer of **crappie** at Lake Isabella. (pg. 85)

Eastern Sierra
- Big **brown trout** are very hungry and unusually careless during bad weather, early season days. Get out there and bag yourself a trophy! (pg. 126)
- The opening stampede is over but the **trout** fishing will really turn on later this month. (pg. 137, 146)
- The **Sacramento perch** bite picks up steam late this month at Lake Crowley and Pleasant Valley Reservoir. (pg. 88)

So. Calif. Lakes & Streams
- Big **striped bass** usually go on a tear at Lake Silverwood sometime from late April to mid-May. (pg. 62)
- The Nacimiento **white bass** spawning frenzy is still keeping anglers hopping early this month. (pg. 74)
- **Crappie** fisherman hit payload at Silverwood, Irvine, Henshaw, El Capitan, Wohlford, Hodges. (pg. 85)
- The **largemouth bass** are still in the shallows. Get there before the summer doldrums. (pg. 25)

Colorado River & Salton Sea
- Western Outdoor News holds its big Lake Havasu striper derby this month. (pg. 73)
- **Striped bass** come alive at Lake Mead later this month. It's the start of great summer fishing. (pg. 62)
- The Salton Sea still has some sizable **corvina** and this is the best time for the big ones. (pg. 82)

JUNE
- The summer heat makes those **catfish** hungry. They turn active when the sun goes down. (pg. 76)

Fresno/Bakersfield Region
- Flyfishermen should consider fishing the Kings River above Cedar Grove for **rainbow trout**. (pg. 137)
- The Kern River, the main fork above Isabella and the south fork, can yield some good **trout** fishing when waters aren't roiled and high from runoffs. (pg. 137, 166?)

Eastern Sierra
- **Sacramento perch** provide great light tackle action and tasty eating fillets for anglers working Lake Crowley and Pleasant Valley Reservoir. (pg. 88)
- The high country is open. Mountain lakes yield many pan-sized tasty **trout**. (pg. 137, 146)

So. Calif. Lakes & Streams
- Anglers are pulling linesides (**striped bass**) from Lake Silverwood. Action will slow next month. (pg. 62)
- **Catfishing** will soon heat up with the summer heat. (pg. 76)

Colorado River & Salton Sea
- The Salton Sea still has some sizable **corvina** and this is the best time for the big ones. (pg. 82)
- **Striped bass** boils are happening at Mead, Mohave and Havasu Lakes. Laughlin has the gambling and behind the casinos, good **trout** fishing in the Colorado River. (pg. 62, 137, 72)

JULY
- Night time fishing for **catfish** will heat up this month. (pg. 76)

Fresno/Bakersfield Region
- Warm summer nights and a hot **catfish** bite make a great combination. (pg. 76)
- Look for some good **kokanee** salmon action at Shaver and Huntington Reservoirs. (pg. 97?)
- The high country is open. Mountain lakes yield many pan-sized tasty **trout**. (pg. 137, 146)

Eastern Sierra

- **Sacramento perch** provide great light tackle action and tasty eating fillets for anglers working Lake Crowley and Pleasant Valley Reservoir. (pg. 88)
- The high country is open. Mountain lakes yield many pan-sized tasty **trout**. (pg. 137, 146)

So. Calif. Lakes & Streams

- The **catfish** season starts in earnest this month. Do you like fried catfish fillets? (pg. 76)
- Lake fishing is slow. You might want to go saltwater fishing where the action is heating up. See FISHING CALIFORNIA-SALTWATER.

Colorado River & Salton Sea

- Topwater **striped bass** action is here! The waters are boiling at Mead, Mohave and Havasu. (pg. 62)
- The Salton Sea still has some sizable **corvina** and this is the best time for the big ones. (pg. 82)

AUGUST

Fresno/Bakersfield Region

- Warm summer nights and a hot **catfish** bite make a great combination. (pg. 76)
- Look for some good **kokanee** salmon action at Shaver and Huntington Reservoirs. (pg. 97)
- The high country is open. Mountain lakes yield many pan-sized tasty **trout**. Take a pack trip out of Edison Lake. (pg. 137, 166)

Eastern Sierra

- The high country is open. Mountain lakes yield many pan-sized tasty **trout**. (pg. 137, 146)

So. Calif. Lakes & Streams

- The night time **catfish** bite is hot! Some lakes hold fish over 50 pounds! (pg. 76)
- Lake Pyramid **striped bass** start busting top water shad schools. (pg. 62)
- Fishing is slow. Go saltwater fishing, the action is heating up. See FISHING CALIFORNIA-SALTWATER.

Colorado River & Salton Sea

- Topwater **striped bass** action is here! The waters are boiling at Mead, Mohave and Havasu. Get out early or stay out late for some heart-thumping action. (pg. 62)
- **Striper** fishing can be good now at Willow Beach and Laughlin or go **trout** fishing. (pg. 62, 137, 72)
- Like a challenge? This is the best time to try for **flathad catfish** on the lower Colorado River. (pg. 79)
- The **channel catfish** evening bite gets serious later this month in the Colorado River. (pg. 76)

SEPTEMBER

Fresno/Bakersfield Region

- Fish the Kern River above Kernville. The fall **trout** bite will liven up later this month. (pg. 137, 166)
- Warm summer nights and a hot **catfish** bite make a great combination. (pg. 76)
- The high country is open. Mountain lakes yield beautiful **golden trout**. Take a pack trip out of Edison Lake. (pg. 131)

Eastern Sierra

- The high country is open. Mountain lakes yield many pan-sized tasty **trout**. (pg. 137, 146)

So. Calif. Lakes & Streams

- The night time **catfish** bite is hot! Some lakes hold fish over 50 pounds! (pg. 76)
- Lake Pyramid **striped bass** are smashing surface lures cast to top water boils. (pg. 62)
- **Crappie** will move into the shallows later this month and aggressively feed. (pg. 85)

Colorado River & Salton Sea

- Topwater **striped bass** are still bending rods at Mead, Mohave and Havasu. (pg. 62)
- It's top-water season for **stripers**. Get out early or stay late for some heart-thumping action. (pg. 62)
- **Striper** fishing can be good now at Willow Beach and Laughlin or go **trout** fishing. (pg. 62, 72)
- The **channel catfish** evening bite is hot from Lake Mead to the lower Colorado. (pg. 76)
- This is the best time to try for **flathad catfish** on the lower Colorado River. (pg. 79)

OCTOBER
Fresno/Bakersfield Region
- Flyfisherman should think about fishing the Kings River near Cedar Grove. The crowds are gone and the **trout** are up! (pg. 137, 166)
- **Trout** catching is great on the Kern River! (pg. 137, 166)
- It's the last month for fishing the high country. Mountain lakes yield many pan-sized **trout**. (pg. 146)
- There's big **stripers** at Santa Margarita Lake near San Luis Obispo. Bring your heavy tackle. (pg. 62)
- Warm summer nights and a hot **catfish** bite make a great combination. (pg. 76)
- Look for a good **spotted bass** bite at Millerton. (pg. 25) **Striped bass** can be bonus attraction. (pg. 62)

Eastern Sierra
- Big **brown trout** are fattening up for the spawn and winter and they get careless during bad weather, late season days. Get out there and bag yourself a trophy! (pg. 126)

So. Calif. Lakes & Streams
- **Crappie** will move into the shallows this month and feed aggressively. (pg. 85)
- The waters have cooled and the **largemouth bass** are back in the shallows. (pg. 25)
- The top water **striped bass** bite continues at Lake Pyramid early this month. Later on the trout plants will turn on the bite at the marina. (pg. 62)
- Great **catfishing** continues. Go to Lake Irvine for "Moonlight Madness" and fill your stringer. (pg. 76)
- Lake Silverwood **striped bass** will turn on this month. (pg. 62)

Colorado River & Salton Sea
- Topwater **stripers** are still bending rods at Mead, Mohave and Havasu and the crowds are gone.(pg. 62)
- **Striper** fishing can be good now at Willow Beach and Laughlin or go **trout** fishing. (pg. 62, 137, 72)
- Like a challenge? This is the best time to try for **flathead catfish** on the lower Colorado River. (pg. 79)
- The **channel catfish** evening bite is hot from Lake Mead to the lower Colorado. (pg. 76)

NOVEMBER
Fresno/Bakersfield Region
- Lake Evans will be loaded with planter **trout** the middle of November. (pg. 137, 166)
- Kern River **trout** are hungry and striking with a vengence. You'd better go trout fishing now before the bad weather comes. (pg. 137, 166)
- There are some big **stripers** at Santa Margarita Lake near San Luis Obispo. They turn on with the trout plants. Better bring your heavier tackle. (pg. 62)
- The **catfish** bite can still be good early this month. (pg. 76)
- There's usually a good **spotted bass** bite this month at Millerton. (pg. 25)
- The Pine Flat winter **trout** fishing begins this month. (pg. 137) **Crappie** may also be on a tear in the shallow brush. (pg. 85, 166)

Eastern Sierra
- Diaz Lake (pg. 132), Pleasant Valley Res. (pg. 165), and parts of the lower Owens River (pg. 165) are open all year for **trout**.
- Later this month the **cutthroat trout** bite will stir at Nevada's Walker Lake. (pg. 129)
- Fly fish the Nevada East Walker River trophy **trout** area—open all year! (pg. 161)

So. Calif. Lakes & Streams
- The DFG starts their massive southern California **trout** plantings this month. Lake fishing will be good until the winter rains muddy the waters. (pg. 137, 146)
- The **catfish** bite can still be good early this month. (pg. 76)
- Hungry **crappie** will still be in the shallows early this month. (pg. 85)
- **Striped bass** action erupts at Lake Silverwood as the trout planting season begins. (pg. 62)

Colorado River & Salton Sea
- This is the last month to experience some of that great top water **striped bass** fun at Lake Mead and Lake Mohave. (pg. 62)

DECEMBER
Fresno/Bakersfield Region
- Lake Evans **trout** are biting. Get out there before the weather turns bad. (pg. 137, 166)
- You'll have to find the good weather windows but the **trout** fishing is still good on the Kern River early this month. (pg. 137, 166)
- There's usually a good **spotted bass** bite this month at Millerton. (pg. 25, 166)
- The good **trout** fishing continues at Pine Flat. (pg. 137, 166)

Eastern Sierra
- Diaz Lake (pg. 132), Pleasant Valley Res. (pg. 165), and parts of the lower Owens River (pg. 165) are open all year for **trout**.
- The **cutthroat trout** bite is picking up steam at Nevada's Walker Lake. (pg. 129)
- Fly fish the Nevada East Walker River trophy **trout** area—open all year! (pg. 161)

So. Calif. Lakes & Streams
- The heavy **trout** plants continue and the lakes remain clear so be prepared to haul in some trout. (pg. 137, 146)
- Pyramid Lake trout plants will attract the big **striped bass**. Toss a large trout-imitation lure for the catch of your life. (pg. 62)
- **Striped bass** action erupts at Lake Silverwood as the trout planting season begins. (pg. 62)
- There's record sized **spotted bass** in Lake Perris. They'll start their hot spawn bite this month! (pg. 25, 78)

Colorado River & Salton Sea
- **Trout** fishing can be good at Willow Beach and Laughlin when the weather clears. (pg. 137, 72)

THE BASICS

As in sports, if the team doesn't thoroughly know the basics, it's in trouble from the start. The following are the basics you must follow for every fishing trip. Although all the following are important, they are in priority order, the most important listed first.

Work For Results

The average person thinks of fishing as liesurely and often boring. They picture someone sitting in a boat on a warm sunny day and either being half asleep or drinking a beer. I've heard people say, fishing is ok but I want something more active.

These people may be talking about fishing, but they certainly aren't talking about catching. The successful angler will catch 2 to 3 times the fish by being aggressive, attentive, inventive and knowledgeable. The stream fisherman that hikes upstream from the road crossing and then uses agressive wading to reach the best lies will catch that trophy trout. If you want "active" try hiking and wading a sizable stream! I have to admit, there are some successful techniques that are "boring". However these can still demand alertness and prolonged, demanding attention. Sturgeon fishing can involve hours of waiting for only one or two pumps on your bait. The successful angler must have his attention focused on that rod tip constantly. Any diversion—talking, eating, etc. can make him miss his brief opportunity for success.

Here are some examples of "working": Keep in touch with your bait, know what it's doing. You need to concentrate to determine a pickup from wave or wind movement. Watch the line entry at the water for a pickup. Watch for bird activity that indicates fish locations. Note the details of any catch—depth, speed of retreive, shade, current, sluggish or active fight, etc. Watch for anyone catching fish and exactly how they're catching them. Watch hatches carefully, are fish dimpling the surface (emergers) or breaking the surface (adults).

Fish in the Right Spot and Depth

It's a fact, 90% of the fish are concentrated in less than 10% of the water. Unless you are fishing in that 10%, you are wasting time.

a. Look in this book for known hot spots in your area.
b. If you own a boat, invest in the best fish finder you can afford and use it. Many professional fishermen use paper graphs for it's superior resolution. Do not waste time fishing blind.
c. A matter of feet can spell success or failure. If you are fishing 5 feet away from a suspended school of crappie and your buddy is dropping his lure straight through the school, you'll be the spectator, he'll catch the fish.

Fish at the Right Time

a. Different fish species have different active seasons. Look under individual species for specifics.
b. Get current information. The maps list local information sources and their phone numbers.

Use the Freshest, Liviest Bait Possible

Be selective in buying bait. Get the freshest bait. Be gentle and quick handling live bait.

Fish Your Lure or Bait with the Right Action

Pay special attention to lure action and bait movement. The right action will generate a strike. This is a tough skill to teach in a book. Watch the good fishermen and imitate them. Specific sections will describe the correct action in more detail. Here are a few examples;

a. Every lure has a best speed where it generates the best action. Test a lure alongside the boat at different speeds before letting it out to troll. Many anglers work lures too fast.

b. When retrieving a cast lure, often a small change in speed can spell success. Another trick is to stop reeling, let the lure fall as if wounded, and than start reeling again to provoke a strike.
c. The rate of fall can spell success or failure when fishing for bass with a worm or jig.

Use the Right Line

a. Use the lightest line possible. This varies considerably by the type of fish and the fishing conditions but, if the bite is slow, go to lighter line. Old line gets brittle and weak—respool with fresh, quality mono.
b. Use high quality line. The following brands have limp, flexible line that has the maximum strength for the minimum line diameter—Ande, Maxima, Izor, Stren, Trilene, Berkeley XT, Berkeley Trilene Big Game.
c. Check your line. After every fish caught, run the last 3 feet of line between your index finger and thumb. If you feel any abrasions or kinks, cut off the length and retie the hook. Test the hook/lure knot by pulling stiffly on the line while holding the hook stationary.

Use Sharp Hooks

Buy lazer sharp hooks or use a sharpener tool. Also sharpen your lure hooks. This is critically important. A simple and inexpensive sharpening tool can do the job. Form a sharp diamond cross-section point by first forming the sides of the diamond by running the hook point down the file groove. Eliminate the burr by filing the bottom of the point with the flat side of the tool. A properly sharpened hook should cut a groove in your fingernail when lightly pulled across it. Ideally, the point should catch as it digs in.

Chumming

Whenever and wherever legal, chum. Chumming is restricted to the Colorado River and in the Sacramento downstream of the highway 80 crossing and in the Carquinez and Suisun Bays. See regs. for allowed chum.

Make a Plan

Develop a plan that concentrates on the fish you are targeting, but also covers the "what if" situations. The plan should consider other kinds of fish in the area should your target species not be active, such as striped bass on a sturgeon trip. It should include the tackle and rigging for the chance meeting with a large fish, i.e. a big striped bass on an trout fishing trip. Remember, "Luck is where preparation meets opportunity".

Pay Attention to Details

This is all important. A very minor detail often can make the difference between catching a limit or being skunked. If someone is catching a lot of fish, find out exactly what they are doing and start doing it!

Noise

Avoid making noise. Any noise in contact with the water should be minimized such as banging things on the bottom of the boat, stomping along a stream bank, etc. In a boat either use a quiet electric motor to approach target areas or position the boat upwind and drift toward the fishing area.

Vary Your Technique and Location

There are no sure fire techniques or spots. The techniques that work most of the time and the spots that most often hold fish are listed in this book, however if you aren't catching fish CHANGE. Some people picture fishing as a person asleep holding a cane pole. This is fine if it's what you want but if you want to catch fish, lots of fish, you need to actively search for feeding fish, you need to work at it.

Big Fish

Often you must change your techniques to catch big fish. What works for the average sized fish of a species stands little chance of catching a jackpot fish. See the **Big Fish** details for specific fish in the alphabetic listings.

Key to Alphabetic Sport Fish Listings

All sport fish listings have the following standard format

FISH VARIETY (Alternate name)

Where

Often the categories Where and When are interdependent and are detailed under the combined title of Where/When.

Hot Spots are revealed on detailed maps. Proven spots are marked by fish symbols (➤). **The maps are NOT too be used for navigation. There are many boating hazards which are not included on this book's maps.**

Structure This section outlines environmental factors that create preferred fish holding areas for this fish species. It will indicate preferred water temperature, water depths and cover, etc.

When

Only the good fishing periods are listed. Fish usually can be caught at other times and seasons but the success rate is much lower. Most of the times given in this book are very reliable, however they can vary from year to year. When planning a trip, you should monitor info sources for current conditions.

Bait/Lures

Baits and lures are again listed generally in order of effectiveness and popularity. If one bait or lure isn't working, try a different color or try a different bait or lure. In general "match the hatch" by choosing a lure that mimics the water's prevalent forage both in size and color. The lures listed and pictured are ideal choices but sometimes difficult to find. If using a substitute, try hard to match action, size and color.

Rig

General rig recommendations are made indicating rod & reel class and reel capacities. Specific examples are given for both rod and reel. Note that the examples given are based on the authors experience and are NOT the only reliable, quality brands available on the market. Terminal rigging is usually diagrammed on a separate page.

Technique

Critical techniques and rigs are in bold type. You MUST use these techniques to catch more than an occasional fish! Often more than one technique will be listed. These are in order of proven effectiveness. If one technique doesn't work try one of the others. If special techniques catch bigger fish, those techniques will be described here under **Big Fish**.

The Law

California fishing regulations are revised every 2 years and are effective from March 1 to the end of February 2 years later. Only general regulations information will be given here. There are many special Department of Fish & Game regulations that change each season. You must consult a current DFG regulations booklet.

Records

All-tackle state and IGFA records

Info

Reliable, current information sources are listed on the area maps.

Access

The detailed area maps give phone numbers for guides and rental boats. Launch ramps are indicated on the maps.

See Also

This area lists other sport fish that are found in the same area. The interested angler should carry recommended bait, lures, rigs and tackle so that luck will be with them if those fish show up (luck = where preparation meets opportunity).

LARGEMOUTH BASS (Also Smallmouth, Spotted):

This largemouth bass section is organized as follows:

1. General Information .... Pg. 25-27

This section explains structure peculiarities for smallmouth and spotted bass, general rig recommendations, bass fishing tools, the law, records, and other sport fish found in the same lakes.

2. Seasonal Patterns .... Pg. 28-37

Tournament bass pros base their winning success largely on finding prevalent bass patterns and then working those patterns hard. The following information is organized to give you the ability to quickly determine a winning pattern and to select the optimum bait or baits for exploiting that pattern. The Seasonal Patterns section splits the year into 7 seasons. Knowledge of bass location and behavior during these seasons allows you to eliminate 80 percent of the lake immediately. Once on the lake the seasonal pattern knowledge determines your search pattern for the remaining 20% of the lake and gives you clues to the best class of lures and techniques.

3. Lure Techniques................................. Pg. 38-50

The Lure Techniques section guides you on selecting lure and techniques to exploit either active or passive bass based on the structure type, forage, holding depth, etc.

4. Maps of big bass lakes........................ Pg. 51-61

Guide Larry Hemphill specializes in nighttime techniques to catch big Clear Lake largemouth.

General Information

There are two strains of largemouth bass in California, the northern and the southern. You'll find the northern strain in lakes north of Lake Isabella (Bakersfield). The southern strain (Florida strain) is a larger bass of the southern California area.

Smallmouth bass are more commonly found in northern California lakes and rivers. Notable lakes: Trinity Lake, Clear Lake, Lake Shasta, Millerton (near Fresno), Lake Almanor, and Pine Flat. Notable rivers: The lower Russian and the Feather. Smallmouth fishing techniques are similar to largemouth techniques.

There also is a spotted bass that is considered a separate species. Spotted bass are prevalent at Pine Flat Reservoir, Millerton Lake, Shasta, Lake Oroville and Lake Perris.

Where/When   See the Seasonal Patterns section for "Where" and "When" details .

Bass fishing is the easiest in spring, from late March through early May, and in the fall before the lake turnover. See Early Fall, Late Fall sections. You will catch the most fish in the early morning. For specifics see the Seasonal Patterns section.

Smallmouth bass differ from largemouth in the following ways:

- They prefer colder water.
- Are seldom found below 20 feet.
- Will spawn in deeper water.
- Eat mostly crayfish, but drifted minnows can be effective.
- Prefer shady areas of rocky ledges, riprap and points.

Spotted bass (Alabama) differ from largemouth in the following ways:
- They spawn earlier (mid-December to mid-to-late January at Lake Perris).
- Spotted bass prefer rocky structure.
- You must be fishing on bottom to be effective.
- In summer, fish at night with a small plastic worm or single spin small spinnerbait.
- Grub jigging is effective in deeper water structure. Color: green, watermelon.
- Live crayfish are the best bait.

Rig

These two rigs will suffice, however, see the Techniques section for more specialized rigs.

1. A conventional freshwater casting reel combined with a 5 1/2 to 6 foot medium action graphite rod for working crankbaits, surface baits, spinnerbaits, Jig and Pigs, spoons and for doodling.

2. A medium weight spinning reel with a 5 1/2 foot medium-to-stiff action rod for working splitshot worms, darter jigs, tube baits and Gitzits.

However, if you are a serious bass fisherman seeking the most fish in the least time, special rigs can be helpful for flipping, pitching, cranking, etc. See the Lure Techniques section for more specific recommendations.

Tools

Fish finders like LCRs (liquid crystal recorders), paper graphs, and flashers are essential for finding the 10% payoff water. They locate structure, bait, the targeted fish and the more sensitive instruments can detect the thermocline.

Water temperature gauges are not widely used by California bass anglers. However they can be useful in locating warmer, bass holding areas in the pre-spawn season, and the cooler holding areas or thermocline in the summer and early fall seasons.

Markers can greatly facilitate working invisible underwater structure, whether it is a submerged mound, rock pile, breakline (drop-off), or deep weedline. First meter the structure and then mark it with one or more floating markers. Then you can concentrate on using your electric trolling motor to maneuver the boat and effectively and accurately work the area.

Techniques

See Lure Techniques section

Big Bass Techniques Of the 25 largest bass ever recorded, 21 of them were caught in southern California. Nineteen of those 21 bass were caught in January, February or March. Certainly the most prominent of the big bass lakes is Lake Castaic. Castaic yielded the state record 21.74 lb.in 1991. This was the second largest bass in history. In that same year an even bigger bass of 22.1 lbs. was caught and released! The Lake Castaic Marina is the only place where you can apply instantly via FAX for the Bassin' magazine $1 million Big Bass World Championship. Lake Casitas is also famous for big bass. The former state record, a 21 lbs. 3 oz. bass was pulled from the lake in 1980.

Southern California big bass lakes have one critical thing in common, the DFG plants them with trout during the late fall through spring months. Big bass become giant bass by eating trout.

Big bass fishing requires different techniques. The current top tournament winner with multiple BassMaster Classic wins has only caught one (1) bass over 10 pounds! Whereas the producers of the video *Bodacious Bass* have caught over 100 bass over 10 pounds and even a few over 20 pounds!

The two most effective big bass techniques are:

1. Still fishing with crayfish.

Careful selection of prime point structure with sharp drop-offs to deep water is critical. Successful anglers use paper graphs to pinpoint and record subtle bottom structure. They return days or hours later being careful to use quiet, precise positioning a long-casting-distance from the fish-holding structure. This careful double anchoring inshore of deeper holding structure allows precise presentation and ultimate sensitivity to bait action. Practitioners use sensitive graphite rods or ultra-slow stitching techniques to detect lure or bait action, bottom characteristics and fish pickups. A good day may yield one or two bites to a patient, persistent angler.

For a guided trip from the renown big bass fisherman Bob Crupi, call (805) 257-0860. To learn more see Bob Crupi and Dan Kadota's big bass video *Bodacious Bass* or read *In Pursuit of Giant Bass* by Bill Murphy.

2. Slow trolling with large, trout-imitation lures.

This technique involves trolling Trout-Imitation Lures: A.C. Lure, Z-Plug, Day Lure, or large Rapalas. The angler slow trolls the lure using leadcore line over bottom structure at depths of 30 to 40+ feet. Prime deep structure is thoroughly worked over using different trolling speeds and different trolling paths. This technique is best during trout forage season from the beginning of planting in November to early March.

Other big bass techniques include vertically fishing deep metered fish using Rapala Ice Jigs, Tora Tubes, Rubber Trout, etc. These techniques mimic crayfish fishing in requiring precise positioning over known bass holding spots.

The Law	Generally the limit is 5 fish 12" or longer, however several exceptions occur. Check current DFG regulations for "black bass" that includes largemouth, smallmouth, and spotted bass.
Records	State Record: 21 lb. 3 oz.; Lake Casitas, 1980, a 22.1 lb. fish was caught at Lake Castaic in 1991. Pending: 9 lbs. 7 oz., Pine Flat Res., Feb. 1994. World Record: 22 lbs. 4 oz.; Georgia; 1932. Smallmouth: 9 lbs. 1 oz., Trinity Lake, 1976. Spotted: 9 lbs. 4.5 oz., Lake Perris.
See Also	Rainbow trout, striped bass, crappie, catfish.

SEASONAL PATTERNS

Bass behavior can be conveniently categorized by seasons. The savvy angler who knows the seasons can eliminate 80% of the lake as unproductive just by knowing the general season and surface water temperature. The seasonal patterns are also a good general guide to fish mood. Knowing whether the fish are active or passive can lead to the selection of active, fast working lures and techniques or passive, finesse lures and techniques. This knowledge is the first step to establishing a winning, bass-catching pattern on any lake or river, in any season.

Note that there may be more than one pattern depending on water depth, time of day, etc. Look for different early morning, mid-day and deep water patterns.

There is a definite overlap of these "seasons". For example during late pre-spawn significant numbers of fish will still be schooled deep in a winter pattern, others will be in the spawning pattern. The spawning pattern may occur 3 weeks earlier in the protected,

California Bass Seasons			
Season Months	Surface Water Temp	Season	Page
November to early February	Less than 55	Winter	28
January to early March	50 to 60	Pre-Spawn	30
March, April, early May	60 to 70	Spawn	32
Late May	70 to 75	Post-Spawn	33
June to September	60 to 70	Summer	33
September	70 to 75	Early Fall	37
October	55 to 65	Late Fall	37

northwest coves of a lake than in the wind-cooled flats of the lake's southern shoreline. Over the course of the seasons, the main bass forage changes. Choose lures and techniques that match-the-hatch. Forage seasons will vary somewhat by area and altitude.

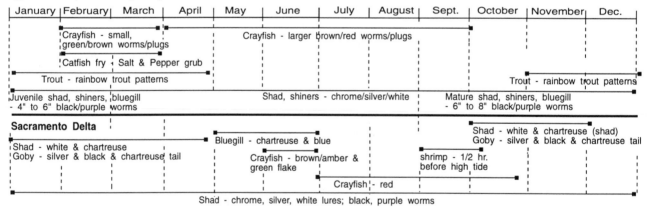

Winter to early Pre-spawn (surface water temperature less than 55 degrees): Generally late November, December, January & early February.

Where
Fish school in deeper water from 25 - 55+ feet. Fish are usually close to the bottom and near some bottom structure. Around January, fish are still in deep water, but become more concentrated outside spawning areas next to deep water. The schools will gradually move along the easiest paths of structure toward shallower waters as the waters warm. Warmer days, especially a series of clear, calm days can move fish to 10 feet deep or less.

Technique
Fish are very passive and deep. Therefore either use quick sinking lures such as spoons or use the spoons to find willing biters and then switch to even slower techniques such as doodling.   All bait/lure presentations must be very slow in this cold water. This translates to short lift jigging when using spoons off the bottom. During this slow movement season, a big bass might watch 25+ strokes before striking. Be patient. Work slow then work slower. See page 26 for Big Bass techniques.

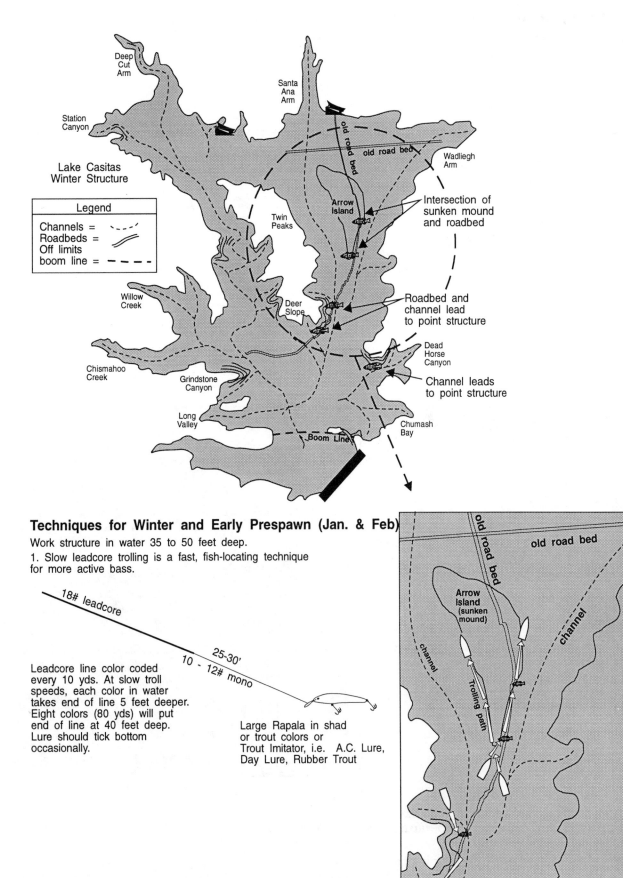

Lake Casitas
Winter Structure

Legend

Channels =	------
Roadbeds =	
Off limits	
boom line =	— — —

Deep Cut Arm

Santa Ana Arm

Station Canyon

old road bed

old road bed

Wadliegh Arm

Twin Peaks

Arrow island

Intersection of sunken mound and roadbed

Willow Creek

Deer Slope

Roadbed and channel lead to point structure

Chismahoo Creek

Grindstone Canyon

Dead Horse Canyon

Channel leads to point structure

Long Valley

Boom Line

Chumash Bay

Techniques for Winter and Early Prespawn (Jan. & Feb)

Work structure in water 35 to 50 feet deep.

1. Slow leadcore trolling is a fast, fish-locating technique for more active bass.

18# leadcore

25-30'
10 - 12# mono

Leadcore line color coded every 10 yds. At slow troll speeds, each color in water takes end of line 5 feet deeper. Eight colors (80 yds) will put end of line at 40 feet deep. Lure should tick bottom occasionally.

Large Rapala in shad or trout colors or Trout Imitator, i.e. A.C. Lure, Day Lure, Rubber Trout

old road bed

old road bed

Arrow island (sunken mound)

channel

channel

Trolling path

Techniques for Winter and Early Prespawn (Jan. & Feb.) continued:

2. Vertical Spoon jigging, Rapala Ice jig over graphed fish or prime structure
Spoon jigging works on neutral fish. Ice jigs are finesse lures for passive fish.

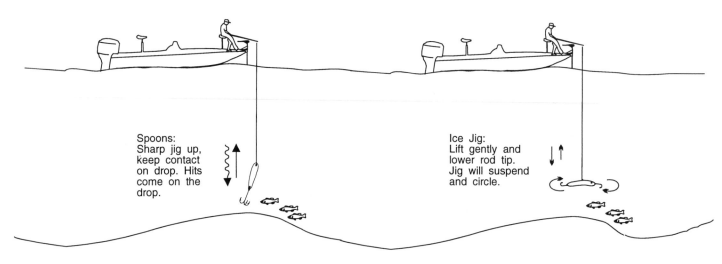

Spoons:
Sharp jig up,
keep contact
on drop. Hits
come on the
drop.

Ice Jig:
Lift gently and
lower rod tip.
Jig will suspend
and circle.

3. Jig 'N Pig and live crayfish over outside structure.
Work crayfish uphill and over points. Work near rocky
structure. Work Jig 'N Pig downhill through structure.
Jig 'N Pig targets neutral fish. Crayfish work on passive bass.

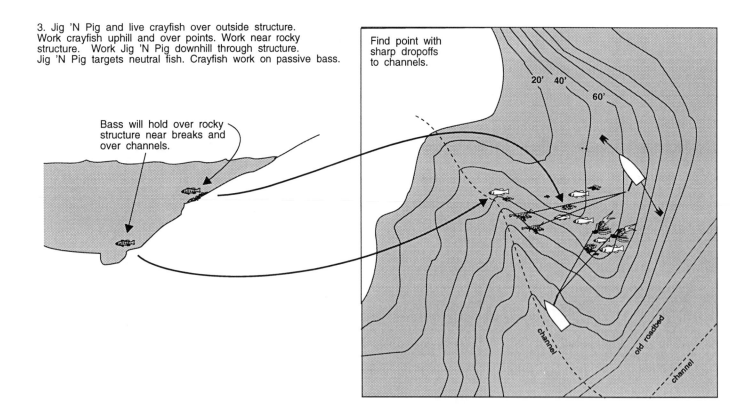

Bass will hold over rocky
structure near breaks and
over channels.

Find point with
sharp dropoffs
to channels.

20'   40'

60'

channel

old roadbed

channel

Late Pre-spawn (surface water temperature = 50-60 degrees): Generally occurs from early to mid-March.

This season varies somewhat by specific lake as some lakes, especially at higher elevations, are earlier then others. This movement is accelerated by a trend of warm, calm days. Best time of day: 10 AM to 4 PM when the sunny, protected shallows warm.

Where The bass will be staging for their move into the shallow water spawning flats. The sunny sides of northwestern and northern bays warm first and see the first action. During the early stage of prespawn, the bass will be in deep water, on the bottom, at 25 to 50+ feet deep. They will be close to protected northern bays, coves, or inlets with sand, gravel or hard bottom shallow flats, especially over darker (heat holding) bottoms.

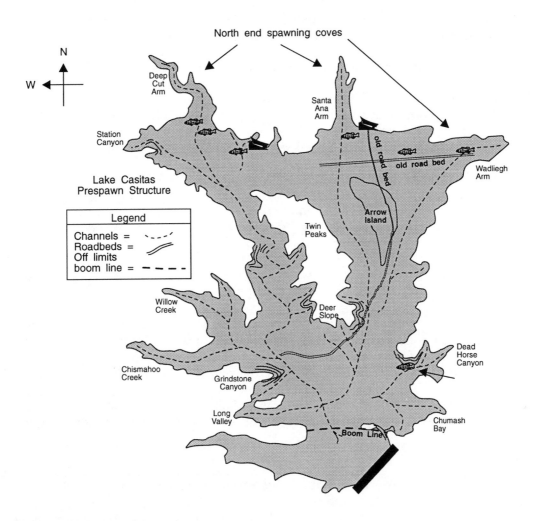

North end spawning coves

N
W

Deep Cut Arm

Santa Ana Arm

Station Canyon

old road bed
old road bed

Wadliegh Arm

Lake Casitas Prespawn Structure

Arrow Island

Legend

Channels = – –
Roadbeds =
Off limits
boom line = – – –

Twin Peaks

Willow Creek

Deer Slope

Dead Horse Canyon

Chismahoo Creek

Grindstone Canyon

Long Valley

Chumash Bay

Boom Line

Techniques for late Prespawn (March).
Work structure in water 15 to 35 feet deep.

Slow drag and twitch splitshot worms & grubs, Pig 'N Jigs, Gitzits.
jig head worms and live crayfish.

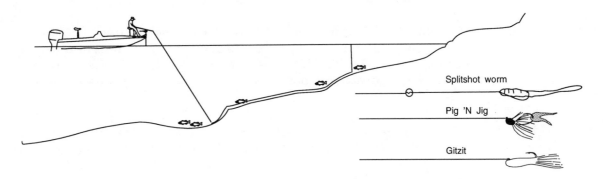

Splitshot worm

Pig 'N Jig

Gitzit

As this stage moves toward the spawn period, the fish will move to shallower holding positions in water 10 to 25 feet deep. Cold fronts will move them a little deeper, a series of warm days will even move them up into the sunny, 5+ foot shallows. Note that the northern coves of lakes with cold water inflow such as Silverwood and the Ski Arm of Castaic Lake, will not have the north bay spawning activity.

This book's lake maps show spawning areas with a dark bass ( ). Pre-spawn areas are in deeper water structure next to the spawning flats.

In deeper water areas (10'- 35') next to spawning areas.

In or near structure in the above areas such as:
* Creek channel ledges and bends (especially outside bends)
* Stumps & stickups
* Vertical cover leading from deeper water to spawning shallows

Bass will move along paths defined by structure. The structure will include anything that affords protection in moving from the deeper water toward the spawning flats. Structure can be old submerged river channels, raised roadbeds, tree or stump lines, or combinations of structure especially in the north end of the lake. When searching for the bass follow the structure paths until you find the fish concentration.

They will move to the shallow water flats with warmer weather. They will hold their depth or move slightly deeper if a storm comes through.

| **Technique** | The fish are almost all in a passive mode. Work all baits and lures very slowly in these cold water conditions. However after a series of warm calm days, especially late in this season, many bass may become active and move shallower. Also shallow bass may become active later in day, from 10 am to 4 pm when the shallows have warmed. |

Crayfish (2-4"), Shiners, Jigs and Pigs, Gitzit and finesse worm techniques are effective during pre-spawn. Crayfish are especially effective for lunker bass during this time of the year.

Spawn (Surface water temperature = 60 - 70 degrees): March, April, early May.

During spawn the smaller male fish will hit your lure first, you can keep casting or come back for the big female. Bass are vulnerable during this season and can be easily stressed. Heavy angling during this period can severely damage angling success on the lake for the rest of the year. I recommend that the caring angler refrain from pursuing bass on the spawn but concentrate on the outside pre- and post-spawn structure. At least practice quick and careful release.

| **Where** | Usually on north end, especially western side of lake on sunny flats in protected coves. In 3' to 8' deep water, especially on the flats close to a channel or other structure leading to deep water. This book's lake maps show bass spawning areas with a black bass ( ). They will NOT be in areas of moving water currents such as the back of coves with running streams. |

| **Technique** | Spawning fish are generally in a passive mood but will strike lures to protect the nest. The smaller male is the most aggressive defender and will be the first one hooked. |

Look for These Patterns:
* In spawning beds and shallow cover use a split-shot plastic worm, 4", black, purple, or brown. Cast past the nest and move it into the nest and wait for the bass to pick it up. Use a stiff 5 1/2' graphite rod with 14# - 20# mono.

- In spawning beds, if no wind, early mornings and late evenings; use a #11 Floating Rapala:
  1. Cast 2-3 feet past the spawning bed.
  2. Let plug sit motionless for 10-25 seconds.
  3. Twitch it once or twice.
  4. Run it under the water 2 - 3 feet toward the bed.
  5. Let float to surface.
  6. Repeat.
- In spawning areas, in tules, over grass, in the trees during early mornings and late evenings use the flipping technique, especially if a wind is breaking up the surface and allowing a close enough approach to the shallows. Flip with Jig and Pig or spinnerbait.

Post-spawn / pre-summer (surface water temperature = 70-75 degrees): Late May, early June.

There is a post-spawn season where the spawning bass move out of the shallows and are reluctant to feed. This short season comes between spawning and pre-summer. In northern lakes, the pre-summer season is quite short and can produce excellent fishing. In southern reservoirs this season is less noticeable.

Where   In weedy lakes, the fish move out of the spawning areas and into the newly developing weed beds on gradually or gently sloping banks and points. The fish will spread out in the lake. If you are unfamiliar with the lake, using a fast fish-locator technique is imperative. In reservoirs with minimal weed/reed cover, the bass will move along structure from shallow areas near spawning flats down to structure in 15 to 20 feet of water. Typically this means movement along secondary creek channels toward junctions with the main lake channel. They will tend to cluster at brush or tree covered areas along the creek channel.

This book's lake maps show spawning areas with a black bass symbol (). Early post-spawn areas are in deeper water structure next to the spawning flats. The first post-spawn structure is the same as pre-spawn (see pre-spawn structure map).

Technique   Fish moods vary all over the scale from aggressive to very passive. Start your search with a fast, active technique. Switch to more passive lures and techniques if few active fish found.

Look for these patterns:
- In the mornings and late evenings use a top water lure—Zara Spook, Torpedo, Pop-R. This is the best season for top water fishing.
- Along isolated weedbeds, or weed line structure—points or coves use a crankbait, and work parallel with the weed line. Use a #7 Countdown Rapala, especially if the fish are holding deeper than can be reached easily with a crankbait.
- If fish are not aggressive try more subtle baits such as p-heads or darter heads on small plastic worms.

Summer (surface water temperature = 75+ degrees): Generally June to September.

The fish are spread throughout the lake. The best time of day for aggressive fish is early morning until sunlight hits the water and dusk.

Where   In the early morning and evening hours, active bass can be found in shallow water structure. As the sun comes up they will become less active while fish at deeper, outside structure will still be catchable.

Starting in summer, bass depth is limited by the thermocline that develops in deeper lakes from early summer and last until early fall. You can find the thermocline depth by either turning up the sensitivity on your fish finder until you detect a lightly shaded, uniform depth area located between the surface and the bottom or by metering fish and bait to find their maximum holding depth. Bass will always be above the thermocline. Look for lake areas where good fish holding structure is at a depth just above the thermocline.

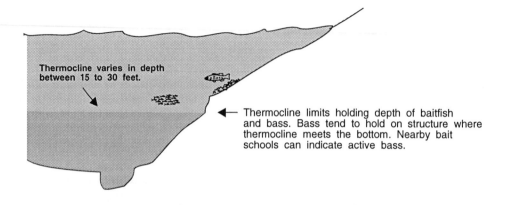

Thermocline varies in depth between 15 to 30 feet.

Thermocline limits holding depth of baitfish and bass. Bass tend to hold on structure where thermocline meets the bottom. Nearby bait schools can indicate active bass.

On lakes with weed banks, summer bass are in the weeds. See above diagram explaining bass holding areas. Weed structure areas include points, sharp inlets in the reeds, or channels cutting through the reeds. The best weed areas are near a slight drop-off, even as small as 1 foot in 3 feet of water.

In reservoirs without extensive weed/reed cover, the bass will be moving down the secondary creek channels to the junction with the main channel. Often they will hold at concentrations of submerged brush or trees situated along this route. In the summer the bass are usually on the bottom. The following structures in less than 30 feet of water are prime summer spots:

- Creek channel junctions with the main channel
- Roadbed/creek junctions
- Outside bends in the main river channel
- Sharp bends in the main channel
- Points with rock structure near channels
- Sunken mounds

Fish will generally be on the up-current, windy side of such structures. They will be active near the surface and shallows in the early morning and late evening.

There also can be mid-day, surface action caused by bass chasing shad schools to the surface. In August and September be on the lookout for this action and have a setup pre-rigged. These bass will be small.

Summer & Fall Structure

From June through November bass are spread throughout the lake on windy main points and where channels lead to shoreline structure in water from 5 to 15 feet deep.

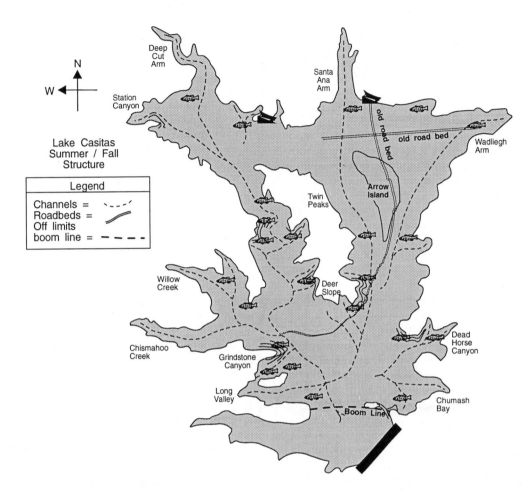

Technique   Fish are active at dusk and dawn. Mid-day fish are more passive. Some mid-day fish are available in deep shade under low docks or on deeper structure at 10 to 25 feet.

Multiple environmental factors can affect bass, influencing whether they are aggressive or passive. Use the following diagram to guide your pattern search.

Factors impacting shallow to mid-depth bass behavior:

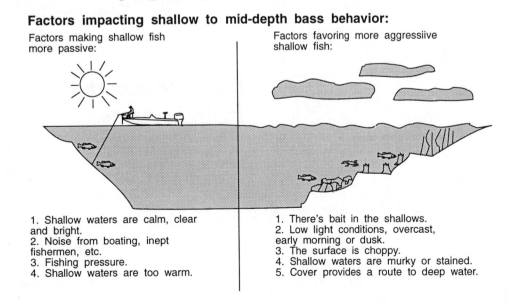

Factors making shallow fish more passive:	Factors favoring more aggressiive shallow fish:
1. Shallow waters are calm, clear and bright.	1. There's bait in the shallows.
2. Noise from boating, inept fishermen, etc.	2. Low light conditions, overcast, early morning or dusk.
3. Fishing pressure.	3. The surface is choppy.
4. Shallow waters are too warm.	4. Shallow waters are murky or stained.
	5. Cover provides a route to deep water.

Bass affinity to structure will vary with their mood, either active or passive. Active bass will prowl 10, 15 or 20 feet away from structure. Less active bass will hold on structure outer boundaries. Passive bass will be tight to and inside structure boundaries. Search the outer perimeters first with active techniques and lures. Proceed to finesse techniques if you don't find active fish.

Working Summer Structure: Trees, stumps, weeds, reeds, etc.

First try faster working techniques for active bass. Progress to slower, finesse techniques until you find a winning pattern.

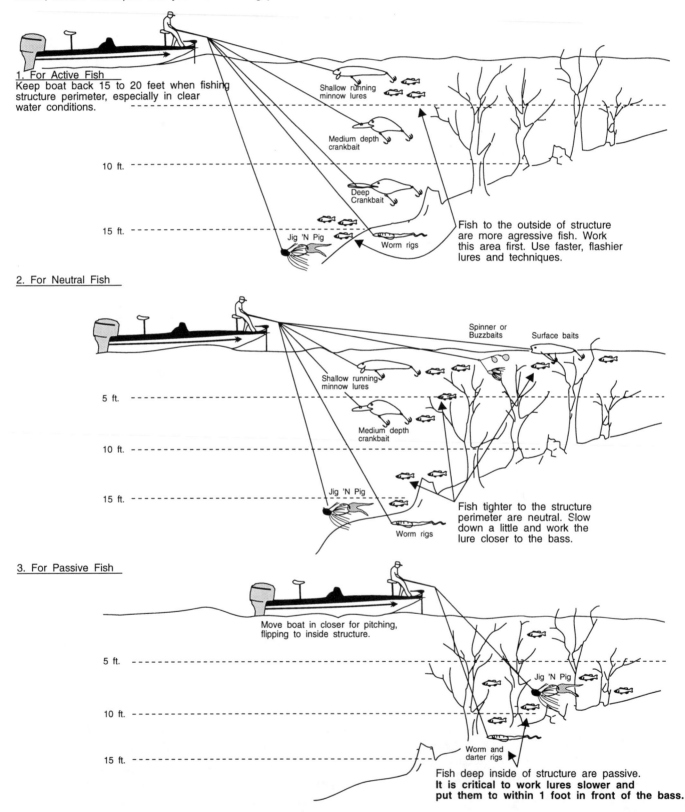

1. For Active Fish
Keep boat back 15 to 20 feet when fishing structure perimeter, especially in clear water conditions.

Shallow running minnow lures

Medium depth crankbait

10 ft.

Deep Crankbait

15 ft.

Jig 'N Pig

Worm rigs

Fish to the outside of structure are more agressive fish. Work this area first. Use faster, flashier lures and techniques.

2. For Neutral Fish

Spinner or Buzzbaits   Surface baits

Shallow running minnow lures

5 ft.

Medium depth crankbait

10 ft.

Jig 'N Pig

15 ft.

Worm rigs

Fish tighter to the structure perimeter are neutral. Slow down a little and work the lure closer to the bass.

3. For Passive Fish

Move boat in closer for pitching, flipping to inside structure.

5 ft.

Jig 'N Pig

10 ft.

15 ft.

Worm and darter rigs

Fish deep inside of structure are passive. **It is critical to work lures slower and put them to within 1 foot in front of the bass.**

In some lakes, notably some of the San Diego lakes like Hodges, there can be significant surface boiling as schooled bass chase shad to the surface. Fish these boils by cautiously approaching to within casting distance and casting to the action with a small, 1/4 oz. Kastmaster, or Hopkins spoon.

Early fall (surface water temperature = 65-75 degrees): September

This is a time when the lake shallows are still too warm to be ideal for bass activity but fishing action picks up when the water cools.

Therefore, fish in the morning hours while the shallows are still cool or after cool windy days, or one or two days after a cooling storm.

Where	Look for fish around:
	• the shallows in the back end of coves and secondary channels and bank areas with cover near these channels.
	• points that are slow tapering on the main lake near drop-offs or remaining weeds.
	• in deep water, off points with cover near channels.
	• if there is little lake cover, try creek channel intersections with the main channel, or sharp, outside bends in main channels in water 5 to 15 feet deep.

Technique	The bass are still scattered. Use a fast working lure to cover area quickly and locate fish. Use a deep running crankbait or a small blade spinnerbait.
	Look for these patterns:
	• In the early AM look for aggressive fish in the shallows. Use buzzbaits, spinnerbaits, and crankbaits like the Fat Rap, and Rapala. Try jerking the Rapala. Continue to work this pattern until the bite dies off.
	• After the morning active bite dies, work deeper with more finesse using reapers and larger 6 to 8" worms. This works well on breaks where 5 foot deep shelves drop to around 15 feet.

Late fall (surface water temperature = 55-65 degrees): Early October

In early October water temperatures remain stratified before turnover. This is a time when the lake shallows have cooled below the ideal for bass activity but after warm weather periods the shallows attract aggressive fish.

Therefore, fish during the mid-day hours, from 10 am to 2 pm, especially after a trend of warm, calm days.

Where	Bass will move deeper with the cooling weather. They will school in 10 - 30 ft. deep water.
	Look for fish:
	• on the steep side of points.
	• in deeper water channel intersections.
	• off rocky bluffs near channels.

Technique	As the water cools, crayfish will move out of the dying weed areas to rocky bottoms, riprap. If the lake has shad, they are the main forage.
	If the weather has been warm, try for more active fish in the shallows. If its been colder, seek less aggressive fish in deeper water. Use shad colored, smaller lures and retrieve at a slower speed. For example, Bill Norman crankbaits, Fat Raps, and Bomber lures or large blade or double spinnerbaits worked just below the surface are effective now.

LURE TECHNIQUES

I've organized the following lure families from fast working, run-and-gun techniques for active bass to passive/finesse techniques. Competitive anglers look for aggressive patterns first—aggressive patterns mean more fish quicker. Finesse techniques work on aggressive fish too, but cover ground so much slower. Depending on your search results, you need to select a lure and technique that is the optimum compromise between speed and finesse.

Within each lure family, specific lures may be suited more for active or passive fish depending on such factors as size, color, retrieve speed, etc. The following diagram shows the general lure features and techniques. After your initial lure selection, analyze each fish caught to further hone your technique and lure selection. Ask these questions. Was it an active or lethargic fight (is he active or passive)? What was my speed of retrieve?

General Guide to
Lure and Technique Selection

Active Fish	Neutral Fish	Passive Fish
Bigger Lures		Smaller Lures
Action lures		Slow lure action
Noisy / Splashing		Quiet
Bright Colors		Dull, dark Colors
Added Trailers		

Fast retreive ———————————————————————— Slow retreive
Fast drop (shape & heavier) — Slow drop (shape & lighter)
Place within several feet — Place within 1 foot of
of fish — fish mouth

Where was the fish positioned in the cover, inside/outside/top/edge/in shade? What was the color and size of the lure? Did he hit on the fall or retrieve? What was the holding depth of the fish?

No matter what lure you use **it is critical that you don't spook the fish.** A spooked bass is uncatchable. A bass will spook if he sees or hears you or if he is startled by your lure. Of course this becomes much more of a concern when you are working in the shallows, 15' or less. In clear, calm water conditions, stay at least 20 feet out from the perimeter of fish holding structure for your initial casts. Keep a low profile for both your body and your fishing rod. Choppy, stained or muddy water allows much closer initial approaches. After working the outer structure move closer to fish for less aggressive fish holding closer to the structure. Unless you are flipping or pitching, cast your lure up to 10 feet past the fish holding structure and retrieve it back to the prime spot. When pitching or flipping, take especial care to place the lure as gently as possible with minimal splash. Practice in your living room until you can pitch a jig into a cocktail glass without making a noise!

In addition to selecting lures and techniques based on fish moods, you need to pick lures depending on the cover you are working. Use the following table as a guide:

Lure Type & Cover Type Combinations	
Lure Type	**Cover Type & Depth**
Crankbaits	Open water, 1-15 feet deep if cranked, up to 30 feet if trolled
Surface plugs, poppers, stickbaits	Surface over submerged weeds or open water
Spinnerbaits and buzzbaits	Near surface in open water or through timber
Zara Spook	Surface over submerged weeds or open water
Flipping with a Jig and Pig	In and around weed cover. Lure is heavy enough to penetrate cover.
Jig and Pig	Shallow to deep water jigging
Plastic worms, grubs, reapers	In and around stumps, trees, light weeds and open cover. Shallow to deep water.
Tube baits, p-heads, darter jigs	Open water, Shallow to deep.
Spoons	Open water. Shallow to deep.
Bait	Light cover. Shallow to deep.

Crankbaits

When   Crankbaits are fast working and good for searching techniques, especially for active bass in post spawn and summer seasons when the bass are scattered.

Rig

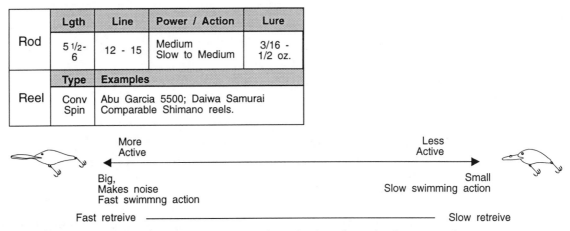

Rod	Lgth	Line	Power / Action	Lure
	5 1/2-6	12 - 15	Medium Slow to Medium	3/16 - 1/2 oz.

Reel	Type	Examples
	Conv Spin	Abu Garcia 5500; Daiwa Samurai Comparable Shimano reels.

More Active ◄──────────────────────► Less Active

Big, Makes noise Fast swimmng action   Small Slow swimming action

Fast retreive ─────────────────────── Slow retreive

Make sure the lure runs true, straight. Adjust by bending the lure attachment ring opposite to the direction the lure is running.

Colors: Match size and color to the forage, i.e. crayfish color for spring crayfish, chrome or Tennessee shad colors for small spring shad and larger summer shad.

Technique   Different lures work best at different speeds. If unfamiliar with the lure, test it within sight to see the retrieve that gives the best action. Vary retrieve speed based on fish aggressiveness. If hooked fish are sluggish, use a medium to slow retrieve. If hooked fish are active, use a medium to fast retrieve.

Always cast 10 to 20 feet past the target and bring the lure back to the prime spot. It **is critical with crankbaits to occasionally run into structure, bump a stump, tick the bottom.** Never retrieve a crankbait with a regular, steady retrieve. Give lifelike action to the lure with irregular retrieves, pauses, jerks, brief periods of rapid retrieves, etc.

Successful floating lure techniques are twitching, & jerking (pulling).

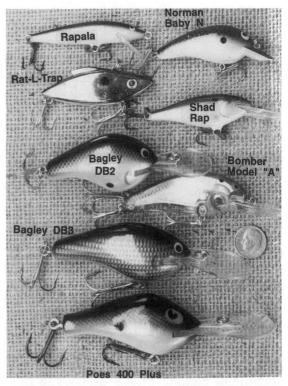

Twitching Cast the lure past the structure. Let it sit quietly for a few seconds and retrieve up to the structure area. Twitch lightly, let it sit, twitch again and retrieve. This is more of a passive technique than either stroking or ripping.

Stroking employs 2 to 3 foot downward pulls/retrieves, in cooler waters—March or April.

Jerking Jerk the lure below the surface with a backward sweep of the rod. Reel in the slack while letting the lure float part way back toward the surface. Jerk again. Jerking is more effective in the warmer months.

Surface Plugs, Poppers, Chuggers, Stickbaits

When   These active lures are best during warm water, summer months, especially early morning and evening hours with calm surface conditions. Use louder lures such as the Woodchopper, Jitterbug or Torpedo during windier, choppier conditions.

Rig   Use 15 to 20# mono.

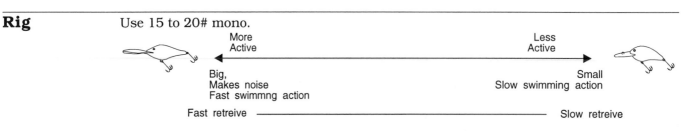

Poppers have a cup shaped head that caused a "pop" when jerked on the surface. Examples: Rebel Pop-R, Rico, Arbogast Hula Popper.

Stickbait examples are Floating Rapala (#7 or #11, silver foil with black back); Bagley Bang-O-Lure; Rebel Floating Minnow.

Technique   Fish points where the water depth drops off (breaks) to deeper holding areas:
- Work from the shallows out past the break
- Work across the face of the point
- Cast parallel to the shore on each side of the point

Always cast past the target 10 to 20 feet and bring the lure back to the prime spot. On a hit, allow fish to submerge the plug before setting the hook. Keep the lure moving after a "miss". Try twitching, stroking and jerking with surface stickbaits.

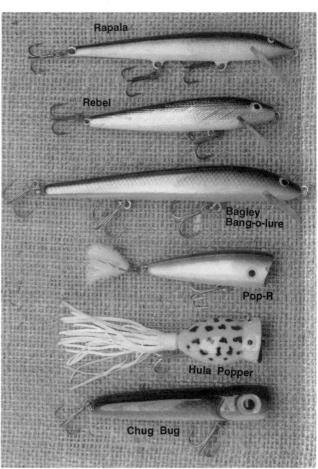

Spinnerbaits & Buzz Baits

When/Where Spinnerbaits are usually used as shallow water lures for active bass in the spring through fall seasons. However spinnerbaits can be effective at greater depths worked slower like Jig and Pigs. They can be fished with heavy 14 to 20 or even 25 pound mono.

Rig Use a 5 1/2 to 6 foot, medium action rod with a conventional bass reel with 14 to 20# lb. line. Rubber skirts are best. Blade Size: #4 or #5. Brands: Turnabout, Haddock, Eagle, Strike King.

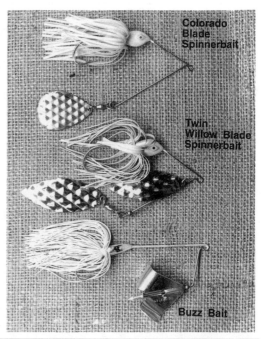

More Active ←———————————→ Less Active

Big, tandem, chrome blades or Buzzbait 1/2 - 3/4 oz. Added trailer   Single Colorado blade 1/8 - 1/4 oz.

Fast retreive ———————————————— Slow retreive

Note for stained, muddy water use more active, noisy baits, with copper or gold blades and retreive slower.

For shallow to mid-depth retrieves, use a 3/8 to 1/2 oz. lure. In stained, dirty water use a single Colorado blade for slower retrieves. Use copper or gold colored blades. Single Colorado blades work slower.

In clear, shallow water use tandem willow blades with nickel or silver blades. Tandem, willow blades can be worked faster.

In deeper water use 1/2 to 3/4 oz. spinners. A single Colorado blade spins better on the fall. Colors: White, chartreuse & white, chartreuse.

Add a pork rind trailer to get a slower lure or an action-tailed plastic worm for bigger fish.

Buzz Baits are good for windy conditions.

Colorado Blade Spinnerbait

Twin Willow Blade Spinnerbait

Buzz Bait

Technique **Spinnerbaits and Buzzbaits** Since these are fast working lures, they are effective for locating active fish concentrations. These are good "weedless" lures for working heavy cover, i.e., stickups, etc. **It is critical with spinnerbaits to work the lure to bump cover than give it a short fall.** Many hits come on the fall.

Spinnerbaits can be effective in muddy, shallow water. Work past points, structure junctions, along fallen tree trunks. Spinnerbaits are also very effective worked like a Jig and Pig in deeper waters.

Buzz Baits When casting, you must retrieve immediately to keep the buzz bait at the surface. Try to keep your line on or near the surface by holding your rod tip high. The buzz bait blade(s) should be breaking the surface.

Zara Spook

When

The Spook is an active-bass surface lure for smooth surface waters. It can be effective all day but works especially well in the early morning and evening.

Rig

Use a long handled trigger stick, a light 6 1/2 to 7 foot casting rod with a flexible tip. Use fifteen to 20 lb. line which floats better making it easier to work the Spook.

Best lure colors are striper, shad, clear patterns.

Add a split ring to the nose eye. This maximizes lure action. If the lure does not properly move from left to right on alternate jerks, it may need to be tuned.

Technique

Work Spooks with a technique called the "dog walk", that results in alternate left and right, side-to-side slides, not splashes. This action is accomplished by casting out, turning 90 degrees to the direction of the cast, placing the rod butt end against the inside wrist and pointing the rod tip down. Retrieve the lure with sharp wrist action jerks.

On a hit, let the lure go under before setting the hook. After a missed strike, slow down the retrieve, using shorter small sideward moves.

Jig and Pig

When

This versatile lure is effective in intermediate and deeper waters for passive or semi-active bass. Jig and Pigs are especially effective during the pre-spawn season and winter months. Because of their weight they can be worked faster than other "finesse lures" and are easier to work in deeper water to 20+ feet.

Rig

Use a medium action casting rod with 12# mono.

More Active → Less Active

Faster sinking 5/8 oz. Added trailer

Slower sinking 1/4 oz.

Swim ———————————— Bottom bouncing ———————————— Flipping, Pitching

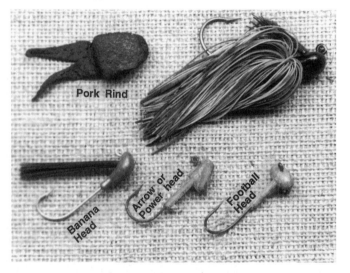

Pork Rind

Banana Head

Arrow or Power head

Football Head

Leadhead Banana heads and football heads are relatively snagless for hopping off the bottom since they land hook up. Banana heads are the most popular jig shape and are good for sinking techniques such as flipping. Lighter weights fall slower for more subtle presentation. Heavier weights are better for penetrating weeds.

Football heads are good for working on the bottom. It sinks fast and doesn't turnover on the sink or when it hits the bottom. Use lighter weights (3/16, 1/4, 5/16, & 3/8 oz.) for shallower depths. Use heavier weights up to 5/8 oz. for penetrating heavy surface weed cover or for sinking to deeper winter depths of 40 to 60 feet.

Arrow shaped or power head jigs sink slower and drift on the drop giving more action but causing more hangups. This jig type will usually land properly with the hook up.

Skirt Live rubber skirts tend to give more action than plastic skirts.

Trailer Pork trailers are best in cooler water. The standard trailer is an Uncle Josh #11 Bait Frog. Use crayfish colors in early season. Hook the trailer "meat down". Use plastic trailers in warm water over 65 degrees or in depths greater than 20 feet. **Brands:** Stanley Jigs, Bobby Garland Spider Jig. Best colors are brown, black, blue & black. In clear water use pumpkin, black, purple, brown or combinations of these colors. In stained or muddy water use brown & orange, black & chartreuse.

Technique

How to swim a jig:
1. Cast beyond the target
2. Count down to the desired depth or drop to the bottom
3. Crank up with several rapid turns
4. Stop
5. Repeat crank and stop until lure is close to boat

Other methods with the Jig and Pig are:

• vertical jigging. Hits occur on the crank or the fall after the stop. Work sharp breaks next to deep water. Bass will usually hold on the edge of a break, 20 to 40 foot depths are easiest to work. Use marker buoys. Move your boat directly over the fish, winter bass won't move very far. Work lures straight up and down, vertically.

• bouncing along the bottom.

• flipping.

Flipping works best when a wind is breaking up the surface, reducing visibility, and not spooking shallow fish. Flip if you can see only half way to the bottom or less or you can't see your lure past 5 feet deep. Also use this technique to fish areas of heavy grass, cattail cover, etc. where you flip the jig to small open areas and allowed to fall.

Rod	Lgth	Line	Power / Action	Lure
	7 1/2	15 - 25	Heavy Fast	3/8 - 2 oz.

Reel	Type	Examples		
	Conv	A regular casting reel with the drag buttoned down or a special reel with a 'flipping switch'		

1. Let out enough line so that the lure is hanging just below knee level, with the rod tip held high and a length of line being held out, down and to the side with your left hand.

2. Swing the lure backward then forward by lowering the rod and then lifting the rod, extending the arms, and finally flipping the wrist. Your left hand should at the same time move forward toward the right hand releasing the length of line.

3. While the lure flies toward the target let line freespool through the left hand. Just before the lure hits the water, grip the line and lift the rod tip slightly. This action stops the lure in mid-air and minimizes the splash.

Pitching is a modification of flipping for reaching targets beyond flipping range. Let out line so that lure hangs about 6" above reel. Set the magnetic drag to minimum. Put the reel in freespool. Hold the lure in your left hand (watch those hooks!) and with the rod tip pointing downward, flip the rod toward the target with your right wrist and arm and simultaneously release the lure. Don't engage the reel allowing the lure to free fall vertically to the bottom. With practice this technique can be very accurate at intermediate distances.

With both pitching and flipping, allow the lure to drop to the bottom, let sit, move slightly, repeat.

To get a soft, quiet lure entry use your wrist and forearm to give a quick, upward lift with the rod tip just before the jig hits the water. Applied correctly, this slight lifting motion will minimize the splash.

Plastic Worms, Grubs, Reapers

When

Plastic worms are very versatile finesse lures. They can be used effectively all seasons and in shallow water to deep water structure. Worms colors, sizes, and rigs can be modified to imitate the current bait forage. Split-shot worms, worked downwind in the summer will be more horizontal, imitating the dominant shad forage. Slip, bullet sinker rigged worms worked off the bottom will have a more vertical orientation imitating a crayfish, the dominant spring forage.

In general, use a longer worm when the bass are actively feeding; use a shorter worm when fish are inactive. The next thing to be determined is the position of the fish. If they are shallow or near the surface of the water, they usually are feeding actively. A slow dropping worm (with a light weight) gives them more time to look over the lure. A fast dropping worm (with a heavier weight) is more effective for the line control and feel necessary to fish for bass that are near the bottom.

Rig

Use a 5 1/2 to 6 foot medium action spinning rod with a sensitive tip for working splitshot worms, Carolina and Texas rigs. Use a conventional reel and casting rod for vertical doodling and swimming a grub or Slug-Go.

	Lgth	Line	Power / Action	Lure	
Rod	5 1/2-6 1/2	4 - 8	Light to Medium Fast	1/8 - 3/8 oz.	

	Type	Examples
Reel	Conv Spin	Use spin for plastic worms, conventional for doodling & grub swimming. Conv: Abu Garcia 2500; Comparable Daiwa and Shimano reels. Spin: Daiwa 1300; Comparable Shimano and Abu Garcia reels.

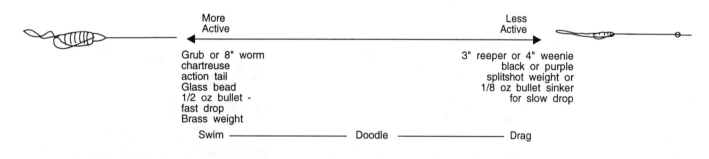

More Active → Less Active

Grub or 8" worm
chartreuse
action tail
Glass bead
1/2 oz bullet -
fast drop
Brass weight

3" reeper or 4" weenie
black or purple
splitshot weight or
1/8 oz bullet sinker
for slow drop

Swim ——————— Doodle ——————— Drag

Worms 4 - 6", Examples: Culprit, Super Floater, Kalins Weenies, Don Iovino worms, reapers, grubs, etc. Worm Colors: Black, purple, brown, cinnamon, and cinnamon combinations.

Grubs Yamamoto, Kalin. Grub Colors: Salt and pepper, salt and pepper/chartreuse, also worm colors above.

Hooks 4" Worms: Use a #1 to 1/0 hook for 4" worms. Use a 1/0 to 2/0 for 6" to 8" worms. For grubs use a 2/0 hook. For reapers use a #2 hook. Use a 2X or 3X long-shank sproat hook with baitholder barbs on the shank. Quality brands are Grey Shadow (fine wire), Black Weapon, Gamakatsu.

Bullet Weights Non-lead, environmentally safe weights are new. Iovino markets a brass weight that is claimed to make fish attracting noise when used with a faceted glass bead. 3/16 oz. is standard. Use heavier for deeper.

To keep the worm from slipping down the hook shank, insert a piece of 70-80# mono through the head of the worm and the eye of the hook. Cut off any excess.

If a seam is visible, embed the hook and penetrate along the seam. If the worm has a flat side, reinsert the hook through the middle of that side. It is important that the worm is straight on the hook. This will minimize unnatural spin on the retrieve. This is especially true when using curly-tailed, action worms when they are drifted or reeled in for action.

Technique

There are many techniques for working a worm. Probably the most common technique used with split-shot, Carolina & Texas rigged worms is:

1. Cast out and let the rig sink to the bottom. Keep the slack out of the line on the drop and watch the line for indications of a pickup, hesitations in the drop, sudden slack in the line, etc. **Important: 95% of the pickups can't be felt, you must constantly watch the line for unexplained movements. When in doubt, strike!**
2. Once the lure reaches the bottom, retrieve moving the rod tip **slowly** and erratically.
3. Using only the wrists, move slowly from almost a horizontal position to short of vertical. If you are working slowly enough, the lure will maintain contact with the bottom.
4. Lower the rod tip again to almost horizontal while reeling in the slack line and repeat.
5. If you either know or can feel that the lure has dropped over a break or ledge, try to let the lure fall naturally by releasing line tension. Many hits will come on such a drop.
6. If you get a pickup, set the hook by swinging back up sharply with both hands. By working the rod only between 9 and 11 o'clock, you will have room to strike on any hit.

Doodling requires a rod with a flexible, sensitive rod tip but stiff back and a medium weight conventional reel such as an Ambassadeur 2500, 3400 or 3500 reel. When the sinking worm is in the fish holding area, start shaking the rod tip with light, short, rapid movements. Make the worm wiggle. Take up line to keep the worm off the bottom. Experiment with different depths. Watch the bouncing rod tip carefully. A hit will be a slight pull or weight on the rod tip. Vertical doodling is limited to fishing deeper water over 20 feet.

Dragging a worm very slowly across the bottom by reeling in slowly is also effective for very passive fish. The special Do-Nothin rig can be combined with this technique.

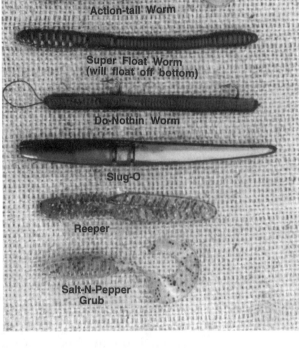

Green Weenie

Action-tail Worm

Super Float Worm
(will float off bottom)

Do-Nothin Worm

Slug-O

Reeper

Salt-N-Pepper
Grub

Stitching is a variation of dragging where you retrieve the line slowly by hand. After the cast, with the spinning reel bail open, pinch the line between your thumb and forefinger. To retrieve line, while still pinching the line, reach up with the last three fingers and pull the line down slowly into the palm. Pause and wait for a pickup. Release the forefinger and thumb hold and re-pinch up the line. Repeat this procedure very slowly and methodically. Retreive loose line periodically by closing the bail and winding in.

Swimming a worm by slowly drifting a worm or by casting and reeling in is especially effective with curly-tailed, action type worms, grubs, or reapers. This technique is good for shallow waters.

More Info

For more detail see the video *Finesse Fishing for Bass* by Don Iovino.

Worm, Grub, and Reeper Rigs and Techniques:

1. Shake & Swim / Doodle Slide for shallow water fish in sparse or heavy cover.

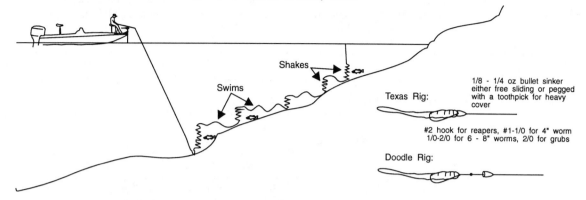

Shakes

Swims

Texas Rig:

1/8 - 1/4 oz bullet sinker
either free sliding or pegged
with a toothpick for heavy
cover

#2 hook for reapers, #1-1/0 for 4" worm
1/0-2/0 for 6 - 8" worms, 2/0 for grubs

Doodle Rig:

2. Shaking / Doodling for graphed fish in water 15 feet and deeper.

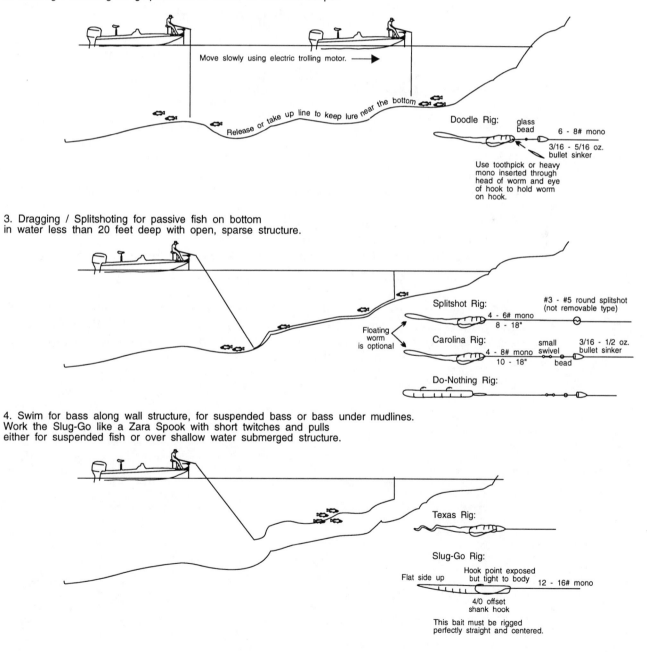

Move slowly using electric trolling motor. ➡

Release or take up line to keep lure near the bottom

Doodle Rig:

glass
bead

6 - 8# mono

3/16 - 5/16 oz.
bullet sinker

Use toothpick or heavy
mono inserted through
head of worm and eye
of hook to hold worm
on hook.

3. Dragging / Splitshoting for passive fish on bottom
in water less than 20 feet deep with open, sparse structure.

Splitshot Rig:

#3 - #5 round splitshot
(not removable type)

4 - 6# mono

8 - 18"

Floating
worm
is optional

Carolina Rig:

small
swivel

3/16 - 1/2 oz.
bullet sinker

4 - 8# mono

10 - 18"

bead

Do-Nothing Rig:

4. Swim for bass along wall structure, for suspended bass or bass under mudlines.
Work the Slug-Go like a Zara Spook with short twitches and pulls
either for suspended fish or over shallow water submerged structure.

Texas Rig:

Slug-Go Rig:

Flat side up

Hook point exposed
but tight to body

12 - 16# mono

4/0 offset
shank hook

This bait must be rigged
perfectly straight and centered.

Tube Baits (Gitzits), Darter Jigs, P-Heads

When   These are passive-bass lures especially effective during the pre-spawn, early spawn and the post-spawn period.

Rig   Use a medium weight spinning reel on a 6 to 7 foot graphite rod with a sensitive tip. Fish these lures on 4# to 6# line. Use a 1/16 oz. weight in water around 5' to 6' deep. Use a 1/8 to 1/4 oz. weight in water > 6' deep. Colors: Shad colors are smoke, smoke sparkle, clear; crawfish colors are pumpkin, motor oil, smoke & red flake, green & orange flake.

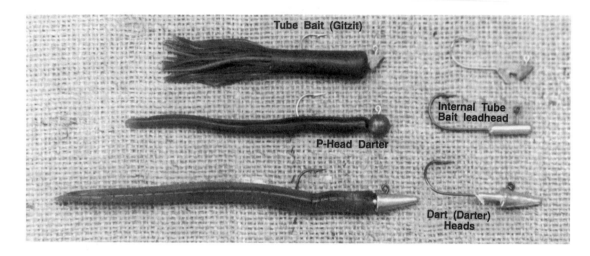

Technique   These are subtle lures for fishing medium depths during tough fishing conditions requiring smaller baits & lighter lines. Tube baits are especially effective during pre-spawn. Darter heads and p-heads catch fish during the tough post-spawn season.

Most hits come on the fall. The goal is to keep the bait swimming just off the bottom. On pickups, reel in to the drag. To fish this bait you:
• Cast into the wind, let the lure fall on a slack line, reel in some line and let fall again or
• Let the lure fall to the bottom and pop it making the lure jump.

You can also rig tube baits (Gitzits) with the plastic worm splitshot technique. Cast out and work it back slowly on the bottom or drag it on a slow drift. A number 2 or 3 long-shank, light wire hook is pegged to the inside of the bait with a flat toothpick. Rig a 1/8 oz. bullet sinker 18" ahead of the bait.

Jigging Spoons

When   This is a winter technique used for metered deep water fish. However, spoons are also effective for summer, surface shad boils.

Rig   Spoon examples are Hopkins #075 "Shorty" (3/4 oz.), Kastmaster, 1/2 oz., Haddock Jig 'N Spoon, 3/8 oz., Mann-O-Lure. Fish on 10 to 12# mono. Add an "O" ring to the lure. Optional: Replace factory hook with larger hook for better results, i.e., a 2/0 treble.

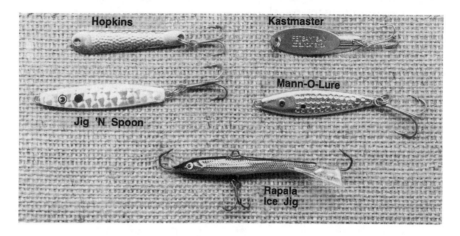

Technique   Work vertically over graphed fish, especially fish suspended near breaks or around suspended shad schools or work the lure just below the shad or bottom graphed bass. See the winter techniques diagram in the Seasonal Patterns section. Let the spoon drop to the bottom. Jig the spoon vertically so that at bottom of jig, the spoon is laying on the lake bottom. Use short, 1 foot, slow jigs. On the fall, don't allow slack in the line. Strikes usually come on the fall. Watch for any hesitation in the line. Be patient, it often takes 25+ jigs in one spot to get a strike. Try dragging or stitching a worm or crawfish if the spoon isn't working.

Live Bait

Some baits, notably crayfish and shiners, are illegal to use at some lakes.

Live bait is the ultimate finesse technique. When winter fishing for big bass, you can sit for hours soaking a crayfish, waiting for just one bite. That's finesse! Use small 2" crayfish. Nose hooking is most effective but requires a gentle cast to avoid tearing loose. When hooking through the bony nose, work the hook gently to avoid breakage. Or hook the crayfish through the tail end. Slow dragging, stitching or even still fishing a crayfish can catch monster bass!

For nightcrawler worms use a worm inflator to inject air into worm. This makes the worm float off the bottom. Add a #5 or smaller split shot for better control especially at greater depths. Run the hook through the worm collar and re-embed in the body to make weedless.

Work shiners (minnows) by:
- casting lip-hooked shiners to shallow water structures. Keep the minnow in the bait well between casts. The minnow will only stay lively 5 to 6 casts.
- Fishing it below a bobber near tules, lily pads, etc. Hook it lightly above the spine, behind the dorsal fin.
- Flylining it near shallow structure.

Bass Map Index

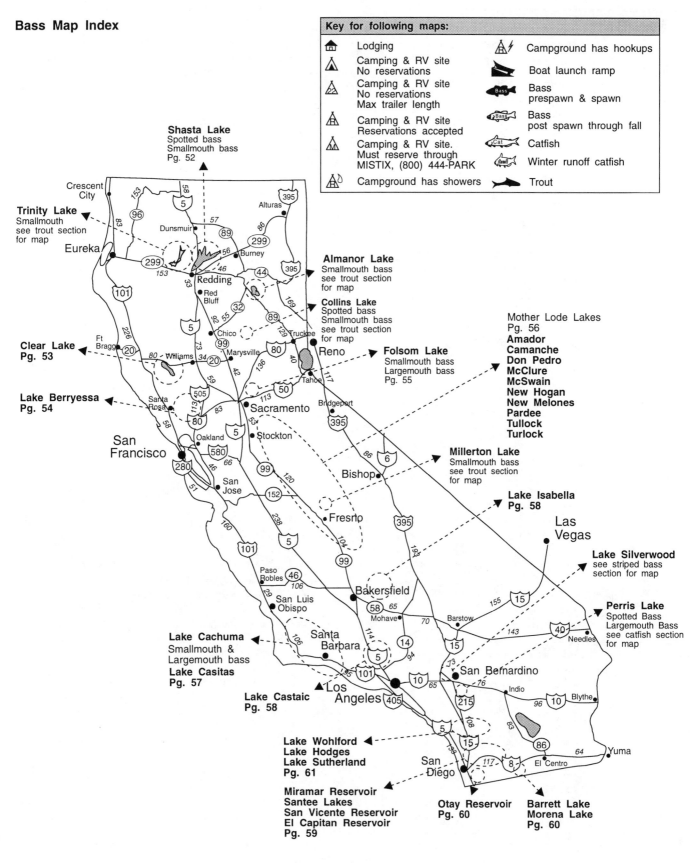

Key for following maps:

Lodging		Campground has hookups	
Camping & RV site No reservations		Boat launch ramp	
Camping & RV site No reservations Max trailer length		Bass prespawn & spawn	
Camping & RV site Reservations accepted		Bass post spawn through fall	
Camping & RV site. Must reserve through MISTIX, (800) 444-PARK		Catfish	
Campground has showers		Winter runoff catfish	
		Trout	

Shasta Lake
Spotted bass
Smallmouth bass
Pg. 52

Trinity Lake
Smallmouth
see trout section
for map

Almanor Lake
Smallmouth bass
see trout section
for map

Collins Lake
Spotted bass
Smallmouth bass
see trout section
for map

Mother Lode Lakes
Pg. 56
Amador
Camanche
Don Pedro
McClure
McSwain
New Hogan
New Melones
Pardee
Tullock
Turlock

Clear Lake
Pg. 53

Folsom Lake
Smallmouth bass
Largemouth bass
Pg. 55

Lake Berryessa
Pg. 54

Millerton Lake
Smallmouth bass
see trout section
for map

Lake Isabella
Pg. 58

Lake Silverwood
see striped bass
section for map

Perris Lake
Spotted Bass
Largemouth Bass
see catfish section
for map

Lake Cachuma
Smallmouth &
Largemouth bass
Lake Casitas
Pg. 57

Lake Castaic
Pg. 58

Lake Wohlford
Lake Hodges
Lake Sutherland
Pg. 61

Miramar Reservoir
Santee Lakes
San Vicente Reservoir
El Capitan Reservoir
Pg. 59

Otay Reservoir
Pg. 60

Barrett Lake
Morena Lake
Pg. 60

Shasta Lake

> CAUTION: Not to be used for navigation

Season: All year. Limit 5, min. size 12"
Bass best from March through May.
Brown Trout best February and March.
Trout best deep trolled in June and after lake turnover,
late November and early December.
Catfish in back coves July and August.

Fishing Info:
Trout Plants, (916) 225-2146
Trout Guides:
Gary Manies, (916) 347-5494
Shasta Lake Sportfishing, (916) 275-2278
Bass Guides:
Gary Manies - see above
Russ Meyer, (916) 275-0513
General Info:
Redding Chamber of Commerce, (916) 225-4433
Shasta Cascade Assoc., (800) 4-SHASTA
Houseboats:
Holiday Flotels, Redding
(916) 275-5570

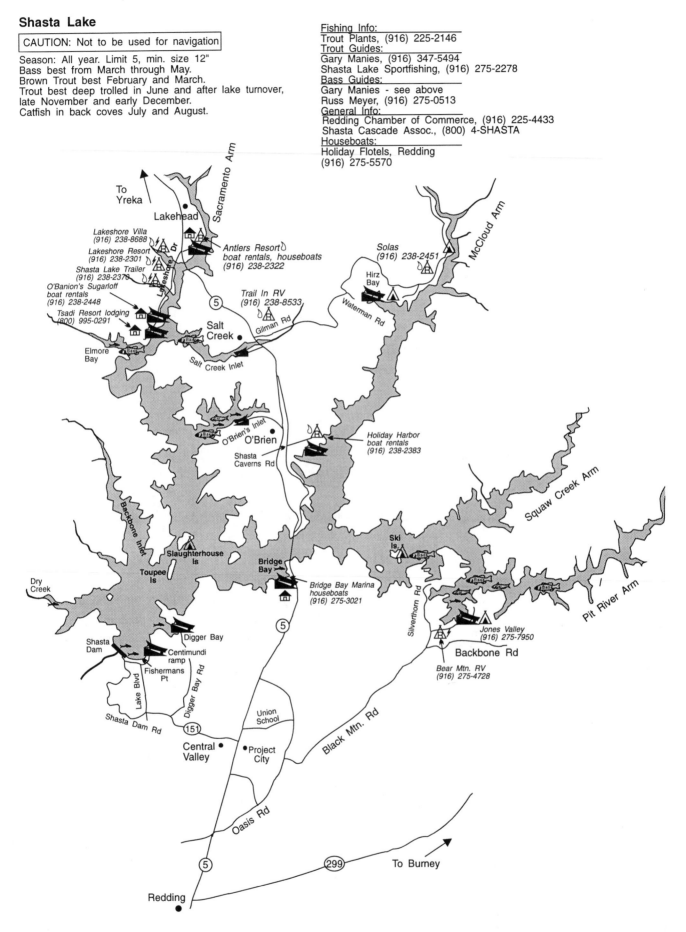

Clear Lake

CAUTION! Not to be used for navigation.

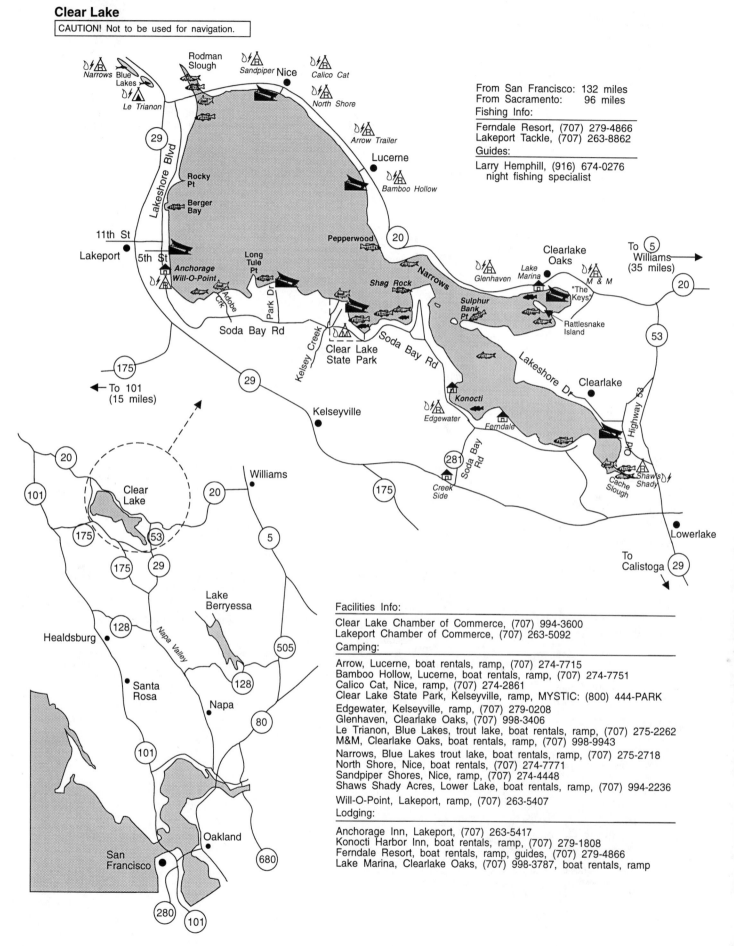

From San Francisco: 132 miles
From Sacramento: 96 miles
Fishing Info:

Ferndale Resort, (707) 279-4866
Lakeport Tackle, (707) 263-8862
Guides:

Larry Hemphill, (916) 674-0276
night fishing specialist

Facilities Info:

Clear Lake Chamber of Commerce, (707) 994-3600
Lakeport Chamber of Commerce, (707) 263-5092
Camping:

Arrow, Lucerne, boat rentals, ramp, (707) 274-7715
Bamboo Hollow, Lucerne, boat rentals, ramp, (707) 274-7751
Calico Cat, Nice, ramp, (707) 274-2861
Clear Lake State Park, Kelseyville, ramp, MYSTIC: (800) 444-PARK
Edgewater, Kelseyville, ramp, (707) 279-0208
Glenhaven, Clearlake Oaks, (707) 998-3406
Le Trianon, Blue Lakes, trout lake, boat rentals, ramp, (707) 275-2262
M&M, Clearlake Oaks, boat rentals, ramp, (707) 998-9943
Narrows, Blue Lakes trout lake, boat rentals, ramp, (707) 275-2718
North Shore, Nice, boat rentals, (707) 274-7771
Sandpiper Shores, Nice, ramp, (707) 274-4448
Shaws Shady Acres, Lower Lake, boat rentals, ramp, (707) 994-2236

Will-O-Point, Lakeport, ramp, (707) 263-5407
Lodging:

Anchorage Inn, Lakeport, (707) 263-5417
Konocti Harbor Inn, boat rentals, ramp, (707) 279-1808
Ferndale Resort, boat rentals, ramp, guides, (707) 279-4866
Lake Marina, Clearlake Oaks, (707) 998-3787, boat rentals, ramp

Lake Berryessa

CAUTION! Not to be used for navigation.

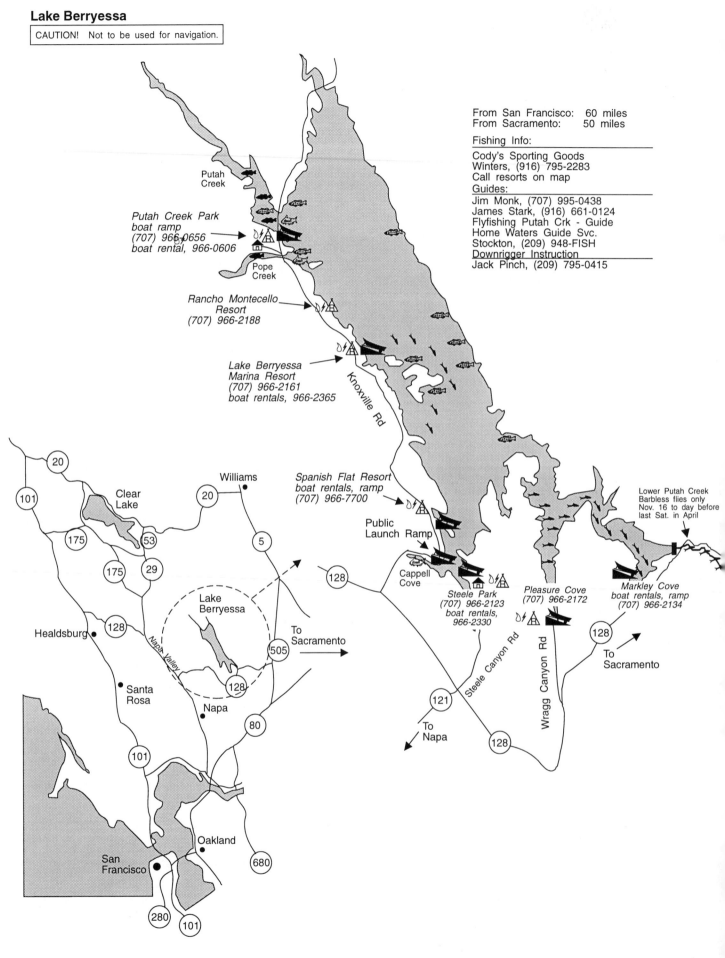

From San Francisco: 60 miles
From Sacramento: 50 miles

Fishing Info:

Cody's Sporting Goods
Winters, (916) 795-2283
Call resorts on map
Guides:
Jim Monk, (707) 995-0438
James Stark, (916) 661-0124
Flyfishing Putah Crk - Guide
Home Waters Guide Svc.
Stockton, (209) 948-FISH
Downrigger Instruction
Jack Pinch, (209) 795-0415

Putah
Creek

Putah Creek Park
boat ramp
(707) 966-0656
boat rental, 966-0606

Pope
Creek

Rancho Montecello
Resort
(707) 966-2188

Lake Berryessa
Marina Resort
(707) 966-2161
boat rentals, 966-2365

Knoxville Rd

Spanish Flat Resort
boat rentals, ramp
(707) 966-7700

Public
Launch Ramp

Cappell
Cove

Steele Park
(707) 966-2123
boat rentals,
966-2330

Pleasure Cove
(707) 966-2172

Lower Putah Creek
Barbless flies only
Nov. 16 to day before
last Sat. in April

Markley Cove
boat rentals, ramp
(707) 966-2134

Steele Canyon Rd

Wragg Canyon Rd

To
Sacramento

Clear
Lake

Williams

Lake
Berryessa

To
Sacramento

Healdsburg

Napa Valley

Santa
Rosa

Napa

To
Napa

Oakland

San
Francisco

Folsom Lake

Bass best from mid-March to early May.
Trout best from early March with clearing waters
to deep water trolling in early June.

Fishing Info:
The Fish'N Hole, (916) 791-2248
Sacramento Pro Tackle, (916) 925-0529
Folsom Lake Marina, (916) 933-1300
Jon Walton, (510) 782-3932
General Info:
Folsom Lake, (916) 988-0205

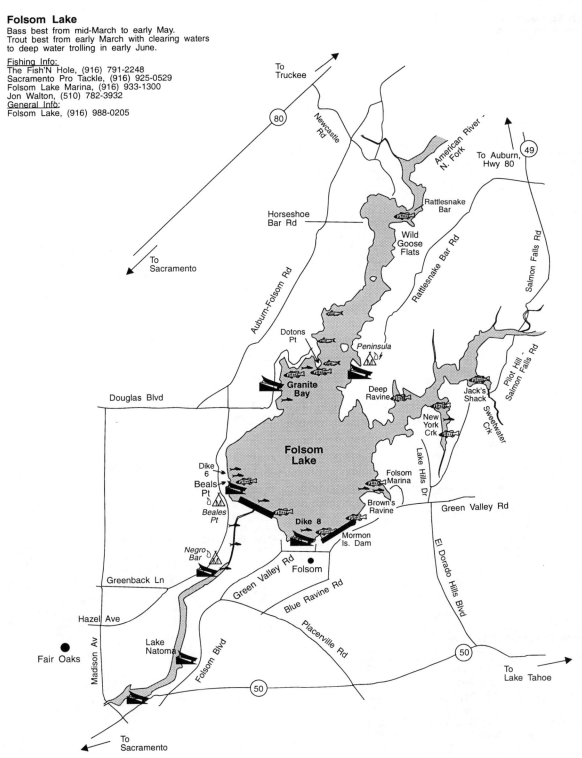

Motherload Bass & Trout Lakes
Phone Area Code is 209

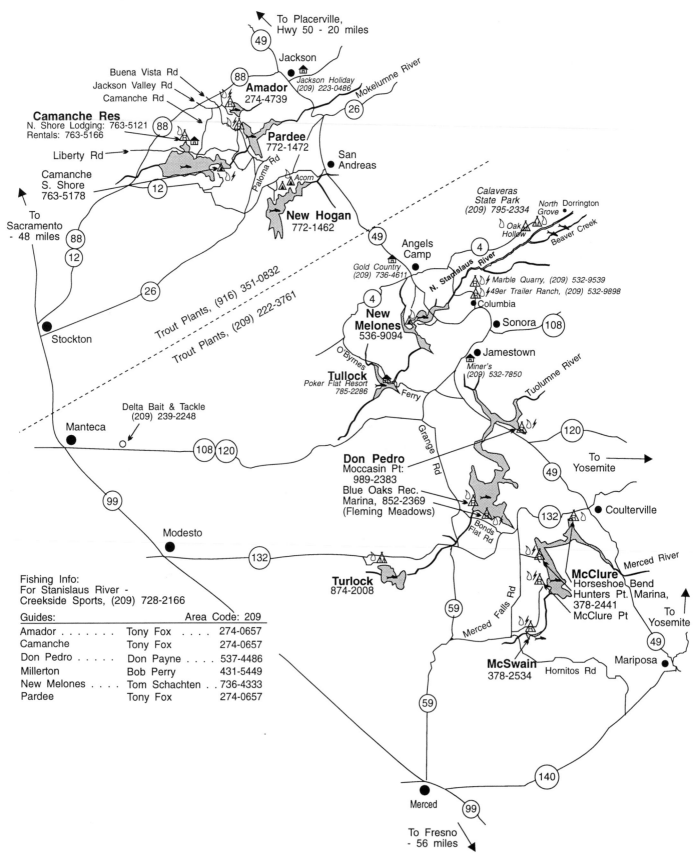

Fishing Info:
For Stanislaus River -
Creekside Sports, (209) 728-2166

Guides:		Area Code: 209
Amador	Tony Fox	274-0657
Camanche	Tony Fox	274-0657
Don Pedro	Don Payne	537-4486
Millerton	Bob Perry	431-5449
New Melones	Tom Schachten . .	736-4333
Pardee	Tony Fox	274-0657

Southern California Big Bass Lakes, Map 1
Call about private boat type and size restrictions

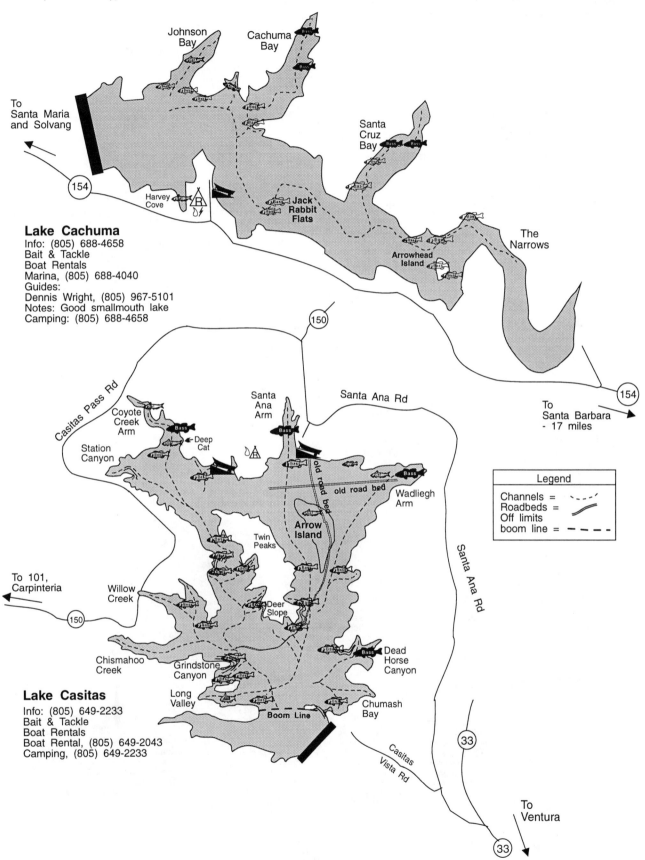

To
Santa Maria
and Solvang

154

Johnson
Bay

Cachuma
Bay

Santa
Cruz
Bay

The
Narrows

Harvey
Cove

Jack
Rabbit
Flats

Arrowhead
Island

Lake Cachuma
Info: (805) 688-4658
Bait & Tackle
Boat Rentals
Marina, (805) 688-4040
Guides:
Dennis Wright, (805) 967-5101
Notes: Good smallmouth lake
Camping: (805) 688-4658

150

Casitas Pass Rd

Coyote
Creek
Arm

Deep
Cat

Station
Canyon

Santa
Ana
Arm

Santa Ana Rd

154

To
Santa Barbara
- 17 miles

Santa Ana Rd

old road bed

old road bed

Wadliegh
Arm

Arrow
Island

Twin
Peaks

Legend

Channels =
Roadbeds =
Off limits
boom line =

To 101,
Carpinteria

150

Willow
Creek

Deer
Slope

Chismahoo
Creek

Grindstone
Canyon

Long
Valley

Dead
Horse
Canyon

Chumash
Bay

Boom Line

Lake Casitas
Info: (805) 649-2233
Bait & Tackle
Boat Rentals
Boat Rental, (805) 649-2043
Camping, (805) 649-2233

Casitas
Vista Rd

33

To
Ventura

33

Southern California Big Bass Lakes, Map 2
Call about private boat type and size restrictions

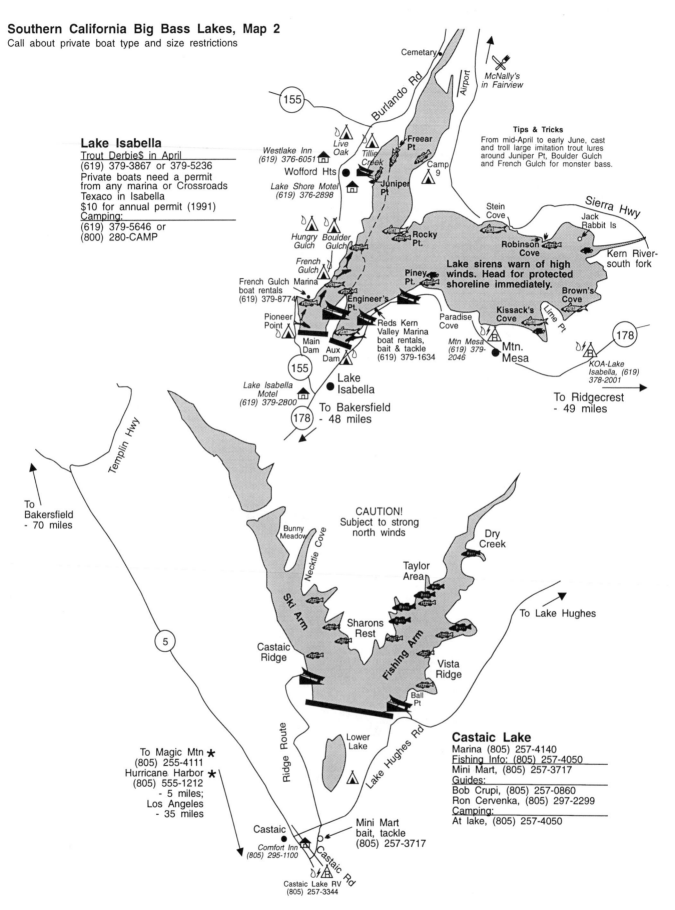

Lake Isabella
Trout Derbie$ in April
(619) 379-3867 or 379-5236
Private boats need a permit
from any marina or Crossroads
Texaco in Isabella
$10 for annual permit (1991)
Camping:
(619) 379-5646 or
(800) 280-CAMP

Cemetary
Airport
McNally's
in Fairview

155
Burlando Rd

Tips & Tricks
From mid-April to early June, cast
and troll large imitation trout lures
around Juniper Pt, Boulder Gulch
and French Gulch for monster bass.

Westlake Inn
(619) 376-6051
Wofford Hts
Lake Shore Motel
(619) 376-2898

Live
Oak
Tillie
Creek
Freear
Pt
Camp
9
Juniper
Pt

Sierra Hwy
Stein
Cove
Jack
Rabbit Is
Kern River-
south fork
Robinson
Cove
Rocky
Pt.
Hungry
Gulch
Boulder
Gulch
French
Gulch
French Gulch Marina
boat rentals
(619) 379-8774
Engineer's
Pt.
Piney
Pt.
**Lake sirens warn of high
winds. Head for protected
shoreline immediately.**
Brown's
Cove
Lime Pt.
Kissack's
Cove

Pioneer
Point
Reds Kern
Valley Marina
boat rentals,
bait & tackle
(619) 379-1634
Paradise
Cove
Main
Dam
Aux
Dam
Mtn Mesa
(619) 379-
2046
Mtn.
Mesa
178
KOA-Lake
Isabella, (619)
378-2001

155
Lake Isabella
Motel
(619) 379-2800
Lake
Isabella
To Bakersfield
- 48 miles
178
To Ridgecrest
- 49 miles

Templin Hwy
To
Bakersfield
- 70 miles

CAUTION!
Subject to strong
north winds
Dry
Creek
Bunny
Meadow
Necktie Cove
Taylor
Area
To Lake Hughes
Ski Arm
Sharons
Rest
Fishing Arm
Castaic
Ridge
Vista
Ridge
Ball
Pt
5
To Magic Mtn ✱
(805) 255-4111
Hurricane Harbor ✱
(805) 555-1212
- 5 miles;
Los Angeles
- 35 miles
Ridge Route
Lower
Lake
Lake Hughes Rd
Mini Mart
bait, tackle
(805) 257-3717

Castaic Lake
Marina (805) 257-4140
Fishing Info: (805) 257-4050
Mini Mart, (805) 257-3717
Guides:
Bob Crupi, (805) 257-0860
Ron Cervenka, (805) 297-2299
Camping:
At lake, (805) 257-4050

Castaic
Comfort Inn
(805) 295-1100
Castaic Rd
Castaic Lake RV
(805) 257-3344

San Diego Area Big Bass Lakes, Map 1

Various San Diego lakes are closed for different periods from mid-September to February.
For all San Diego Lakes not separately listed:
Fishing Info: (619) 465-3474
Boat Rentals: (619) 390-0222

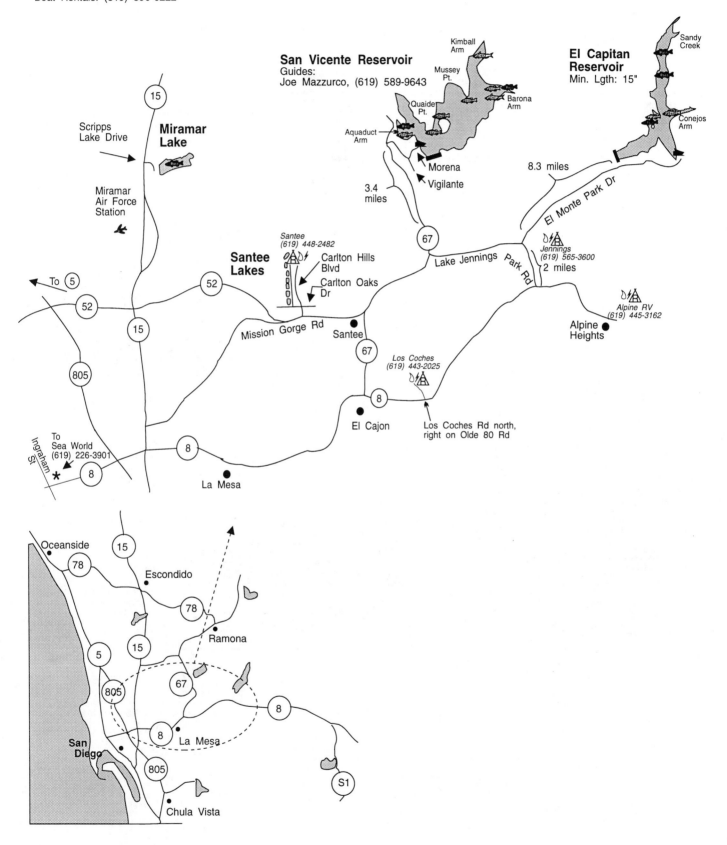

San Vicente Reservoir
Guides:
Joe Mazzurco, (619) 589-9643

El Capitan Reservoir
Min. Lgth: 15"

Kimball Arm

Mussey Pt.

Sandy Creek

Quaide Pt.

Barona Arm

Aquaduct Arm

Conejos Arm

Miramar Lake

Scripps Lake Drive

Miramar Air Force Station

Morena

Vigilante

3.4 miles

8.3 miles

El Monte Park Dr

15

67

Lake Jennings Park Rd

Jennings (619) 565-3600 2 miles

Santee (619) 448-2482

Santee Lakes

Carlton Hills Blvd
Carlton Oaks Dr

52

To 5

52

15

805

Mission Gorge Rd

Santee

Alpine RV (619) 445-3162

Alpine Heights

67

Los Coches (619) 443-2025

8

El Cajon

Los Coches Rd north, right on Olde 80 Rd

To Sea World (619) 226-3901

Ingraham St

8

8

La Mesa

Oceanside

78

15

Escondido

78

Ramona

5

15

805

67

8

8

La Mesa

San Diego

805

Chula Vista

S1

San Diego Area Big Bass Lakes, Map 2

Various San Diego lakes are closed for different periods from mid-September to February.

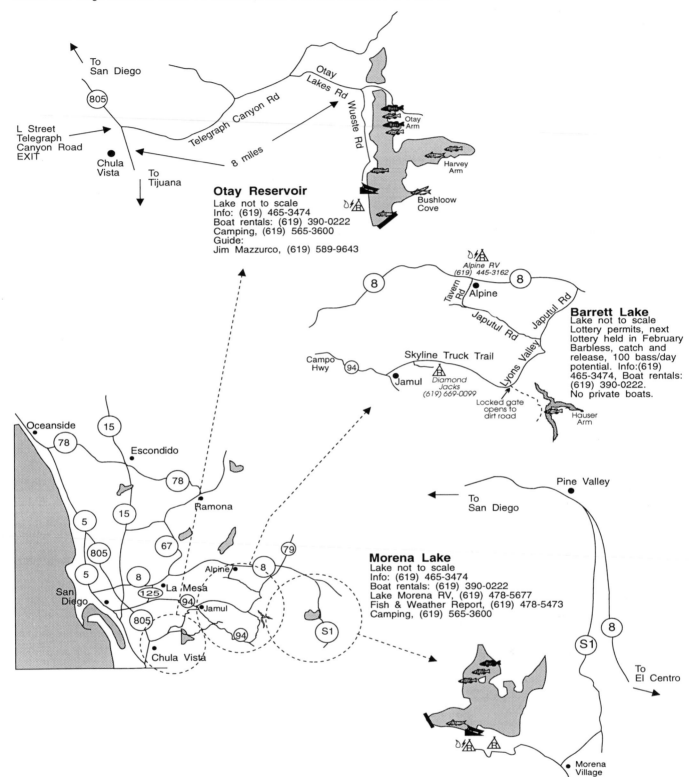

To
San Diego

805

L Street
Telegraph
Canyon Road
EXIT

Chula
Vista

To
Tijuana

Telegraph Canyon Rd

Otay
Lakes Rd

Wueste Rd

8 miles

Bass

Bass
Otay
Arm

Harvey
Arm

Bushloow
Cove

Otay Reservoir
Lake not to scale
Info: (619) 465-3474
Boat rentals: (619) 390-0222
Camping, (619) 565-3600
Guide:
Jim Mazzurco, (619) 589-9643

Alpine RV
(619) 445-3162

8

8

Tavern Rd

Alpine

Japutul Rd

Japutul Rd

Lyons Valley

Barrett Lake
Lake not to scale
Lottery permits, next
lottery held in February
Barbless, catch and
release, 100 bass/day
potential. Info:(619)
465-3474, Boat rentals:
(619) 390-0222.
No private boats.

Campo
Hwy

94

Skyline Truck Trail

Jamul

Diamond
Jacks
(619) 669-0099

Locked gate
opens to
dirt road

Hauser
Arm

Oceanside

15

78

Escondido

78

15

5

Ramona

805

67

Alpine

8

79

5

8

125

La Mesa

94

Jamul

San
Diego

805

94

S1

Chula Vista

Pine Valley

To
San Diego

Morena Lake
Lake not to scale
Info: (619) 465-3474
Boat rentals: (619) 390-0222
Lake Morena RV, (619) 478-5677
Fish & Weather Report, (619) 478-5473
Camping, (619) 565-3600

S1

8

To
El Centro

Morena
Village

San Diego Area Big Bass Lakes, Map 3

Various San Diego lakes are closed for different periods from mid-September to February.

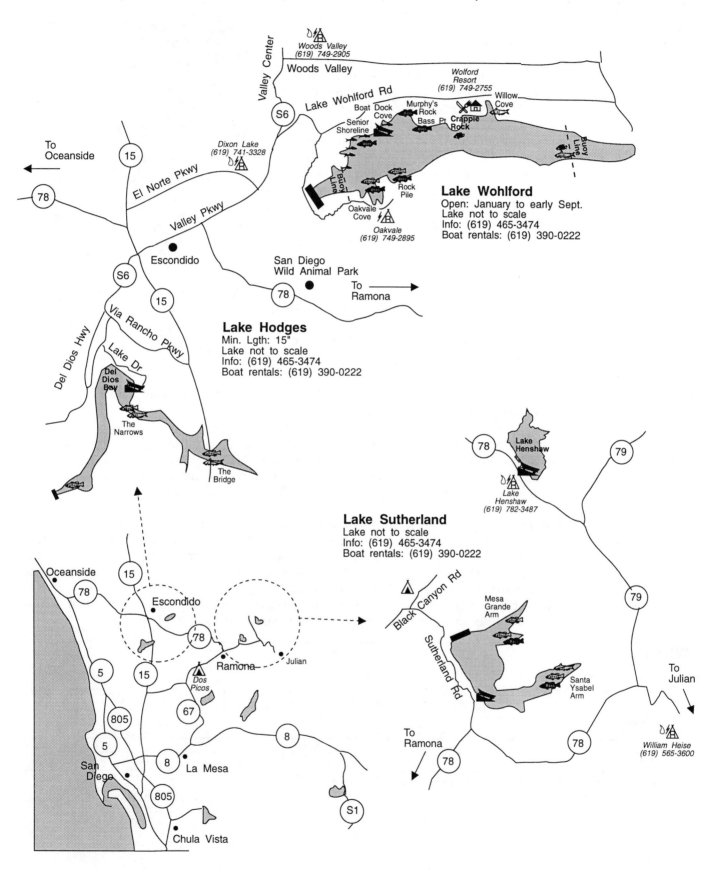

Woods Valley
(619) 749-2905

Woods Valley

Wolford
Resort
(619) 749-2755

Lake Wohlford Rd

Willow
Cove

Boat Dock
Cove

Murphy's
Rock

Bass Pt

Crappie
Rock

Senior
Shoreline

Buoy Line

Valley Center

S6

To
Oceanside

15

78

El Norte Pkwy

Dixon Lake
(619) 741-3328

Valley Pkwy

Buoy Line

Rock
Pile

Lake Wohlford
Open: January to early Sept.
Lake not to scale
Info: (619) 465-3474
Boat rentals: (619) 390-0222

Oakvale
Cove

Oakvale
(619) 749-2895

Escondido

San Diego
Wild Animal Park

To
Ramona

S6

15

78

Via Rancho Pkwy

Del Dios Hwy

Lake Dr

Del
Dios
Bay

The
Narrows

The
Bridge

Lake Hodges
Min. Lgth: 15"
Lake not to scale
Info: (619) 465-3474
Boat rentals: (619) 390-0222

Lake
Henshaw

78

79

Lake
Henshaw
(619) 782-3487

Lake Sutherland
Lake not to scale
Info: (619) 465-3474
Boat rentals: (619) 390-0222

Oceanside

15

78

Escondido

78

Julian

Ramona

Black Canyon Rd

Mesa
Grande
Arm

79

5

15

Dos
Picos

Sutherland Rd

Santa
Ysabel
Arm

To
Julian

805

67

8

To
Ramona

William Heise
(619) 565-3600

5

8

La Mesa

78

78

San
Diego

805

S1

Chula Vista

STRIPED BASS

Where

River Structure

- Structure includes points, submerged trees, pilings, river holes, almost anything that will breakup the current, provide shade and give shelter. Good holes are often found at the mouths of creeks and agricultural inlets.

- If there's a current or tide, stripers will be on the bottom. They'll lurk on the down-current side of structure waiting for the current to bring food. Effective trolling puts the lure near this structure, moving naturally with the current.

Lake Structure

- In the late summer, stripers surface feed in the early morning.
- Bigger fish are often deeper, 25 to 60 feet.
- Stripers congregate near dam spillway whitewater.
- Stripers follow the predominant forage—planted trout in the winter and early spring, shad in the summer and fall.

Tomi Kelley caught this chunky striped bass in April on the Sacramento River

Bob Sparre's Guide Service, Fair Oaks

In the cool months, trout concentrate around the stocking ramp especially within 1 to 3 days of the plant. They'll be near stream inlets and shoreline dropoffs. In the summer months they'll be at the thermocline. They'll gather near dams where the released water causes a current. For more structure see the Rainbow Trout section.

Shad are plankton feeders. Since plankton can grow almost anywhere on a lake near the surface, it is harder to pin-point shad location. Shad tend to be in the shallows and coves in the early morning hours and go deeper and suspend offshore during the rest of the day. Small stripers will follow them into the shallows. The bigger stripers will hold in deeper water toward outside points. The seagulls also follow the shad. Always keep a lookout for working birds. Birds hovering and swooping usually means striper are surface boiling. Several seagulls sitting on a rocky point can mean stripers just offshore.

When

Striped Bass Fishing Calendar:

	January	February	March	April	May	June	July	August	Sept.	October	November	Dec.
Northern California				San Luis & O'Neill Reservoirs			New Hogan Res.			Delta Fall Run		
			Delta Spring Run							San Luis & O'Neill Reservoirs		
				Sac River near Colusa						Lake Mendocino		
Southern California						Lake Mead, Colorado River						
						Lake Mohave, Colorado River						
						Lake Havasu, Colorado River						
		Pyramid Lake								Pyramid Lake		
			Silverwood Lake							Silverwood Lake		
		Skinner Lake								Santa Margarita Lake		
										Skinner Lake		
										Castaic Lake		

The best bite is in the early morning and dusk hours. Top-water boiling is limited to the morning hours in late summer and early fall when water temperatures are above 65 degrees. Generally the bite slows when the sun hits the water. The fish move deeper and to the bottom during the day or congregate at spillways on the edge of the white water. In the winter, the bite turns off when rain run-offs cool and muddy the water.

The delta bite is influenced by the tides. Stripers will hug the bottom and wait for the tides to sweep food by. The bite turns on during strong tidal flows.

Bait/Lures

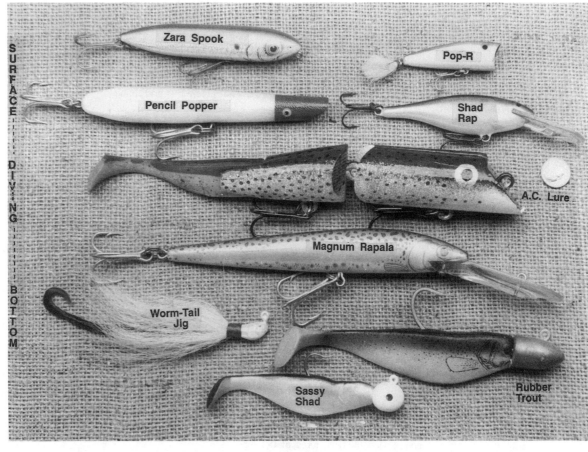

Rig

Striped Bass Casting and Bait

Rod	Lgth	Line	Power / Action	Lure	
	5 1/2 - 6 1/2	10 - 17	Light to Medium Fast	1/4 - 3/4 oz.	
	Type	**Size**	**Examples**		
Reel	Conv Spin	150 - 200 yds 10# mono	Conv: Abu Garcia 5500; Comparable Daiwa and Shimano reels. Spin: Daiwa 1600; Comparable Shimano and Abu Garcia reels.		

Striped Bass Troll

Rod	Lgth	Line	Action	Examples
	6 - 6 1/2	mono or 18 leadcore	Medium	Daiwa EL772
	Type	**Size**	**Examples**	
Reel	Conv	100 - 200 yds mono or 18# leadcore	Penn 209, 309	

Striped Bass Rigs
1. Bait Rigs:

a. Bottom Still Fishing

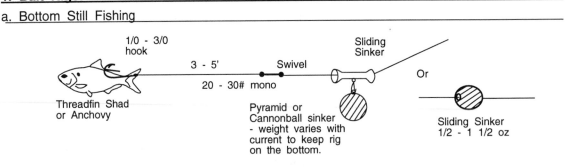

1/0 - 3/0 hook

3 - 5'

Swivel

Sliding Sinker

Or

20 - 30# mono

Threadfin Shad or Anchovy

Pyramid or Cannonball sinker - weight varies with current to keep rig on the bottom.

Sliding Sinker 1/2 - 1 1/2 oz

2. Trolling / Casting Rigs:

Select lures to imitate common forage fish. Use herring and anchovy imitations in San Francisco Bay, use shad imitations in the Sacramento River, use trout and shad imitations in the Colorado river and in lakes. For lakes use shad imitations in the summer and fall, use trout imitations in the winter and spring.

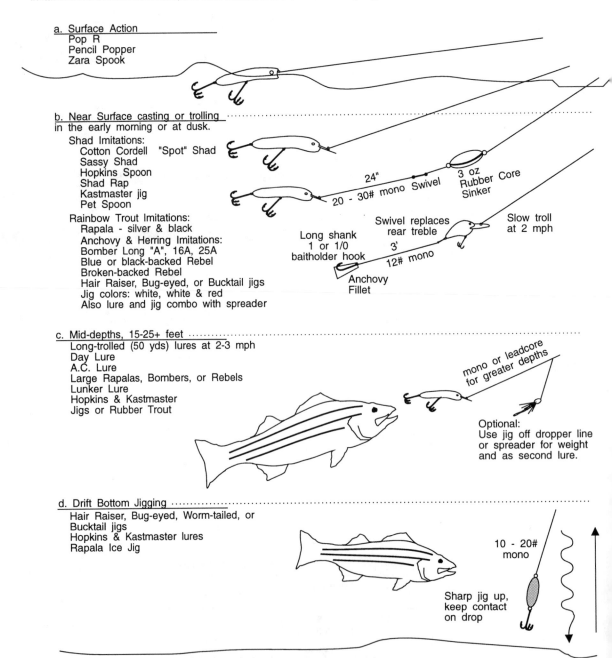

a. Surface Action
   Pop R
   Pencil Popper
   Zara Spook

b. Near Surface casting or trolling
in the early morning or at dusk.
   Shad Imitations:
      Cotton Cordell "Spot" Shad
      Sassy Shad
      Hopkins Spoon
      Shad Rap
      Kastmaster jig
      Pet Spoon
   Rainbow Trout Imitations:
      Rapala - silver & black
      Anchovy & Herring Imitations:
      Bomber Long "A", 16A, 25A
      Blue or black-backed Rebel
      Broken-backed Rebel
      Hair Raiser, Bug-eyed, or Bucktail jigs
      Jig colors: white, white & red
      Also lure and jig combo with spreader

24"
20 - 30# mono   Swivel   3 oz Rubber Core Sinker

Swivel replaces rear treble

Slow troll at 2 mph

Long shank 1 or 1/0 baitholder hook

3'
12# mono

Anchovy Fillet

c. Mid-depths, 15-25+ feet
   Long-trolled (50 yds) lures at 2-3 mph
   Day Lure
   A.C. Lure
   Large Rapalas, Bombers, or Rebels
   Lunker Lure
   Hopkins & Kastmaster
   Jigs or Rubber Trout

mono or leadcore for greater depths

Optional:
Use jig off dropper line or spreader for weight and as second lure.

d. Drift Bottom Jigging
   Hair Raiser, Bug-eyed, Worm-tailed, or Bucktail jigs
   Hopkins & Kastmaster lures
   Rapala Ice Jig

10 - 20# mono

Sharp jig up, keep contact on drop

Technique

1. Cast lures during topwater action in late summer and fall in the early morning and at dusk. **Constantly scan the lake for feeding birds or splashes of white water caused by shad-busting stripers. Take care in approaching surface boils not to scare the action away.** When approaching boils, cut the motor at least 50 yards away from the fish. Position your boat upwind of the fish so you'll drift to the side of the boiling school.

Except for the late summer topwater season, the fish are usually on the bottom. When fishing from the shore, after casting,, retrieve slowly until your lure sinks to bottom. Reel fast near the shore to avoid rocks or brush. If you are not snagging rocks occasionally you are not deep enough. On a boat, locate shad schools and jig fish with a leadhead (hair raiser) or Hopkins spoon bounced along the bottom or fish bait 3 turns off the bottom with a sliding sinker rig.

2. Troll during clear water conditions. Surface troll in the dark early morning or late afternoon hours when fish are near the surface. Trolling is often used to locate striper schools followed by casting lures or fishing bait. Troll the lure 40 to 50+ feet behind the boat.

Stripers will move deeper, and into holes as the day gets brighter. After mid-morning, troll lures near the bottom. **It is critical to troll very close to fish holding structure. If you are not occasionally hitting bottom or getting snagged, you are not trolling effectively.** Use a downrigger or leadcore to reach deeper holding spots.

3. Bait Fishing is better than other techniques during mid-day hours, muddy water or tidal flow conditions. In areas affected by tidal forces, bottom bait techniques work better because the strong water movement causes the fish to hunker down near the bottom. Bait fishing is especially effective for reaching the bottom of holes where stripers hold out during bright, daylight hours. Chumming with cut bait, allowed in the Colorado and some Delta regions, can turn on the bite.

On the Colorado River, if the water temperature is greater than 65°, look for a early morning surface bite. Try drifting anchovies. If the water temperature is less than 65°, try cut anchovies near the bottom.

"Balance Bar" Technique A striped bass will quickly drop a bait if it feels any resistance. The balanced bar technique is used to balance the rod and reel so that when the fish picks up the bait, the balanced rod tips forward easily, releasing the tension on the bait. The angler must then quickly and carefully pick up the rod while lowering the rod tip, put the reel in freespool, and very gently thumb the outgoing line until the fish has moved 10 to 20 feet and has taken the bait. Finally, the reel is engaged and the line allowed to straighten out and tighten before setting the hook.

The Law

The limit is generally 2 fish with a minimum length of 18" but regulations vary widely by area. A separate fee is required for fishing the Colorado River and its reservoirs. San Luis Reservoir, O'Neill Forebay, New Hogan, San Antonio and Santa Margarita lakes have a 5 fish limit and no minimum size. The Colorado River and Castaic, Silverwood and Pyramid lakes have a 10 fish limit and no minimum size. See current regulations.

Records

State: 67 1/2 lbs., O'Neil Forebay, May 1992
IGFA: 78 lbs. 8 oz., New Jersey, 1982

See Also

Trout, bass and catfish in lakes and the Colorado River, sturgeon and catfish in the Sacramento River and Delta.

Striped Bass Map Index

Key for all striped bass maps:

🏠 Lodging

⛺ Camping & RV site
No reservations

⛺ Camping & RV site
Reservations accepted

⛺ Camping & RV site.
Must reserve through
MISTIX, (800) 444-PARK

⛺ Campground has hookups

⛺ Campground has showers

Boat launch ramp

Striped bass

Bass

Catfish

Trout

Lake Mendocino
late Sept. to early Dec.

New Hogan
mid-June through
October
Pg. 69

**Lake Mead, Willow Beach
Laughlin, Davis Dam**
May through
November
Pg. 72

Sacramento River
April through May
Pg. 67

Lake Mohave
June through
November
Pg. 72

Sacramento Delta
April and May
mid-Sept. to mid-Nov.
Pg. 68

San Francisco
Bay & Coast
see FISHING CALIFORNIA - Saltwater

Lake Havasu
June through
October
Pg. 73

**San Luis Res.
O'Neill Forebay**
March to May
late Sept. through Nov.
Pg. 69

Santa Margarita Lake
Oct. through Nov.

Pyramid Lake
Best late Oct. through
May with trout plants.
Surface action August
to early October.
Pg. 70

Lake Silverwood
Oct. through June
Pg. 70

Skinner Lake
Oct. through March
Pg. 71

Striper Fishing - Sacramento River

> CAUTION!   Not to be used for navigation.

Season all year.
No night fishing from 10 PM to 6 AM,   May 1 through June 14.
Limit: 2, 18"

Fishing Info:
Bert's Steelhead Marina
(916) 458-2944

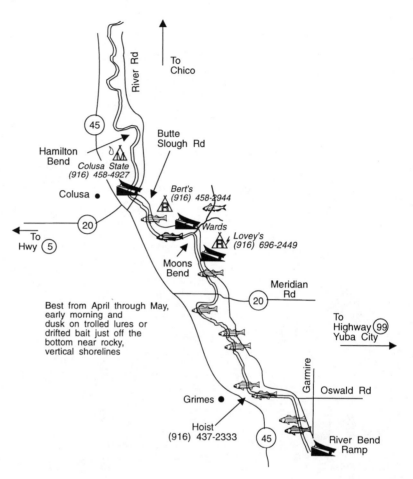

To
Chico

River Rd

45

Butte
Slough Rd

Hamilton
Bend

Colusa State
(916) 458-4927

Colusa ●

Bert's
(916) 458-2944

20

Wards

To
Hwy 5

Lovey's
(916) 696-2449

Moons
Bend

Meridian
Rd

20

To
Highway 99
Yuba City

Best from April through May,
early morning and
dusk on trolled lures or
drifted bait just off the
bottom near rocky,
vertical shorelines

Garmire

Oswald Rd

Grimes ●

Hoist
(916) 437-2333

45

River Bend
Ramp

Striper Fishing - Sacramento Delta

CAUTION! Not to be used for navigation.

Season all year, Limit: 2, 18". Best during "spring run" from March through early May and "fall run" from late October through November.

Fishing Info:
The Trap, Rio Vista
(707) 374-5554, Bait & Tackle
W. Delta, J&B Bait & Tackle
(510) 432-8466
S. Delta, Tony's Sport Goods
(510) 443-9191

E. Delta, Martini Bait & Tackle
(209) 951-1692
Guides:
Jay Sorrenson, (209) 478-6645
Jack Findleton, (916) 487-3392
Barry Canevaro (916) 777-6498
Tim O'Shea, (209) 369-7166

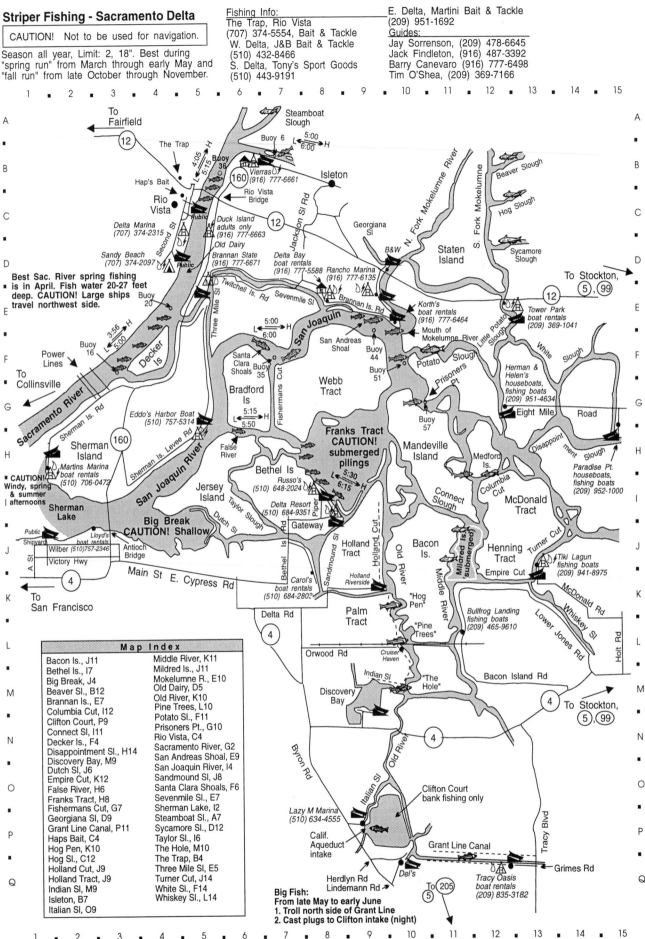

Map Index

Bacon Is., J11
Bethel Is., I7
Big Break, J4
Beaver Sl., B12
Brannan Is., E7
Columbia Cut, I12
Clifton Court, P9
Connect Sl., I11
Decker Is., F4
Disappointment Sl., H14
Discovery Bay, M9
Dutch Sl, J6
Empire Cut, K12
False River, H6
Franks Tract, H8
Fishermans Cut, G7
Georgiana Sl, D9
Grant Line Canal, P11
Haps Bait, C4
Hog Pen, K10
Hog Sl., C12
Holland Cut, J9
Holland Tract, J9
Indian Sl, M9
Isleton, B7
Italian Sl, O9

Middle River, K11
Mildred Is., J11
Mokelumne R., E10
Old Dairy, D5
Old River, K10
Pine Trees, L10
Potato Sl., F11
Prisoners Pt., G10
Rio Vista, C4
Sacramento River, G2
San Andreas Shoal, E9
San Joaquin River, I4
Sandmound Sl, J8
Santa Clara Shoals, F6
Sevenmile Sl., E7
Sherman Lake, I2
Steamboat Sl., A7
Sycamore Sl., D12
Taylor Sl., I6
The Hole, M10
The Trap, B4
Three Mile Sl, E5
Turner Cut, J14
White Sl., F14
Whiskey Sl., L14

Big Fish:
From late May to early June
1. Troll north side of Grant Line
2. Cast plugs to Clifton intake (night)

Striper Lakes - Map 1
Season all year. Limit: 5, no size limit.

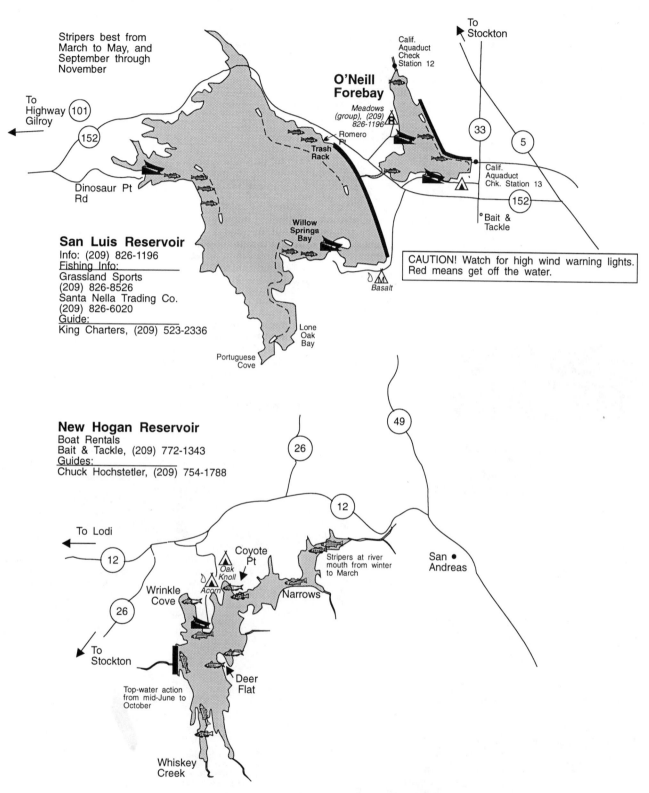

Stripers best from
March to May, and
September through
November

To Highway
Gilroy (101)
(152)

To
Stockton

Calif.
Aquaduct
Check
Station 12

**O'Neill
Forebay**

*Meadows
(group), (209)
826-1196*

Romero
Pt

Trash
Rack

(33) (5)

Calif.
Aquaduct
Chk. Station 13

(152)

°Bait &
Tackle

Dinosaur Pt
Rd

San Luis Reservoir
Info: (209) 826-1196
Fishing Info:
Grassland Sports
(209) 826-8526
Santa Nella Trading Co.
(209) 826-6020
Guide:
King Charters, (209) 523-2336

**Willow
Springs
Bay**

Basalt

CAUTION! Watch for high wind warning lights.
Red means get off the water.

Lone
Oak
Bay

Portuguese
Cove

New Hogan Reservoir
Boat Rentals
Bait & Tackle, (209) 772-1343
Guides:
Chuck Hochstetler, (209) 754-1788

(49)

(26)

(12)

To Lodi

(12)

Coyote
Pt

*Oak
Knoll*

Acorn

Stripers at river
mouth from winter
to March

San ●
Andreas

Wrinkle
Cove

Narrows

(26)

To
Stockton

Deer
Flat

Top-water action
from mid-June to
October

Whiskey
Creek

Striper Lakes - Map 2

Season all year.
Limit: 10, no size limit.

Pyramid Lake

Info: (805) 257-2892
Boat Rentals
Bait & Tackle
Trout Plants, (310) 590-5020

Trout plants have stopped at Pyramid and Silverwood. Shad are now the primary striper forage.

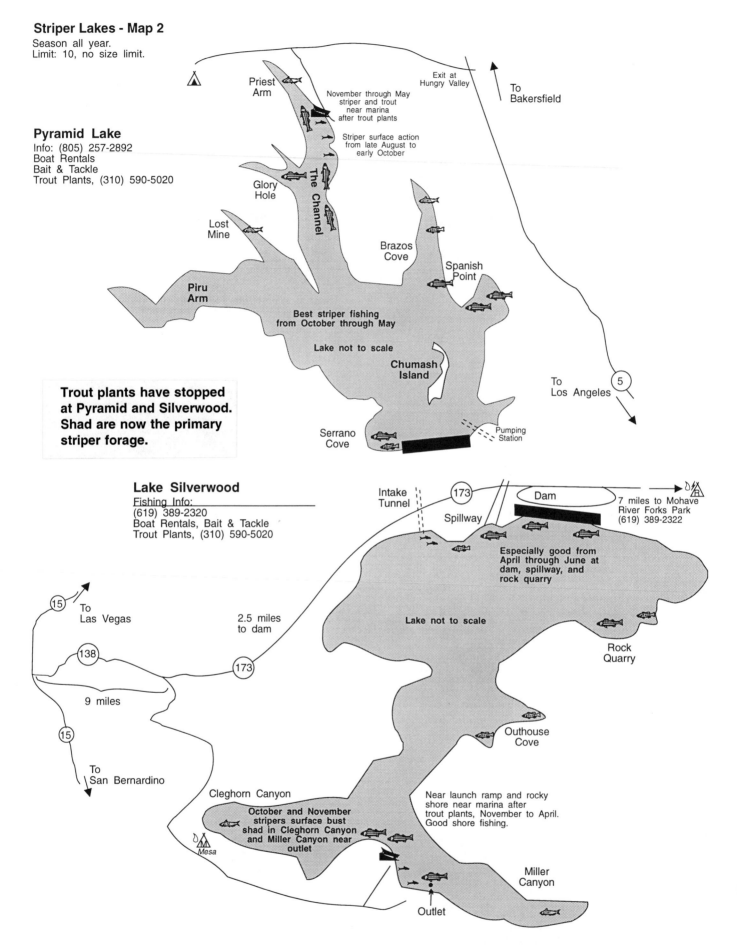

Priest Arm

November through May striper and trout near marina after trout plants

Striper surface action from late August to early October

Exit at Hungry Valley

To Bakersfield

The Channel

Glory Hole

Lost Mine

Brazos Cove

Spanish Point

Piru Arm

Best striper fishing from October through May

Lake not to scale

Chumash Island

To Los Angeles

5

Serrano Cove

Pumping Station

Lake Silverwood

Fishing Info:
(619) 389-2320
Boat Rentals, Bait & Tackle
Trout Plants, (310) 590-5020

Intake Tunnel

173

Dam

Spillway

7 miles to Mohave River Forks Park
(619) 389-2322

Especially good from April through June at dam, spillway, and rock quarry

Lake not to scale

15

To Las Vegas

2.5 miles to dam

138

173

9 miles

Rock Quarry

15

To San Bernardino

Outhouse Cove

Cleghorn Canyon

October and November stripers surface bust shad in Cleghorn Canyon and Miller Canyon near outlet

Mesa

Near launch ramp and rocky shore near marina after trout plants, November to April. Good shore fishing.

Miller Canyon

Outlet

Striper Lakes - Map 3
Season all year.
Limit: 2, over 18"
Stripers best late September through March
If fish not on surface, try bottom-drifted chicken liver
Trout stocked November through June

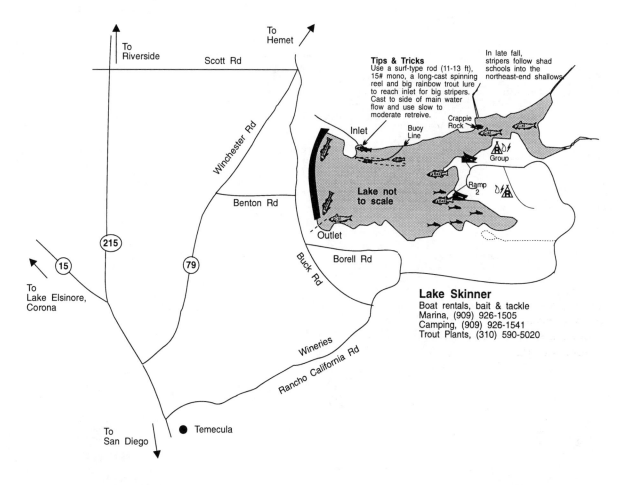

Tips & Tricks
Use a surf-type rod (11-13 ft),
15# mono, a long-cast spinning
reel and big rainbow trout lure
to reach inlet for big stripers.
Cast to side of main water
flow and use slow to
moderate retreive.

In late fall,
stripers follow shad
schools into the
northeast-end shallows

Crappie
Rock

Group

Inlet

Buoy
Line

Ramp
2

Lake not
to scale

Outlet

Borell Rd

Buck Rd

Lake Skinner
Boat rentals, bait & tackle
Marina, (909) 926-1505
Camping, (909) 926-1541
Trout Plants, (310) 590-5020

Winchester Rd

Scott Rd

To
Hemet

To
Riverside

Benton Rd

215

79

15

To
Lake Elsinore,
Corona

Wineries

Rancho California Rd

To
San Diego

● Temecula

Striper Fishing: Colorado River - Lake Mead, Lake Mohave, Willow Beach, Laughlin
Season all year. Limit: 10, no size limit.

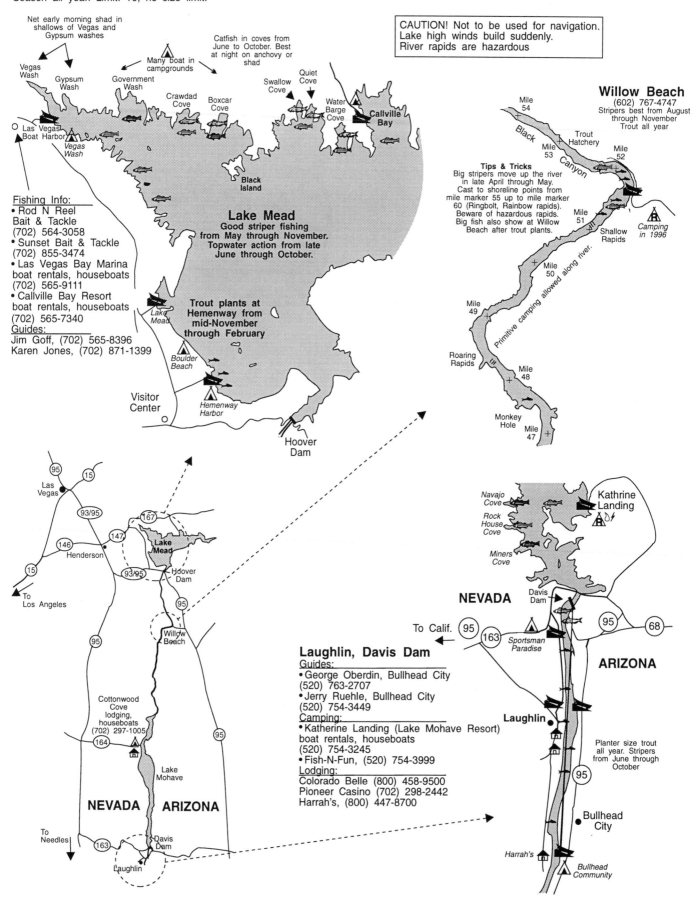

Net early morning shad in shallows of Vegas and Gypsum washes

Catfish in coves from June to October. Best at night on anchovy or shad

Many boat in campgrounds

Vegas Wash

Gypsum Wash

Government Wash

Crawdad Cove

Boxcar Cove

Swallow Cove

Quiet Cove

Water Barge Cove

Callville Bay

Las Vegas Boat Harbor

Vegas Wash

Black Island

Lake Mead
Good striper fishing from May through November. Topwater action from late June through October.

CAUTION! Not to be used for navigation. Lake high winds build suddenly. River rapids are hazardous

Willow Beach
(602) 767-4747
Stripers best from August through November
Trout all year

Mile 54

Mile 53

Mile 52

Black Canyon

Trout Hatchery

Tips & Tricks
Big stripers move up the river in late April through May. Cast to shoreline points from mile marker 55 up to mile marker 60 (Ringbolt, Rainbow rapids). Beware of hazardous rapids. Big fish also show at Willow Beach after trout plants.

Mile 51

Shallow Rapids

Camping in 1996

Mile 50

Primitive camping allowed along river.

Mile 49

Roaring Rapids

Mile 48

Monkey Hole

Mile 47

Fishing Info:
• Rod N Reel Bait & Tackle (702) 564-3058
• Sunset Bait & Tackle (702) 855-3474
• Las Vegas Bay Marina boat rentals, houseboats (702) 565-9111
• Callville Bay Resort boat rentals, houseboats (702) 565-7340
Guides:
Jim Goff, (702) 565-8396
Karen Jones, (702) 871-1399

Lake Mead

Trout plants at Hemenway from mid-November through February

Boulder Beach

Visitor Center

Hemenway Harbor

Hoover Dam

95

15

Las Vegas

93/95

167

147

146

Henderson

15

93/95

Lake Mead

Hoover Dam

95

To Los Angeles

95

Willow Beach

Navajo Cove

Rock House Cove

Miners Cove

Kathrine Landing

NEVADA

Davis Dam

To Calif. 95

163

Sportsman Paradise

95

68

ARIZONA

Cottonwood Cove lodging, houseboats (702) 297-1005

164

Lake Mohave

Laughlin, Davis Dam
Guides:
• George Oberdin, Bullhead City (520) 763-2707
• Jerry Ruehle, Bullhead City (520) 754-3449
Camping:
• Katherine Landing (Lake Mohave Resort) boat rentals, houseboats (520) 754-3245
• Fish-N-Fun, (520) 754-3999
Lodging:
Colorado Belle (800) 458-9500
Pioneer Casino (702) 298-2442
Harrah's, (800) 447-8700

Laughlin

Planter size trout all year. Stripers from June through October

95

NEVADA   **ARIZONA**

To Needles

163

Davis Dam

Laughlin

Bullhead City

Harrah's

Bullhead Community

Striper Fishing: Colorado River - Lake Havasu

CAUTION! Not to be used for navigation

Season all year.
Limit: 10, no size limit.

Lake Havasu City

Guide:
Bob Lee
Lake Havasu City
(520) 855-3406
Camping:
•Crazy Horse
(520) 855-4033
•Havasu Landings Resort
(619) 858-4593
•Islander RV
(520) 855-5005
•Lake Havasu Marina
boat rentals
bait & tackle
(520) 855-2159
Lodging:
Sandman
1700 N. McCulloch
Lake Havasu City
(520) 855-7841
Houseboats:
H20 Boats, (520) 680-1575
Tournaments:
Western Outdoor News
Striper Derby, mid-May
(800) 334-8152

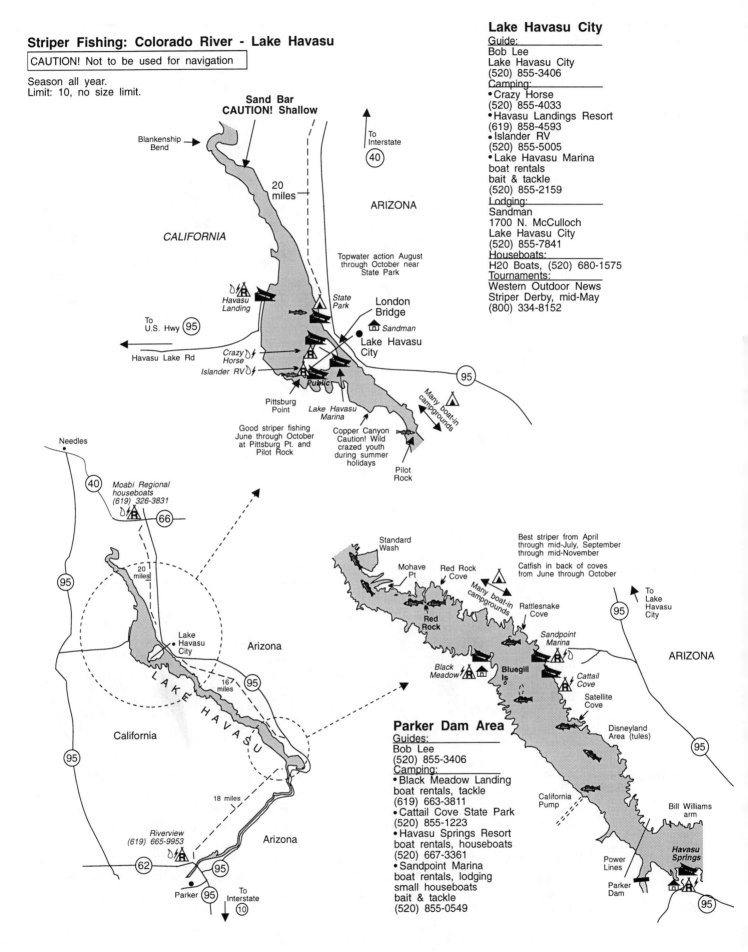

Sand Bar
CAUTION! Shallow

Blankenship Bend

20 miles

To Interstate (40)

ARIZONA

CALIFORNIA

Topwater action August through October near State Park

Havasu Landing

State Park

London Bridge

Sandman

Lake Havasu City

To U.S. Hwy (95)

Havasu Lake Rd

Crazy Horse

Islander RV

Public

Pittsburg Point

Lake Havasu Marina

(95)

Many boat-in campgrounds

Good striper fishing June through October at Pittsburg Pt. and Pilot Rock

Copper Canyon Caution! Wild crazed youth during summer holidays

Pilot Rock

Needles

(40)

Moabi Regional houseboats
(619) 326-3831

(66)

(95)

20 miles

Lake Havasu City

Arizona

LAKE HAVASU

16 miles

(95)

California

18 miles

Riverview
(619) 665-9953

Arizona

(62)

(95)

Parker

(95)

To Interstate (10)

Standard Wash

Best striper from April through mid-July, September through mid-November

Catfish in back of coves from June through October

Mohave Pt

Red Rock Cove

Many boat-in campgrounds

To Lake Havasu City

Red Rock

Rattlesnake Cove

Sandpoint Marina

ARIZONA

Black Meadow

Bluegill Is

Cattail Cove

Satellite Cove

Disneyland Area (tules)

(95)

California Pump

Bill Williams arm

Power Lines

Havasu Springs

Parker Dam

(95)

Parker Dam Area

Guides:
Bob Lee
(520) 855-3406
Camping:
• Black Meadow Landing
boat rentals, tackle
(619) 663-3811
• Cattail Cove State Park
(520) 855-1223
• Havasu Springs Resort
boat rentals, houseboats
(520) 667-3361
• Sandpoint Marina
boat rentals, lodging
small houseboats
bait & tackle
(520) 855-0549

WHITE BASS

Where | Lake Nacimiento

When/Where | The red hot spawning bite occurs from March to early May. The spawn is ignited when a series of calm, warm days start the lake to warm and clear. Fish where Las Tables narrows into Franklin Creek or try up the narrows where the bass are spawning at night. Spawning fish relate to the lake bottom.

Corky Gustafson, Water World Resorts

Fishing is also good during the post spawn period from late May to early June. The action picks up again in the fall from late September to early November. After spawning the white bass follow the shad schools. Look for bird activity, surface boils, or shad concentrations. Fishing is best in the early mornings and towards dusk.

Rig

	Lgth	Line	Lure/Wt.	Power / Action
Rod	5 - 7	2 - 6	1/16 - 1/4 oz.	Light or Ultra Lt. Moderate
	Type	**Size**		
Reel	Conv Spin	150 yds of 4#		

Bait/Lures | Live shad or cut anchovies. To net your own shad, be on the water at daybreak. Look for shad near the shore in the back of coves. **Having live shad can make your day**. Lures: Kastmaster, Roostertail, feather jigs, small surface plugs, crappie jigs, Sassy Shad. Colors: White, silver, chartreuse, yellow.

Roostertail
Sassy Shad
Kastmaster
Marabou Crappie Jig

Technique | While spawning, white bass hold near the bottom. Cast lures out, let sink all the way to the bottom and retrieve. During the rest of the year, cast to surface feeding schools or search for active fish by trolling slowly with the lure well back from the boat. Use light line, 2# - 4#, especially for the surface bite. Similar size fish school together.

The Law | No limit, size or number. No live white bass may be possessed or transported. These fish are aggressive and would endanger other fisheries if released in other lakes or streams.

Records | IGFA: 5 lbs. 14 oz., N. Carolina, 1986

See Also | Largemouth bass, striped bass in San Antonio Reservoir

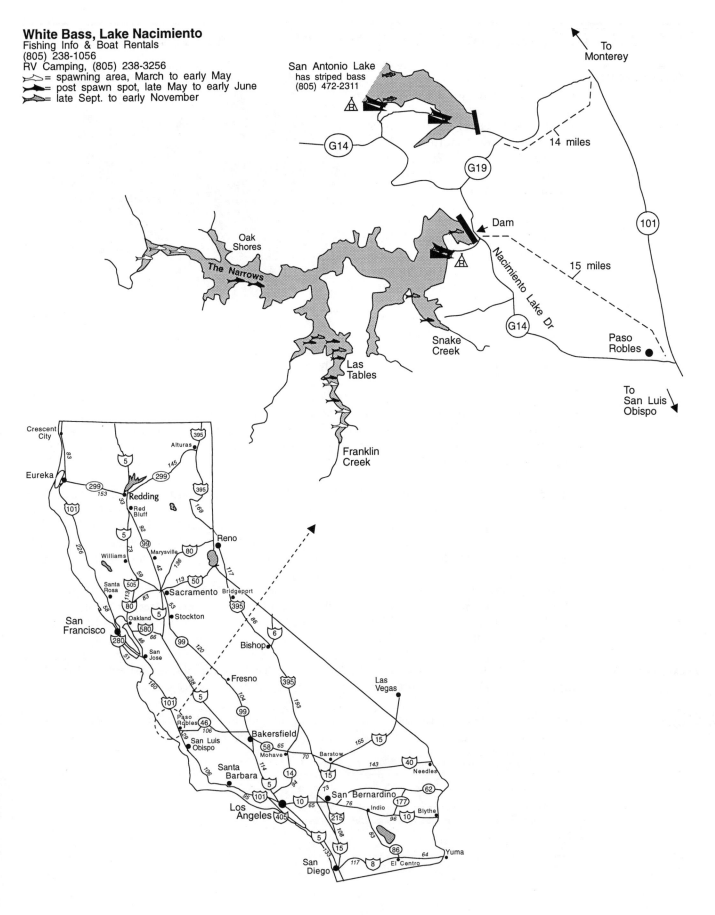

White Bass, Lake Nacimiento
Fishing Info & Boat Rentals
(805) 238-1056
RV Camping, (805) 238-3256

= spawning area, March to early May
= post spawn spot, late May to early June
= late Sept. to early November

San Antonio Lake
has striped bass
(805) 472-2311

To
Monterey

14 miles

101

G14

G19

Dam

Oak
Shores

The Narrows

Nacimiento Lake Dr

15 miles

G14

Paso
Robles

Snake
Creek

Las
Tables

To
San Luis
Obispo

Franklin
Creek

Crescent
City

Alturas   395

83   5

Eureka   299
           153
           299
           395
Redding   33
           Red
           Bluff   92
           5   169
                    Reno
226   73   99
     Williams Marysville 80
     505   42   136
     113   117
Santa 83   113 50
Rosa   Sacramento Bridgeport
58   80   53
     Oakland 5 Stockton 395
San   580 66   86
Francisco 46
280   99   120   6
     San   Bishop
51   Jose
          238
          160   Fresno   395
          101 5
                     104   Las
          99   193 Vegas
     Paso
     Robles 46
          106   155   15
     San Luis Bakersfield
     Obispo 58 65
               Mohave 70   Barstow
          108 14   94   143   40
     Santa   15   Needles
     Barbara   73
          85 101   San Bernardino 62
     Los   10 65   76   177
     Angeles 405   Indio   10 Blythe
               215 96
          5   108 83
          133 15   86
     San   117 8   El Centro 64 Yuma
     Diego

CHANNEL CATFISH, BLUE CATFISH, WHITE CATFISH

Where/When   Catfish can be found in plentiful supplies at many California lakes and rivers. Amador, Clear, and Folsom lakes in northern California provide good fishing. The Feather, Sacramento River, Sacramento Delta and Colorado River are loaded with catfish. The smaller white catfish is quite common in the Sacramento Delta. In southern California some of the more notable lakes are Lake Perris, Casitas Lake, Cachuma, Otay, San Vicente Reservoir, Corona, Santa Ana River Lakes and Irvine Lake. The map shows only 3 top southern California

Dwayne and Lisa Parsons of Parson's Northwater Guide caught these 15 and 20 pound catfish at Clear Lake in early June

catfishing lakes. Since catfish are in almost every lake and river, many maps in other sections of this guide also indicate catfish hotspots (🐟).

In lakes, catfishing is best at night during the warmer weather months, from June through early November. After winter storms, fishing can be great toward the back of coves where catfish forage for food washed in by swollen creeks. These muddy, cold waters don't deter them from active feeding. In rivers, winter fishing for catfish is best during the day in waters muddied by recent rains.

Lake Structure Catfish move into the shallow flats at night to search for food. They follow creek channels from deep water into the shallow flats. They congregate at rocky dam faces, especially in the corners. Catfish hold in deeper, mid-lake bottom depressions during the day. In winter catfish hold in deep water, 50 to 80 feet deep, except after rains when they follow creek channels to the back of coves where creek inlets wash in forage.

River Structure During the day, catfish stay on the bottom in holes found at river bends creek inlets, and wing dams. Holes holding fallen trees are even better. At dusk, some of these catfish become active and wander into the shallower waters to feed, others stay in the holes and wait for food to drift by.

Bait/Lures   Cut mackerel, stinkbait, worms, chicken livers, fresh water clams (especially for white catfish), live & dead minnows, threadfin shad, crayfish, waterdogs, etc.

Rig   Any medium weight spinning or casting reel and rod. For river fishing, a long rod, 9-12 feet, can facilitate placing bait around fallen tree structure.

	Lgth	Line	Lure/Wt.	Power / Action
Rod	7 1/2-9	6 - 12	1/4 - 2 oz.	Medium Moderate
	Type	**Size**		
Reel	Conv Spin	150 yds of 10#		

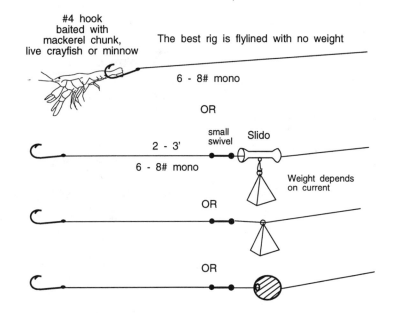

#4 hook baited with mackerel chunk, live crayfish or minnow

The best rig is flylined with no weight

6 - 8# mono

OR

2 - 3'   small swivel   Slido

6 - 8# mono

Weight depends on current

OR

OR

Technique   **It is critical, especially for larger catfish, to have no resistence on the bait.** Flyline the bait with no weight and your spinning reel bail open. When a fish picks up the bait, let him take out about 10 feet of line, engage your reel, reel down to tension and set the hook. In rivers or windy conditions you may have to use a sliding sinker rig. Just release tension as soon as you get a bite. During the day, catfish hold in lake bottom depressions out of the daytime sun. Fish these holes by pulling a bait through through them. Retrieve very slowly, 1/2 foot per minute. When you detect a pickup, immediately release line so the catfish feels no resistance. Let him take the bait and then reel down and set the hook.

In the evening, in late fall, catfish may boil on topwater shad. These fish will hit flylined chunks of mackeral or shad.

If fishing rivers, put the bait upstream of holding structure like stream holes, or fallen timber. Use your long rod to slowly slide the bait into openings in the front and sides of the structure.

The Law   All year and no limit in most lakes. However there are many exceptions. The limit is 10 fish in southern California, Inyo county, Mono county, LaFayette and San Pablo Lakes near San Francisco, and the Colorado River. The limit is 5 fish at Del Valle, Don Castro, Lake Chabot, Contra Loma, Santee, etc.—see regs.

Records   Channel catfish; 48 lbs. 8 oz., Irvine Lake, 1984
IGFA: 58 lbs., S. Carolina, 1964
Blue catfish; 62.3 lbs.; Irvine Lake; November, 1995
IGFA: 97 lbs., S. Dakota, 1959
White catfish; 22.03 lbs., William Land Park, Sacramento; 1995

Catfish Hotspots
Three Southern California Lakes

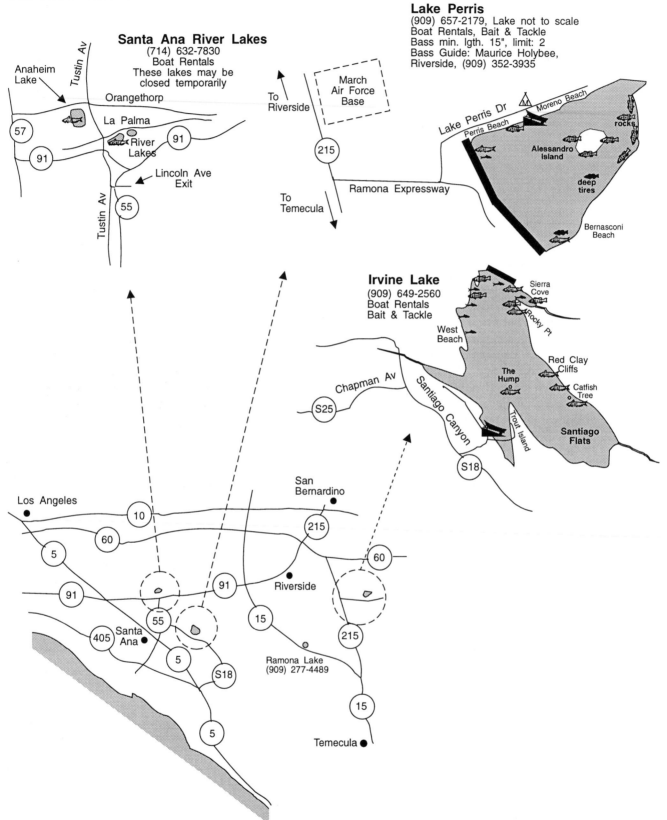

Santa Ana River Lakes
(714) 632-7830
Boat Rentals
These lakes may be closed temporarily

Lake Perris
(909) 657-2179, Lake not to scale
Boat Rentals, Bait & Tackle
Bass min. lgth. 15", limit: 2
Bass Guide: Maurice Holybee,
Riverside, (909) 352-3935

Irvine Lake
(909) 649-2560
Boat Rentals
Bait & Tackle

Ramona Lake
(909) 277-4489

FLATHEAD CATFISH

Where

Structure The ideal structure is an isolated big hole with some snag wood in the middle. The biggest flatheads will be in these holes. Look for good holes at the outside river bends, below shallower, faster riffles. Holes also form where seasonal or permanent tributaries enter the main river and below dams. Smaller holes form in front and behind wing dams and downstream of land points.

Flatheads and channels up to 20 pounds have been pulled from the irrigation canals that are common from Yuma to Palo Verde to Blythe. Here again the fish will hold in the deeper holes of these canals.

When

Flatheads feed at night and in the early morning. The best time is from midnight to just after sunrise. Flatheads are caught all year but the big ones bite in October and November.

Mac's Bait & Tackle, Palo Verde

Bait/Lures

It is critical to use live and lively bait—4 - 6" goldfish, bluegill or thread-

Barbara Bolt caught this giant 46 pound flathead catfish near Palo Verde in October

fin shad. A flathead will not take a dead bait. Hook the bait either through the forward, upper eye socket without puncturing the eye, or in the fleshy part of the tail fin behind the anus. Flatheads also bite on waterdogs, nightcrawlers and crawfish.

Rig

Rod	Lgth	Line	Lure/Wt.	Power / Action
	6 - 6 1/2	20 - 40	1/16 - 1/4 oz.	Heavy

Reel	Type	Size		
	Conv Spin	100 yds of 20#		

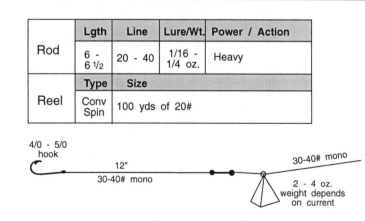

4/0 - 5/0 hook

12"
30-40# mono

30-40# mono

2 - 4 oz.
weight depends
on current

Technique

Position your boat upstream of a fish holding hole. The feeding fish will be near the forward lip of the hole. Position your rig upstream of this forward lip and work your bait back into the hole. You can catch more fish by running and gunning—working many holes. Some holes will have active fish, some not.

Flathead catfish don't swallow a bait outright. They will pick it up and move away 10 to 30 feet. They will be crushing the bait in their jaws while moving and when they stop. With all this bait crunching, you need a big-barbed hook to keep the bait from tearing off. After they stop give them a little time to take the bait. Then reel in or lift your rod to remove the line slack. If the feeling is soft or you can feel the fish still tugging on the bait, give some slack line. If you feel solid weight, quickly reel the line tight and set the hook.

The Law

10 fish limit, no size restrictions. No closures in Colorado River (1990-91). You'll need a California or Arizona license with a Colorado river stamp.

Please consider releasing large flatheads. A flathead of 50 pounds will be over 40 years old. Once taken from the river, it will be hard to replace.

Records

State: 57 lbs. 8 oz., Colorado River, April 1980
IGFA: 98 lbs., Texas, 1986

Flathead Catfish, Lower Colorado River

Key:

🏠	Lodging
⛺	Camping & RV site No reservations
⛺	Camping & RV site Reservations accepted
⚡	Campground has hookups
🚿	Campground has showers
⛵	Boat launch ramp
🐟	Catfish area
🐟	Bass area

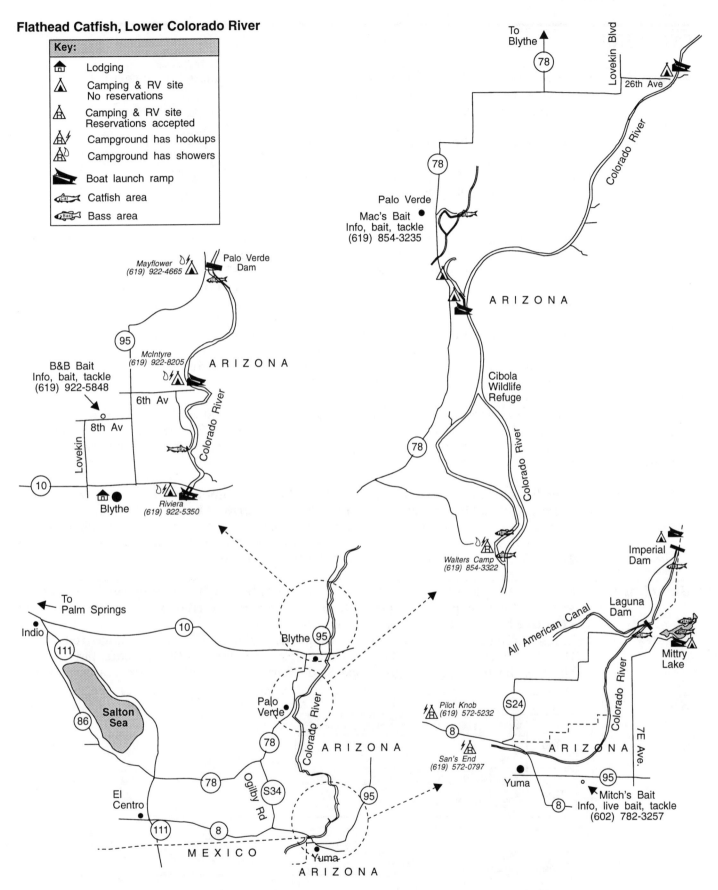

To Blythe 78

Lovekin Blvd
26th Ave

Colorado River

Palo Verde
Mac's Bait
Info, bait, tackle
(619) 854-3235

78

ARIZONA

Mayflower
(619) 922-4665
Palo Verde
Dam

95

B&B Bait
Info, bait, tackle
(619) 922-5848

McIntyre
(619) 922-8205

6th Av

ARIZONA

Colorado River

8th Av

Lovekin

10

Blythe

Riviera
(619) 922-5350

Cibola
Wildlife
Refuge

Colorado River

78

Walters Camp
(619) 854-3322

Imperial
Dam

Laguna
Dam

All American Canal

Mittry
Lake

Colorado River

To Palm Springs

Indio

111

Salton
Sea

86

El
Centro

111

10

78

Blythe 95

Palo
Verde

78

Ogilby Rd

S34

95

Colorado River

ARIZONA

Pilot Knob
(619) 572-5232

8

San's End
(619) 572-0797

Yuma

S24

7E Ave.

95

Mitch's Bait
Info, live bait, tackle
(602) 782-3257

8

8

111

MEXICO

Yuma

ARIZONA

CORVINA

Where/When   There was a fish die off in 1992 which seems to have eliminated the bigger fish in the sea. However the sea is very much alive and fish to over 10 pounds still abound. The Salton Sea is very large—**it is critical to find out exactly where the fish are.** Corvina move considerably from day to day. Therefore you find out where the fish are from the sources listed on the map as close as possible to your planned fishing day.

Structure   Closely observe the color of the water. Almost all of the water is brownish, however this brown takes on different shadings depending on the oxygen content and any plankton bloom. **It is critical to find "brown" or "red" water areas.** Brown water is the best. It indicates plenty of oxygen and plenty of fish. This is pure brown with no sign of the shadings below. Red water is neutral. Green water has low oxygen and no fish

From November through March the fish are in the 3 to 10 foot deep shallows at the south shore. Fishing is good especially during warming trends caused by a series of 70+, wind-less days. Strong winds are common from late January through early April. Don't go fishing on a windy day, watch the forecast.

From April through May larger fish appear in the south end shallows but also arrive near the closed Navy base as the water temperature rises above 70 degrees. Live bait becomes more effective during this period, especially tilapia. The best action is often between 10 AM and early afternoon.

May through July is the best time for big fish. **Fishing is good only in the morning hours in May. Fishing is good only in the VERY early morning hours in June and July.** The best times are typically from 4:30 to approximately 7:30 AM. The bite typically turns off completely around 9 AM when an east wind starts blowing. In June fish are usually around 10 to 15 feet deep. In late June to July they will be 15 to 25 feet deep.

Bait/Lures   Small croaker, less than 6", which can sometimes be caught on jigged Hopkins "Shorty" spoons. Small tilapia or sargo, 2 - 3 inches. **Small live tilapia are by far the most effective bait.** Mudsuckers or minnows.
Lures: ThinFin lures, 3 1/2", sinking (S) model. Colors: silver shad, orange, red, green. Hopkins "shorty" spoon - 1/2 to 3/4 oz. Lunker Lure, 3/8 or 1/2 oz. Colors: pink, orange sparkle, chartreuse, gold & green speckled, chartreuse with black back, orange & black.

Rig

	Lgth	Line	Lure/Wt.	Power / Action
Rod	6 - 7 1/2	10 - 15	3/8 - 2 oz.	Medium Moderate
	Type	**Size**		
Reel	Conv	150 yds of 15#		

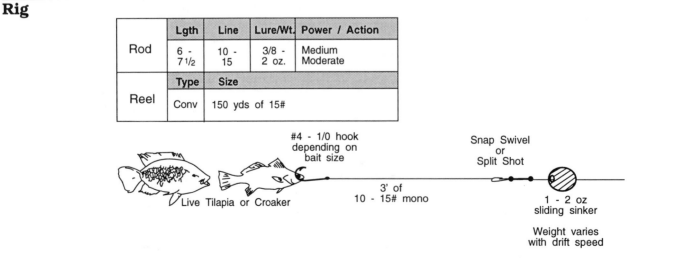

#4 - 1/0 hook depending on bait size

Snap Swivel or Split Shot

Live Tilapia or Croaker

3' of 10 - 15# mono

1 - 2 oz sliding sinker

Weight varies with drift speed

| **Techniques** | **It is critical to troll or drift at a very slow speed.** Control your drift with a sea anchor or trolling motor. While drifting, monitor the fish finder to find out if fish are suspended off the bottom. Adjust your bait to that depth. If fishing mudsuckers, keep the bait moving with an occasional flick of the rod. If hit on bait, lower the rod tip to give slack. When you feel weight on the line set the hook firmly.

From November through May at the south shore shallows cast Lunker lures at right angles to the boat heading and let the lure sink and drift back to the boat's wake and retrieve slowly. Troll Lunker Lures at very slow speeds along the shore. Use your electric motor at the lowest speed. Cast out at right angles from the boat direction and let the lure sink and drift back to the boat's wake. **Avoid making noise**.

From late May to June the when the fish are 8 to 15 feet deep, explore the mapped hot spot areas until you locate a school of fish on your fish finder. If light winds and fish are on the bottom, set the boat up to drift with live bait or Lunker Lures bouncing off the bottom through the area of the located school. With bait fishing, if the fish are suspended off the bottom, use less weight so the bait is pulled up to the fish by the drift. A sea anchor or large bucket may have to be dragged to slow the drift.

In July the fish move to water from 15 to 25 feet deep. If the fish are on the bottom, try dropping a Hopkins to the bottom, sweep the rod tip up, let lure fall to the bottom, repeat. |
|---|---|
| **The Law** | Limit: 5. No size limit |
| **Records** | State: Corvina, 36 1/2 lbs. IGFA: 40 lbs., Ecuador, 1991 |

TILAPIA

When/Where	Best in early summer in the shallows but can be good from Dec. to May from Desert Shores to 81st Av.
Technique	Use a light to medium weight spinning outfit with 4# to 10# mono. Don't cut into the bad smelling stomach when cleaning fish.
The Law	No limit, no closures.

Tilapia
(Averages 1/2 to 1 1/2 lbs.)

Snap Swivel
4 - 10# mono
#6 baitholder hooks
3'
Cut Nightcrawler or Redworm

SARGO

| **When/Where** | Best in November through April. Try the shoreline at Salton Sea State Rec. jetty or Sunken City about 1/4 mile north of Varner Harbor. This area is marked by a partially submerged telephone pole.

Structure Submerged buildings, submerged trees, piers, jetties. |
|---|---|
| **Rig** | Light to medium weight spinning outfit. |
| **Technique** | Chum generously with canned corn. Bring about 3 cans per angler. |
| **The Law** | No limit, no closures. |

Sargo
(Averages 1/2 lb.)

#6 baitholder hooks
4 - 6"
1/2 oz sliding sinker
9 - 12"
4 - 6# mon
Load hooks with corn kernels

The Salton Sea, Corvina

CAUTION!   Not to be used for navigation.

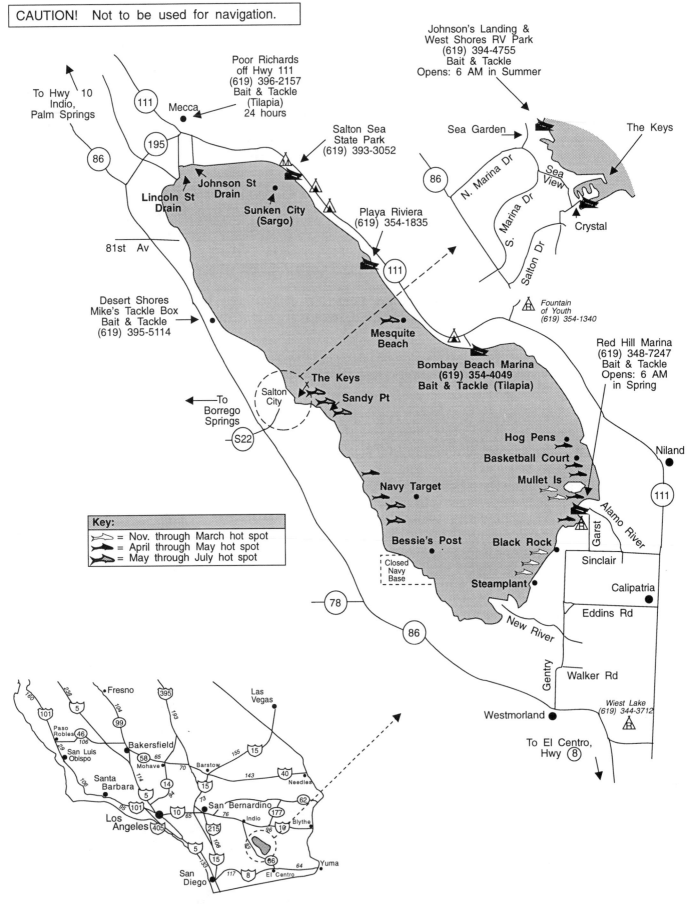

Poor Richards
off Hwy 111
(619) 396-2157
Bait & Tackle
(Tilapia)
24 hours

Johnson's Landing &
West Shores RV Park
(619) 394-4755
Bait & Tackle
Opens: 6 AM in Summer

To Hwy 10
Indio,
Palm Springs

Mecca

Salton Sea
State Park
(619) 393-3052

Sea Garden

The Keys

N. Marina Dr

Johnson St
Drain

Lincoln St
Drain

Sunken City
(Sargo)

Playa Riviera
(619) 354-1835

Sea View

S. Marina Dr

Crystal

Salton Dr

81st Av

Fountain
of Youth
(619) 354-1340

Desert Shores
Mike's Tackle Box
Bait & Tackle
(619) 395-5114

Mesquite
Beach

Bombay Beach Marina
(619) 354-4049
Bait & Tackle (Tilapia)

Red Hill Marina
(619) 348-7247
Bait & Tackle
Opens: 6 AM
in Spring

The Keys

Salton
City

Sandy Pt

To
Borrego
Springs

Hog Pens

Niland

Basketball Court

Mullet Is

Navy Target

Alamo River

Garst

Key:
= Nov. through March hot spot
= April through May hot spot
= May through July hot spot

Bessie's Post

Black Rock

Sinclair

Closed
Navy
Base

Steamplant

Calipatria

Eddins Rd

New River

Walker Rd

Gentry

Wiest Lake
(619) 344-3712

Westmorland

To El Centro,
Hwy 8

Fresno

Las
Vegas

Paso
Robles

Bakersfield

San Luis
Obispo

Mohave

Barstow

Needles

Santa
Barbara

Los
Angeles

San Bernardino

Indio

Blythe

Yuma

San
Diego

El Centro

CRAPPIE (pronounced crop-pee)

Where/When Crappie lake populations are cyclical going from good to bad to good again within a span of 3 to 5 years. Here are a few consistently good lakes; Clear Lake, Berryessa, Uvas, and Black Butte in norhtern California; Isabella in the central state; Silverwood, Irvine, Henshaw, El Capitan, Wohlford and Hodges in southern California.

Jim Niemiec

Structure From late February to early March the fish will be inside of or tight to the edge of shallow water cover in 1 to 12 feet deep water. Look along channels and steep dropoffs outside of protected cove, outside of creek inlets off steeper banks leading to flats with cover and under docks, pilings, floating docks.

From late March through April spawn occurs in areas close to above areas with the heaviest concentrations of reeds, tules, cattails, submerged trees or brush, docks, pilings and underneath floating platforms.

From late April through early May the schools move to nearby deeper structure close to outside weedlines, steeper dropoff breaks, and deeper, outside limbs of sunken trees.

In summer, from June through mid-September, the schools will be suspended from 10 to 20 feet deep in water depths of 15 to 40 feet. Preferred locations will be close to underwater structure like outside weedlines, breaks, submerged trees, underwater rocky mounds. Fish suspended away from structure are usually on the move and hard to follow. Concentrate on schools suspended off structure. Fish will frequent the top of submerged islands or rock piles in the early morning and evening hours. They will move to the deeper, shaded side during the mid-day hours. If there is a current, the fish will concentrate on the protected, down-current side of the mound.

In late September to early Nov. crappie again are tight to the cover and actively feeding.

When Fishing is best in the early morning and at dusk. Cloudy, dark, overcast days can extend the good hours even to the middle of the day. The bite can be good at night, especially the first 2 hours of darkness.

Bait/Lures Live shiners or shad are best at 1 1/2 to 2 1/2 inches. Small jigs from 1/16 to 1/8 oz., i.e. Crappie John finger jigs, Sassy Shad, Mini jigs, micro jigs, finger (tube) jigs. Colors: For all day, all conditions use green & white; for off-color water use black; use white, yellow & white on cloudy days, early mornings and late evenings.

Tube Jigs   Micro Jig

Crappie Jig   Sassy Shad

Rig Use the following spinning rig or in the spring when the fish are inside shallow cover, a special long pole from 10 to 14 feet long for reaching cover pockets.

	Lgth	Line	Lure/Wt.	Power / Action
Rod	5 - 7	2 - 6	1/32 - 1/8 oz.	Light or Ultra Lt. Moderate

	Type	Size		
Reel	Spin	150 yds of 4#		

1. Shallow Water Rigs: 1 - 10+ feet deep

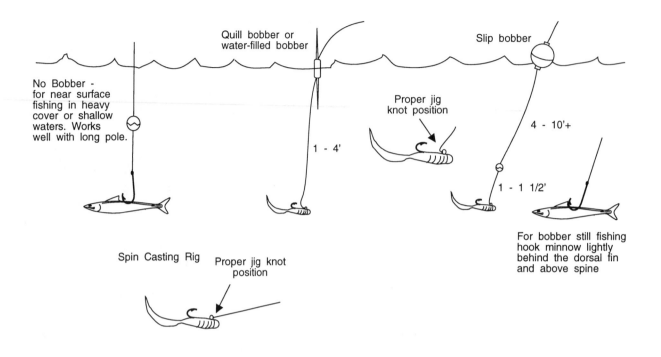

No Bobber - for near surface fishing in heavy cover or shallow waters. Works well with long pole.

Quill bobber or water-filled bobber

Slip bobber

Proper jig knot position

1 - 4'

4 - 10'+

1 - 1 1/2'

For bobber still fishing hook minnow lightly behind the dorsal fin and above spine

Spin Casting Rig   Proper jig knot position

2. Tight Line Rigs for Deeper Water: 10 - 20+ feet deep

Wind Drift or Backtroll

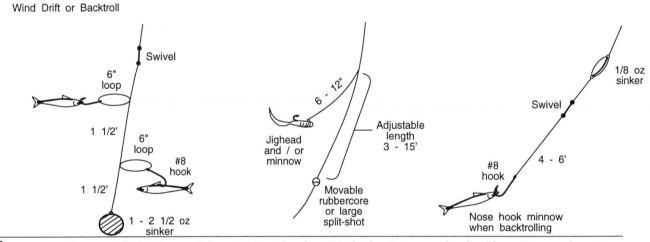

Swivel

6" loop

1 1/2'

6" loop

#8 hook

1 1/2'

1 - 2 1/2 oz sinker

6 - 12"

Jighead and / or minnow

Adjustable length 3 - 15'

Movable rubbercore or large split-shot

1/8 oz sinker

Swivel

#8 hook

4 - 6'

Nose hook minnow when backtrolling

Technique   Use very light line, a 2# or 4# test leader. Work the jig very slowly. If casting and retrieving, retrieve slowly. Extend the index finger of your right hand to intercept the mono as it rolls around the spool on the retrieve. This gives an extra motion to the jig. If using vertical method, move slowly, let sit motionless, twitch occasionally or lift your rod 2 to 3 feet and lower it slowly. Crappies like to attack their prey from below. Work the jig just above and slightly into the fish.

The Law   Limit: 25 fish, no closures

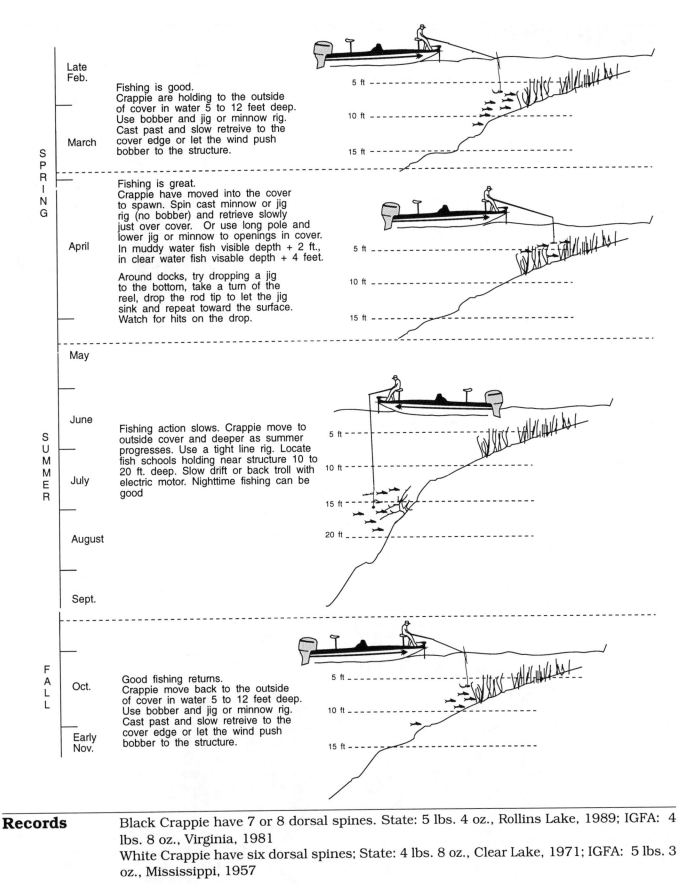

SPRING

Late
Feb.

March

Fishing is good.
Crappie are holding to the outside
of cover in water 5 to 12 feet deep.
Use bobber and jig or minnow rig.
Cast past and slow retreive to the
cover edge or let the wind push
bobber to the structure.

5 ft

10 ft

15 ft

April

Fishing is great.
Crappie have moved into the cover
to spawn. Spin cast minnow or jig
rig (no bobber) and retrieve slowly
just over cover. Or use long pole and
lower jig or minnow to openings in cover.
In muddy water fish visible depth + 2 ft.,
in clear water fish visable depth + 4 feet.

Around docks, try dropping a jig
to the bottom, take a turn of the
reel, drop the rod tip to let the jig
sink and repeat toward the surface.
Watch for hits on the drop.

5 ft

10 ft

15 ft

May

June

SUMMER

July

August

Fishing action slows. Crappie move to
outside cover and deeper as summer
progresses. Use a tight line rig. Locate
fish schools holding near structure 10 to
20 ft. deep. Slow drift or back troll with
electric motor. Nighttime fishing can be
good

5 ft

10 ft

15 ft

20 ft

Sept.

FALL

Oct.

Early
Nov.

Good fishing returns.
Crappie move back to the outside
of cover in water 5 to 12 feet deep.
Use bobber and jig or minnow rig.
Cast past and slow retreive to the
cover edge or let the wind push
bobber to the structure.

5 ft

10 ft

15 ft

Records   Black Crappie have 7 or 8 dorsal spines. State: 5 lbs. 4 oz., Rollins Lake, 1989; IGFA: 4 lbs. 8 oz., Virginia, 1981
White Crappie have six dorsal spines; State: 4 lbs. 8 oz., Clear Lake, 1971; IGFA: 5 lbs. 3 oz., Mississippi, 1957

See Also   Largemouth Bass

SACRAMENTO PERCH

Where/When   Crowley Lake and Pleasant Valley Reservoir. At Crowley, be on the water early as strong winds normally pick up quickly about 11 AM to noon.

Bait/Lures   Small jigs, 1/16 to 1/32 oz. Add a piece of worm or slice of squid. Color: crawdad, red & white, white, purple. See crappie lure picture.

Technique   Use the bobber rig and give the lure some action by flicking rod tip. Or jig very slowly just off the bottom. Action will come in spurts as schools of perch intercept your rig. Watch for other anglers success as best area can shift as the day wears.

Magie Williams shows how big the Sacramento perch get at Crowley Lake

Magie Williams. Vermont Tackle Co.

Rod	Lgth	Line	Lure/Wt.	Power / Action
	6 -7	2 - 6	1/16 - 1/4 oz.	Light or Ultra Lt. Moderate

Reel	Type	Size		
	Conv Spin	150 yds of 4#		

The Law   No Limit. No size restrictions.

Records   State: 3 lbs. 10 oz., Crowley Lake, 1974

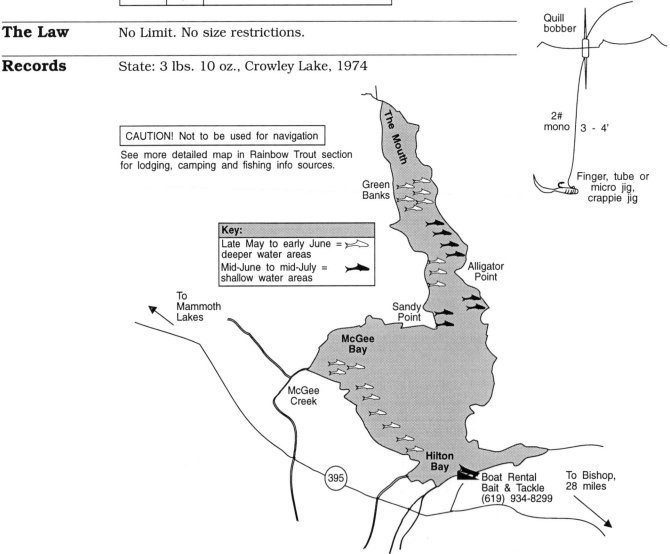

Quill bobber

2# mono | 3 - 4'

Finger, tube or micro jig, crappie jig

CAUTION! Not to be used for navigation

See more detailed map in Rainbow Trout section for lodging, camping and fishing info sources.

The Mouth

Green Banks

Key:
Late May to early June = deeper water areas
Mid-June to mid-July = shallow water areas

To Mammoth Lakes

Alligator Point

Sandy Point

McGee Bay

McGee Creek

Hilton Bay

395

Boat Rental Bait & Tackle (619) 934-8299

To Bishop, 28 miles

SALMON

There are 2 species of salmon commonly caught in California, king salmon and silver salmon. King salmon are also called chinook salmon. The king salmon is the largest salmon species. Fish over 20 lbs. are almost always kings. The biggest spawning run is in the fall but there is a smaller run in the spring. The king spawns principally in the larger rivers. Silver salmon are also called coho salmon. The silver salmon spawns in the fall and winter. They are most common north of San Francisco.

Jim Carter landed this 17 pound king salmon on the Feather River in mid-October

Bob Sparre Guide Service, Sacramento

Where/When   See the Freshwater Index map at end of ths section.

- Fishing is usually best in the morning, 6 AM to 9 AM.
- Avoid full moon periods.
- Moving salmon will follow the deeper and slower water runs. They will often be found along the edges of the main current.
- Resting salmon will hold in the larger holes, especially at the junction of major creeks and rivers. The good holes are well known and all have names, for example: Minnow Hole, Barge Hole, etc.
- Near a river's mouth in the area affected by tidal action, the bite is often better at high tide.

Salmon Fishing Calendar:

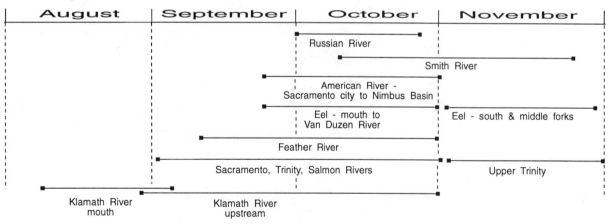

August	September	October	November
		Russian River	
			Smith River
	American River - Sacramento city to Nimbus Basin		
	Eel - mouth to Van Duzen River		Eel - south & middle forks
	Feather River		
	Sacramento, Trinity, Salmon Rivers		Upper Trinity
Klamath River mouth	Klamath River upstream		

Landlocked salmon are stocked in some notable northern lakes such as Lake Shasta, Oroville, Almanor, etc. These fish are found in similar structure and are caught using techniques commonly used for rainbow trout.

Bait/Lures   Anchovies work best near river mouths and for ocean fish. Roe works best upriver near spawning grounds. Tuna balls are oil packed tuna wrapped in maline, a red net material cut to a small square.

Lures: Salmon egg imitations —corkies, yarn. Hot shot, Wee Wart, Krocodile, Little Cleo, Dardevle, Panther Martin, Blue Fox, or Mepps spinners in size 2 to 5, Gold Kastmaster (3/4 oz.), Bear Valley Spinner, Black Roostertail.

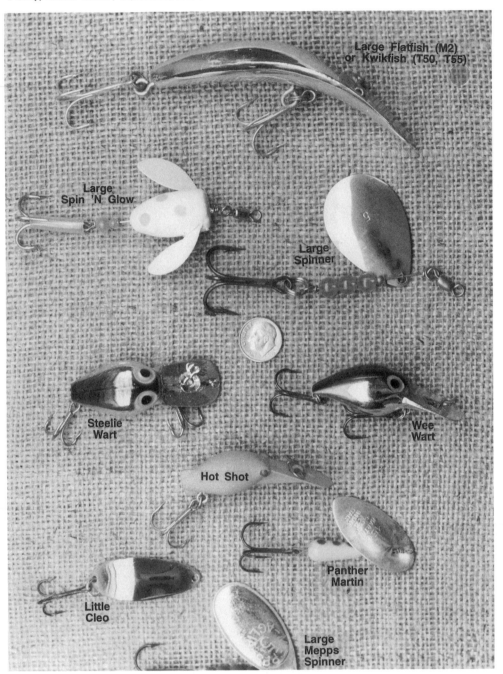

Rig

Back Trolling, Drifting or Casting

Rod	Lgth	Line	Lure/Wt.	Power / Action
	7 1/2 - 8 1/2	15 - 25	1 - 6 oz	Medium Heavy Fast
Reel	Type	Size		
	Conv. Spin	150 yds of 20# mono		

1. Back-Trolling Rig

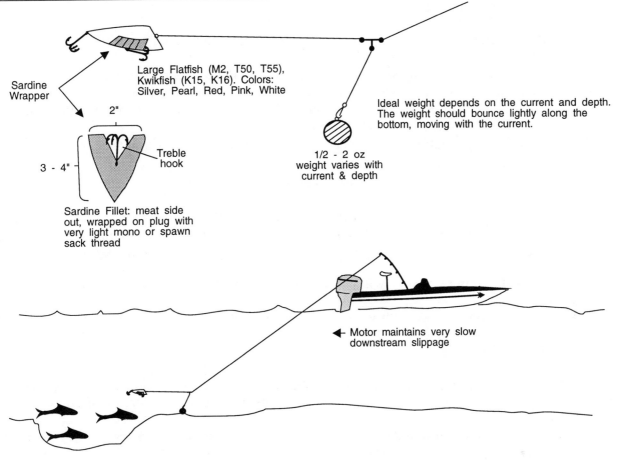

Sardine Wrapper

Large Flatfish (M2, T50, T55), Kwikfish (K15, K16). Colors: Silver, Pearl, Red, Pink, White

2"

3 - 4"

Treble hook

Sardine Fillet: meat side out, wrapped on plug with very light mono or spawn sack thread

Ideal weight depends on the current and depth. The weight should bounce lightly along the bottom, moving with the current.

1/2 - 2 oz weight varies with current & depth

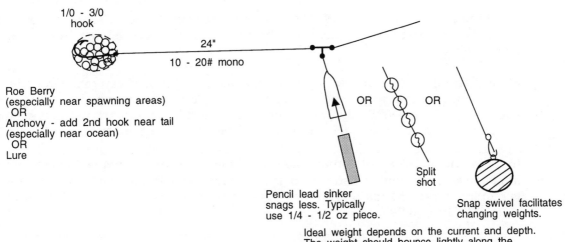

← Motor maintains very slow downstream slippage

2. Back Bouncing Roe, Drift Fishing, Plunking Rig

1/0 - 3/0 hook

24"

10 - 20# mono

Roe Berry (especially near spawning areas)
OR
Anchovy - add 2nd hook near tail (especially near ocean)
OR
Lure

OR   OR

Pencil lead sinker snags less. Typically use 1/4 - 1/2 oz piece.

Split shot

Snap swivel facilitates changing weights.

Ideal weight depends on the current and depth. The weight should bounce lightly along the bottom, moving with the current. Use heavy weights for stationary "Plunking".

Technique

For the following techniques **you MUST have enough weight to be on the bottom**. That's where the salmon are.

Backtrolling with large Flatfish (M2, T50 or T55), Kwikfish (K15 or K16), or roe.

- Run the boat motor just fast enough to keep the boat stationary in the river current above a productive hole.
- Drop your lures back 8 to 20 levelwinds so that the lure goes to the bottom and you feel the weight occasionally hitting bottom.
- Ease slightly off the motor to let the lure slowly move back into the hole.
- Work very slowly downstream.
- Watch carefully for any change in motion and strike!

The objective is to work the lure so that it slowly wobbles downstream toward the salmon's face. Work slowly to give the fish time to get irritated by this thing hanging in their face. Keep the lure working just off the bottom, and drifting slowly downstream.

Back Bouncing Roe differs from back bouncing because you work the bait by

- Pumping the rod to lift your weight off the bottom and let it slip downcurrent while letting some line slip off the reel.
- Repeat this action working different downstream lanes.

Drift Fishing, Bank Fishing or River Wading differ from back bouncing because your are not in a boat. Your must walk or wade into position and cast upstream of prime holes.

- Locate a promising deep hole, such as at the mouth of a feeder creek or stream and cast upstream of the hole.
- Let the current carry the bait through the "run" areas.
- Hold the rod tip high and keep the slack out of the line so you can feel a pickup.
- For lure fishing, systematically work the channels and pools with short casts and retrieves.

Plunking differs from the standard rig with the addition of a heavy sinker to keep the bait from drifting. Used most frequently at the mouth rivers where fish are concentrated and moving upstream.

Float Fishing involves the use of a boat and guide. Techniques can range from fly fishing to throwing plugs with spinning or casting outfits. Prior to big storms fly fishing with flies such as an olive green Woolly Worm is effective. After the rains start, use bait such as roe or nightcrawlers, or lures such as Hot Shots, Wee Warts, or Spin N' Glos (#12 or #14).

The Law

In lakes and streams, salmon are often combined with trout catches to determine daily limits. In lakes the limit is usually a 5 fish combination of salmon and trout. A punch card is required for the Klamath River. See DFG regs. for details or call (707) 445-6493. Silver salmon limit: zero fish.

Records

Chinook, State: 88 lbs., Sacramento River, Nov. 1979. IGFA: 97 lbs. 4 oz., Alaska, 1985
Silver, State: 22 lbs., Paper Mill Creek, January 1959. IGFA: 31 lbs., B.C. Canada, 1947

More Detail

Sacramento River: Complete Atlas & Anglers Guide to the Sacramento River, Shasta Dam to San Pablo Bay; Northern California Angler Publications, Elk Grove, (916) 685-2245. See Streamtime Maps (707) 664-8604 or The Fly Shop, (800) 669-FISH for the Eel, Feather, Gualala/Garcia, Klamath, Matole/Navarro, Russian, Smith and Trinity rivers. These maps accurately describe river access areas and drift boat launch/take-out spots.

Salmon, Freshwater Index

In late fall, the northwest rivers are subject to fishing closures due to low water. Call DFG Eureka for latest info (707) 442-4502

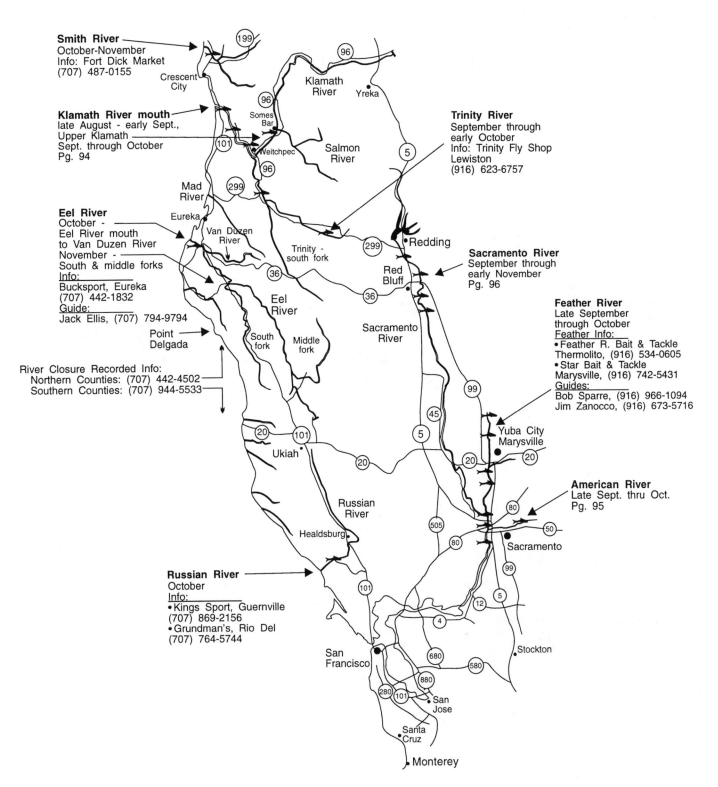

Smith River
October-November
Info: Fort Dick Market
(707) 487-0155

Klamath River mouth
late August - early Sept.,
Upper Klamath
Sept. through October
Pg. 94

Eel River
October -
Eel River mouth
to Van Duzen River
November -
South & middle forks
Info:
Bucksport, Eureka
(707) 442-1832
Guide:
Jack Ellis, (707) 794-9794

River Closure Recorded Info:
Northern Counties: (707) 442-4502
Southern Counties: (707) 944-5533

Russian River
October
Info:
• Kings Sport, Guernville
(707) 869-2156
• Grundman's, Rio Del
(707) 764-5744

Trinity River
September through
early October
Info: Trinity Fly Shop
Lewiston
(916) 623-6757

Sacramento River
September through
early November
Pg. 96

Feather River
Late September
through October
Feather Info:
• Feather R. Bait & Tackle
Thermolito, (916) 534-0605
• Star Bait & Tackle
Marysville, (916) 742-5431
Guides:
Bob Sparre, (916) 966-1094
Jim Zanocco, (916) 673-5716

American River
Late Sept. thru Oct.
Pg. 95

Crescent
City

Klamath
River

Yreka

Somes
Bar

Weitchpec

Salmon
River

Mad
River

Eureka

Van Duzen
River

Trinity -
south fork

Redding

Red
Bluff

Eel
River

Sacramento
River

Point
Delgada

South
fork

Middle
fork

Ukiah

Russian
River

Yuba City
Marysville

Sacramento

Healdsburg

Stockton

San
Francisco

San
Jose

Santa
Cruz

Monterey

Lower Klamath River, Salmon Fishing Areas

> ### CAUTION!   Not to be used for navigation.

Mouth best from August through Sept. Upstream at Pecwan Bar
and Weitchpec best from Sept. through October.
Fishing improves when high tides bring fresh runs into
the river mouth. During outgoing tides cast from shore or
troll   with large Kastmasters or spinners (Mepps #3-#5,
Blue Fox, Panther Martins, etc.). You'll need a 2-4 oz. sinker
A salmon punch card is required. See special regs.
for bag limits and fish over 22 inches.

Fishing Info:
Crivelli's, (707) 482-3713
Guides:
Jack Ellis, (707) 794-9794
Klamath River Outfitters, (916) 469-3349
Ron DeNardi, (916) 842-7655
Dam Drifters, (707) 482-6635

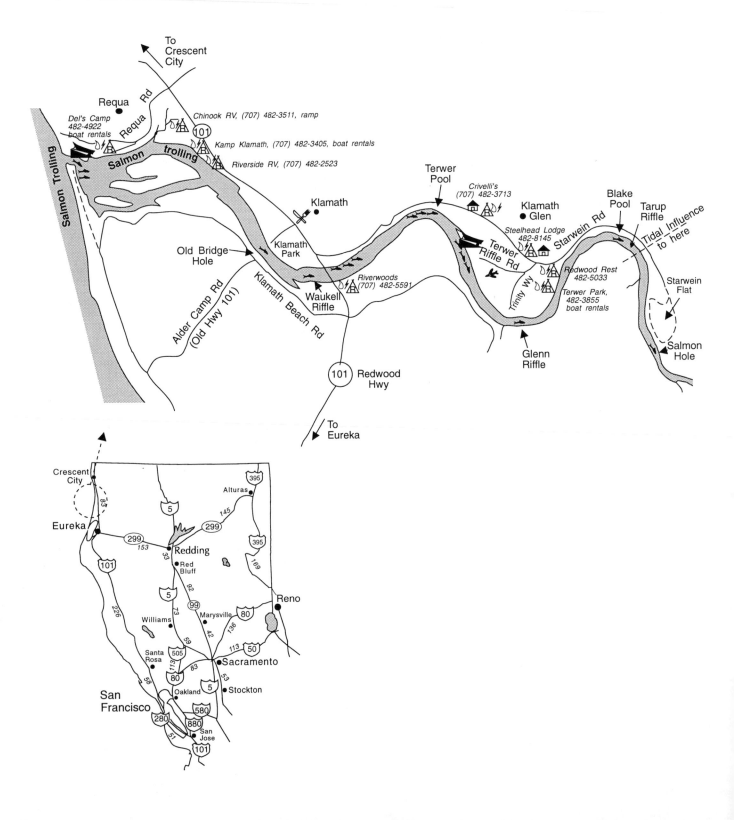

Sacramento City Salmon

| CAUTION! Do NOT use this map for navigation. |

September through October
Fishing Info:
Broadway Rod & Gun, Sacramento
(916) 448-6338
recording (916) 448-7630
Freeport Bait Co., (916) 665-1935
Guides:
Bob Sparre,   (916) 966-1094
John Morrison, (916) 677-3912

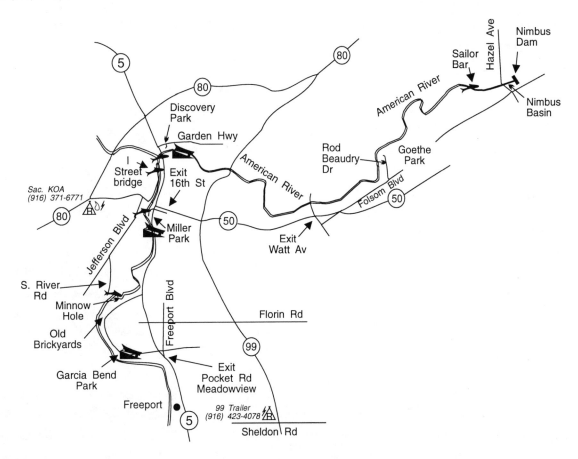

Sacramento River Salmon

> CAUTION! River contains many hazardous riffles & rapids.
> Do NOT use this map for navigation.

Fishing Info:
Red Bluff Diversion Dam fish counts
(916) 527-1408
Guides:
Bob Wigham, (916) 222-8058
Professional Guide Svc., (916) 365-8140
Jack Findleton, (916) 487-3392
Shasta Cascade Wonderland Assoc.
has guide and recreational information
(916) 275-5555
More Detail:
Complete Atlas & Anglers Guide to the Sacramento River
Northern Calif. Angler Publications,
(916) 685-2245

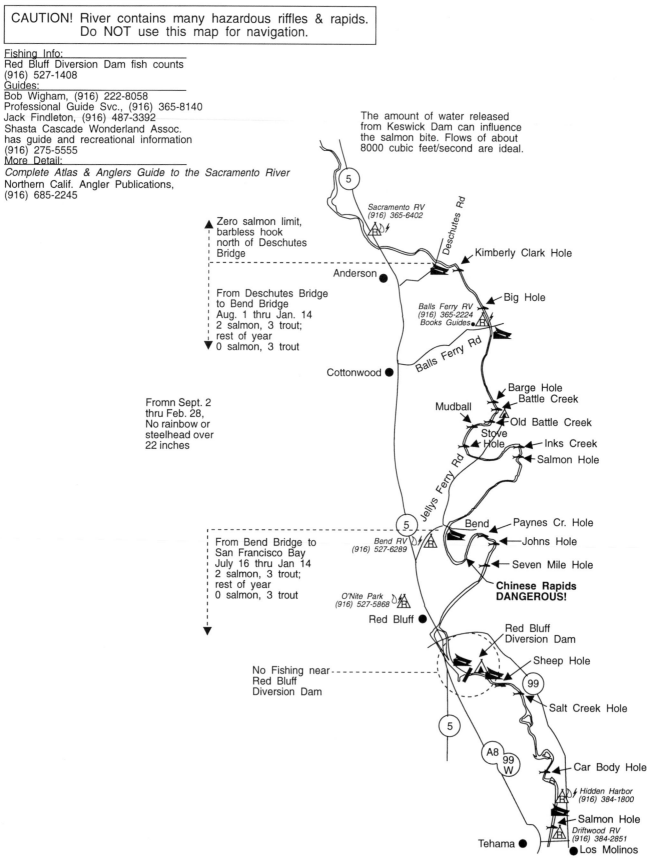

The amount of water released from Keswick Dam can influence the salmon bite. Flows of about 8000 cubic feet/second are ideal.

Zero salmon limit, barbless hook north of Deschutes Bridge

From Deschutes Bridge to Bend Bridge Aug. 1 thru Jan. 14 2 salmon, 3 trout; rest of year 0 salmon, 3 trout

Fromn Sept. 2 thru Feb. 28, No rainbow or steelhead over 22 inches

From Bend Bridge to San Francisco Bay July 16 thru Jan 14 2 salmon, 3 trout; rest of year 0 salmon, 3 trout

No Fishing near Red Bluff Diversion Dam

Sacramento RV (916) 365-6402

Kimberly Clark Hole

Anderson

Balls Ferry RV (916) 365-2224 Books Guides

Big Hole

Cottonwood

Balls Ferry Rd

Barge Hole
Battle Creek

Mudball

Old Battle Creek

Stove Hole

Inks Creek

Salmon Hole

Jellys Ferry Rd

Bend

Paynes Cr. Hole

Johns Hole

Bend RV (916) 527-6289

Seven Mile Hole

Chinese Rapids DANGEROUS!

O'Nite Park (916) 527-5868

Red Bluff

Red Bluff Diversion Dam

Sheep Hole

Salt Creek Hole

Car Body Hole

Hidden Harbor (916) 384-1800

Salmon Hole

Driftwood RV (916) 384-2851

Tehama

Los Molinos

KOKANEE SALMON (Sockeye)

These lake-bound, small (average 1 lb.) salmon exhibit typical salmon characteristics. They congregate near spawning creeks in the fall and spawn in late September and October. As September nears, the kokanee acquire spawning colors and shapes and their flesh becomes less firm and less palatable.

Where/When In Lake Tahoe from June to early September kokanee concentrate in the south-west corner. Look for other fishing boats. In California, if you are fishing alone, you are most probably in the wrong place.

In other lakes, Trinity, Bullards Bar, Stampede, Boca, Donner Lake, Twin Lakes - Bridgeport, Shaver, Pardee, and Bass the best fishing is in August and Sept. when the fish gather for spawning but they can be caught all year. For lakes other than Bullards Bar, Donner, Tahoe and Fallen Leaf, see the maps in the Rainbow Trout section.

Jim Niemiec

Most fish are caught in the early morning hours. Dusk hours can also be a prime time. However, kokanee can be caught at mid-day.

Structure

- Schools of kokanee suspend at depths which vary with the time of day and the season.
- At Lake Tahoe, in early summer and in the fall, kokanee will suspend 40 to 70+ feet deep. In mid-summer, they are deeper, down to 100-120 feet.
- The fish will be shallower in the morning and move deeper toward mid-day. The fish can be quite shallow in the spring, morning hours.
- In Lakes other than Tahoe, during the summer months, the kokanee will be close to the thermocline 40 to 70+ feet deep.

Bait/Lures

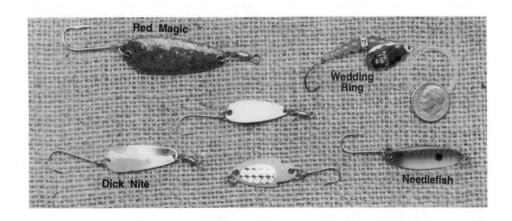

Rig

For trolling use a conventional light to ultra-light reel and rod with a flexible, sensitive tip. When jigging, a faster, stiffer tipped rod is useful for feeling pickups and setting the hook.

Kokanee Salmon, Jigging

	Lgth	Line	Lure/Wt.	Power / Action
Rod	6 - 7	6 - 8	3 - 5 oz.	Light Moderate
	Type	**Size**		
Reel	Conv Spin	150 yds of 6#		

1. Trolling

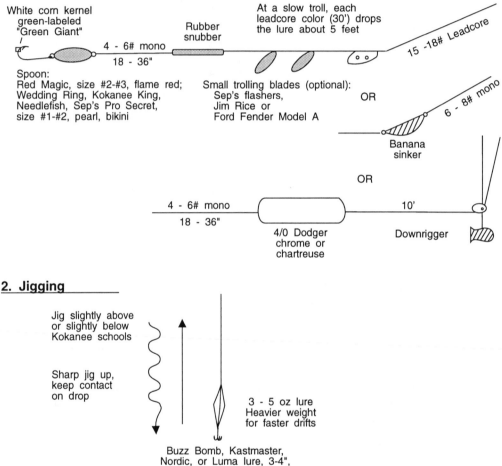

White corn kernel green-labeled "Green Giant"

Spoon:
Red Magic, size #2-#3, flame red; Wedding Ring, Kokanee King, Needlefish, Sep's Pro Secret, size #1-#2, pearl, bikini

Rubber snubber

4 - 6# mono
18 - 36"

At a slow troll, each leadcore color (30') drops the lure about 5 feet

Small trolling blades (optional): Sep's flashers, Jim Rice or Ford Fender Model A

15 -18# Leadcore

OR

6 - 8# mono

Banana sinker

OR

4 - 6# mono
18 - 36"

4/0 Dodger chrome or chartreuse

10'

Downrigger

2. Jigging

Jig slightly above or slightly below Kokanee schools

Sharp jig up, keep contact on drop

3 - 5 oz lure Heavier weight for faster drifts

Buzz Bomb, Kastmaster, Nordic, or Luma lure, 3-4", white or chrome

Technique

Since these fish are not shoreline or structure oriented and essentially wander around the middle parts of the lakes considerably below the surface, a boat with a good fish-finder is essential for locating the suspended schools.

Trolling is the most effective technique when the kokanee are still scattered in June and July. Jigging becomes effective in August when the schools become more concentrated.

For all techniques, you must first locate the correct depth. Call the listed info sources. Troll multiple lines at different depths until successful then change other rigs to the right depth, or the easiest method, use a good fish finder to locate the schools. They will be near the thermocline in summer.

Trolling with downriggers is the most effective fishing method. **It is critical to troll very slowly about 1 mph.** This is equivalent to a slow walk. Kokanee are not spooked by the downrigger ball so you can use a short dropback, about 10 feet. With this short dropback, it is a simple and effective to make many quick swings through a kokanee school until you get a hit. Set your downrigger to troll the lure just above the kokanee depth.

Trolling with leadcore line will not get a lot of fishing action out of a 1 lb. kokanee using leadcore line rigged with blades. For more "sport" use a downrigger or try jigging when appropriate. You need to determine how many colors of lead core to let out. Generally this ranges from 2 colors (early morning, early season) to 8 colors (mid-summer, mid-day). One color will equal about 5 feet of depth.

Jigging with Buzz Bombs or other jig type lures can be effective during mid-day hours. First locate suspended schools with your fish finder. Drop your lure (i.e. Buzz Bomb) straight down and work by jigging either slightly above or below the school depth. The larger males are typically deeper.

The Law	Kokanee salmon are included in the "trout" regulations. Even though the general rule is a 5 trout daily bag limit, many special restrictions apply. See current DFG regulations.
Records	IGFA: 6 lbs. 9 oz., Idaho, 1975
See Also	Rainbow trout, brown trout, and makinaw trout in Lake Tahoe and Donner Lake

Kokanee Salmon, Lake Tahoe, Donner & Fallen Leaf

CAUTION! Not to be used for navigation.

Guides:
Dan Hannum, (916) 541-8801
Bruce Hernandez, (916) 577-2246
Rick Muller, (916) 544-4358
Larry Tomer, (916) 577-4135
For Boat Rentals, Camping and Lodging
see the Mackinaw Trout map.

The Law
for bag limits of kokanee,
mackinaw, brown and rainbow trout
is 5 per day, 10 in possession but
only 2 mackinaw in Lake Tahoe.
See special tributary regs.

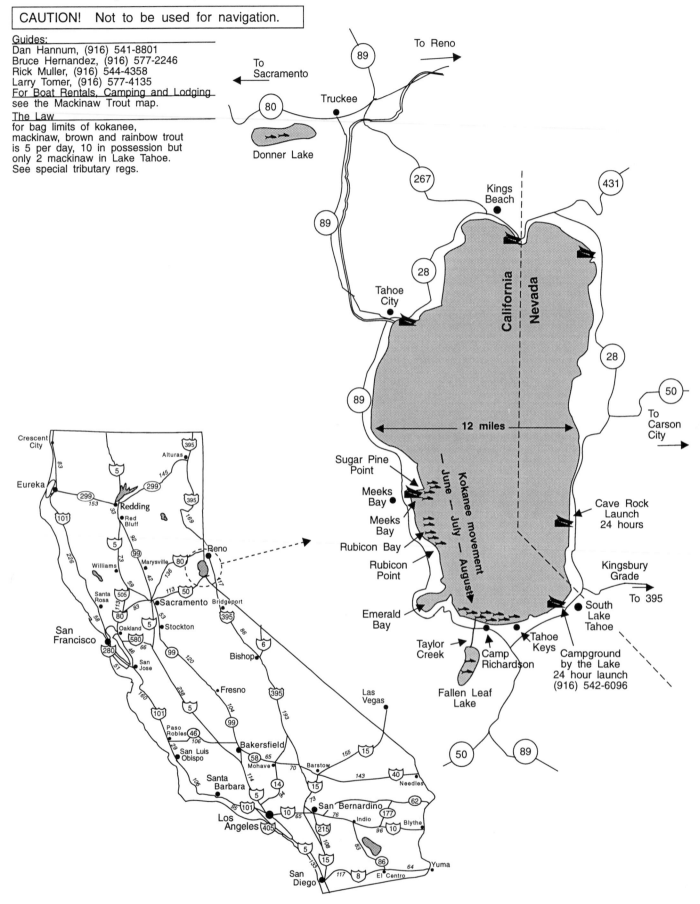

Kokanee Salmon, Bullard's Bar Reservoir

CAUTION!   Not to be used for navigation.

Fishing Info, Rental Boats, Houseboats, Camping
Emerald Cove Marina, (916) 692-3200
= good kokanee spot
= good trout spot

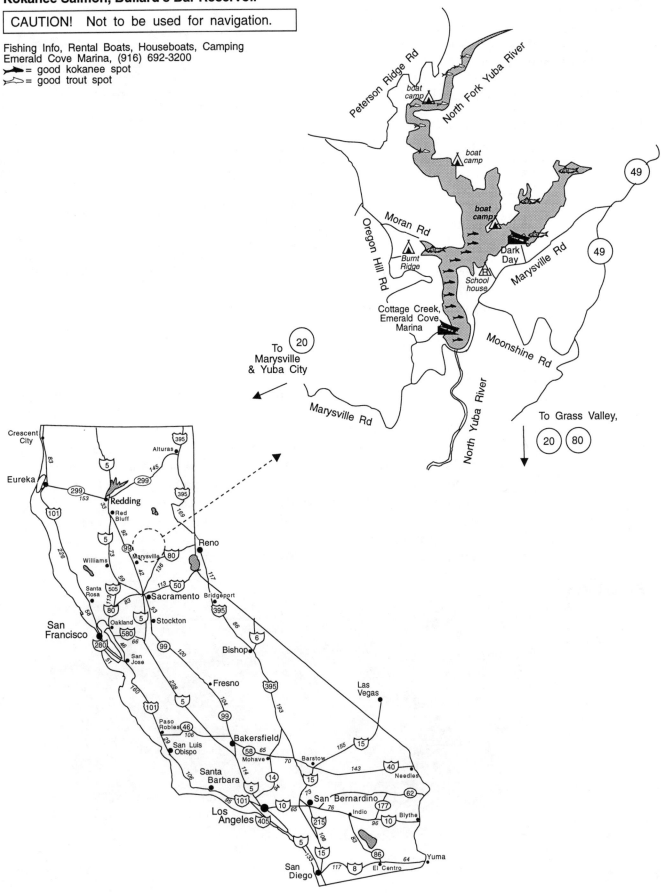

SHAD

Shad are not good eating, although they can be pickled or smoked. Males are smaller and average 2 to 3 pounds. Females average 3 to 5 pounds. Females run later, following males by 2 to 3 weeks.

Guide Bill Adelman produced this fat hen shad for the author on the Sacramento near Verona

Where/When   Sacramento River drainage system including the American, Feather, and Yuba rivers. May to July. Shad runs also occur in the:

- Russian River at the the mouth of Dry Creek and below the rock dam in Healdsburg. from mid-April to mid-June.
- Trinity River at Willow Creek near Hoopa the last half of June.
- Klamath River at Somes Bar and downriver, esp. from Somes Bar to Orleans around mid-June through July.

Structure

- Shad hold in medium to semi-fast current areas that vary from 2 to 10 feet deep. Fish prefer the juncture (seam) of the medium current with adjoining slow currents.
- Shad hold next to the bottom.
- Shad align themselves in long lines oriented upstream/downstream. It is very important to fish the right upstream/downstream line to put your lure in their faces.
- Shad congregate and hold below the junction of major rivers and creeks.
- Shad congregate and hold below dams (Red Bluff Diversion Dam, Nimbus Dam).
- In clear water areas (American River, etc.) shad activity is best in the early morning and early evening hours.
- In muddy waters (Sacramento at Freeport, Verona, etc.) daytime fishing can be good.

Bait/Lures

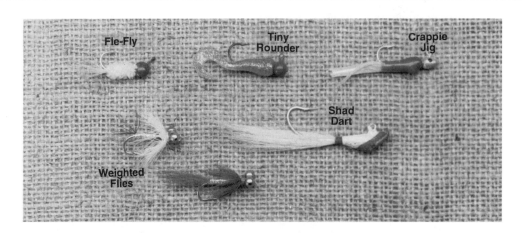

Rig

		Lgth	Line	Lure/Wt.	Power / Action
Rod		5 1/2- 6	4 - 6	1/16 - 1/4 oz.	Light or Ultra Lt. Moderate
Reel		**Type**	**Size**		
		Conv Spin	150 yds of 4#		

Shad Flyfishing

		Lgth	Wt.	Examples
Rod		8 - 8 1/2	6 - 7	Lamiglas G1297-6, G1297-7

1. Bottom Bouncer Rig

For heavier lures, 1/8 - 1/4 oz., a straight rig (no weight) can be used. However lighter lures, 1/16 to 1/32 oz. catch more fish.

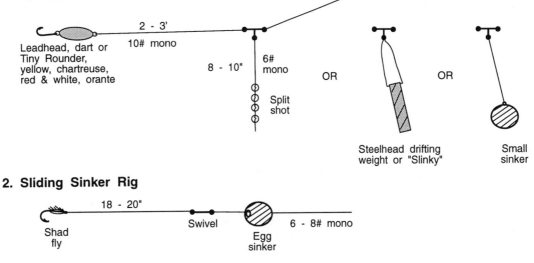

Leadhead, dart or Tiny Rounder, yellow, chartreuse, red & white, orante

2 - 3'
10# mono

8 - 10"   6# mono

Split shot

OR

Steelhead drifting weight or "Slinky"

OR

Small sinker

2. Sliding Sinker Rig

18 - 20"

Shad fly

Swivel

Egg sinker

6 - 8# mono

3. Fly Fishing Rig

Let out about 60 to 80 feet behind anchored boat

Shad fly

8# tippet

6 or 7 weight Hi-speed, Hi-density shooting head

75 feet of "Amnesia" mono (optional)

Backing: 100 yards of 20# dacron

Technique

If wading or bank fishing:

- Cast upstream of a fish holding area.
- Let your lure drift through the prime area.
- Your lure should move with the current occasionally bumping the bottom. Your lure must be hitting the bottom to be effective.
- Shad don't strike, they inhale the lure. Watch for any hesitation in the line movement.

In a boat:

- Let the lure swing with the current directly behind the boat.
- Work the lure by occasional jigging or by jigging and retrieving.

- Try different "lines". Remember that shad hold in long upstream/downstream lines. These lines are not stationary but will shift somewhat. If you are catching fish, stick with your "line". If the action slows try other lines by reaching out one side or the other with your rod and work a different line. If your boat has bow cleats on both the starboard and port sides, simply shifting the anchor line can swing your boat in the current and give you a different, perhaps better line to work. Since the shad lines are long, if you see another boat catching shad, moving a polite distance directly upstream or downstream from that boat can be successful.

Fishing near restricted dam areas may require a surf casting rig or plastic bubble to reach the productive white water.

The Law	Limit, 25; No minimum size.
Records	State: 7 lbs. 5 oz.; Feather River IGFA: 11 lbs. 4 oz., Massachusetts, May 1986
See Also	Sturgeon, striped bass, rainbow trout

Shad Spots, Sacramento City
April and May

Fishing Info:
Broadway Rod & Gun, Sacramento
(916) 448-6338
recording (916) 448-7630
Freeport Bait Co., (916) 665-1935
Guides:
Bill Adelman, (510) 232-9991
Bob Wigham, (916) 222-8058

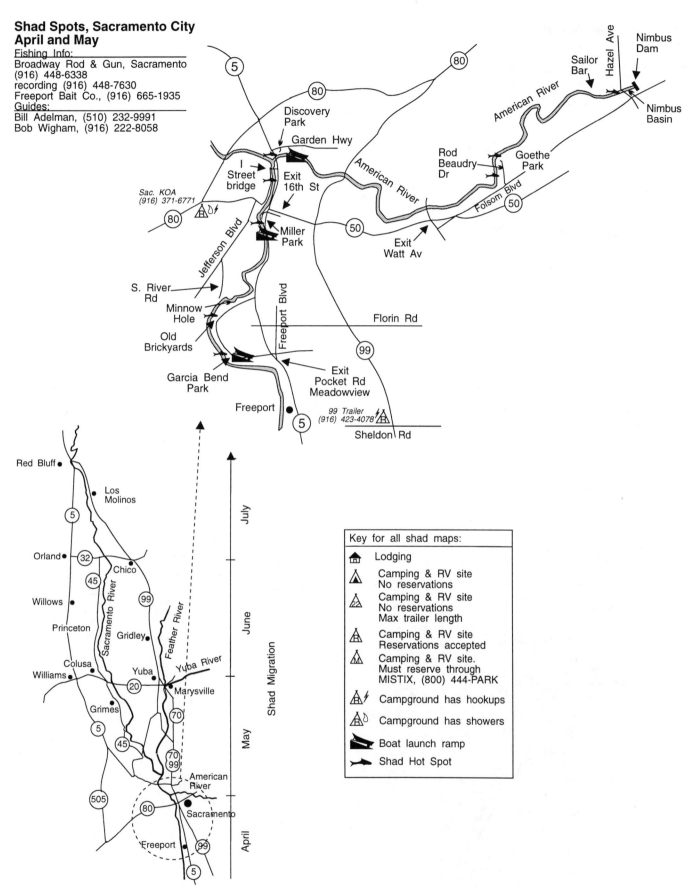

Key for all shad maps:

🏠 Lodging

⛺ Camping & RV site
No reservations

⛺ Camping & RV site
No reservations
Max trailer length

⛺ Camping & RV site
Reservations accepted

⛺ Camping & RV site.
Must reserve through
MISTIX, (800) 444-PARK

⛺⚡ Campground has hookups

⛺💧 Campground has showers

Boat launch ramp

Shad Hot Spot

Shad Spots, May to early June

Fishing Info:
Star Bait & Tackle, Marysville, (916) 742-5431
Guides:
Bill Adelman, (510) 232-9991
Bob Wigam, (916) 222-8058
Flyfishing Guide: Trinity Fly Shop books late May
and early June, Yuba River trips. (916) 623-6757

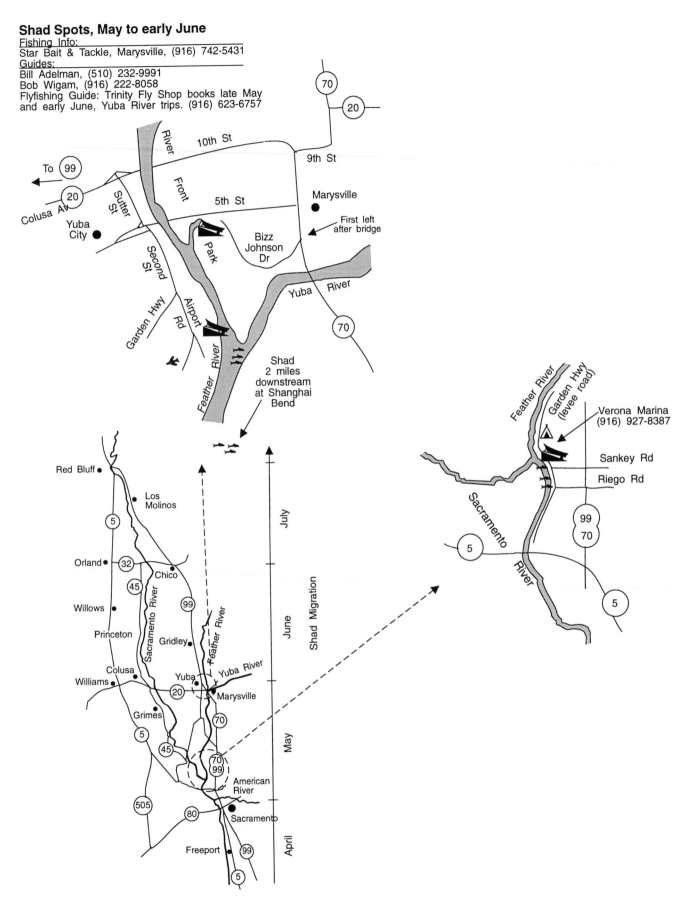

Shad Spots, Red Bluff Area
June through July

Guide:
Professional Guide Svc., (916) 365-8140

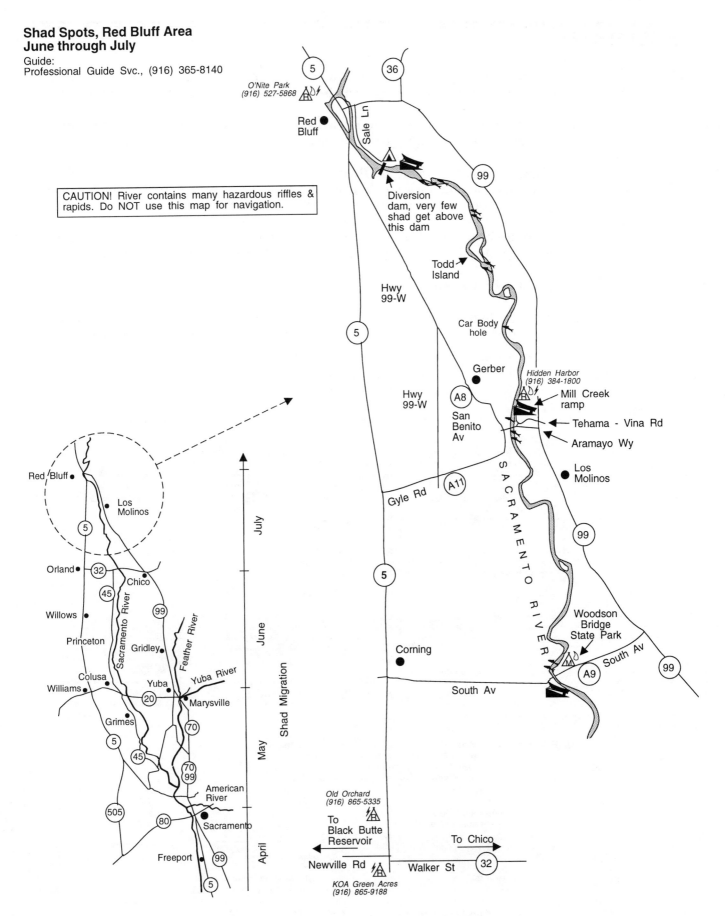

CAUTION! River contains many hazardous riffles & rapids. Do NOT use this map for navigation.

O'Nite Park
(916) 527-5868

Red Bluff

Diversion dam, very few shad get above this dam

Todd Island

Hwy 99-W

Car Body hole

Gerber

Hidden Harbor
(916) 384-1800

Mill Creek ramp

Hwy 99-W

A8

San Benito Av

Tehama - Vina Rd

Aramayo Wy

Los Molinos

Gyle Rd

A11

SACRAMENTO RIVER

Corning

Woodson Bridge State Park

South Av

A9

South Av

Old Orchard
(916) 865-5335

To Black Butte Reservoir

To Chico

Newville Rd

Walker St

32

KOA Green Acres
(916) 865-9188

Red Bluff

Los Molinos

Orland

Chico

Sacramento River

Willows

Princeton

Gridley

Feather River

Colusa

Yuba

Yuba River

Williams

Marysville

Grimes

American River

Sacramento

Freeport

July

June

May

April

Shad Migration

STEELHEAD

Where   The major steelhead rivers are the Klamath and Trinity, Smith, Eel, and Russian. These rivers support sustained runs and can be relied upon to hold steelhead during the season.

The smaller steelhead streams have much shorter runs, and their fishing status can change so quickly that only local anglers can effectively fish them.

As of this writing, the steelhead fishery of the Yuba and American are in bad shape and the Feather and Sacramento are fading fast. Since these areas are close to the major Sacramento populations, some details are provided on these rivers.

Average steelhead size varies considerably between major rivers. A trophy steelhead on the Klamath is 10+ pounds. A trophy steelhead on the Smith is 20+ pounds.

Structure, Winter Season Adults:

Steelhead hold in water that is quieter than surrounding waters. These holding areas are usually adjacent to their runs, or preferred paths of least effort in swimming upstream.

1. Winter Season: Colder water (lower oxygen requirements) and non-feeding status contribute to preference for quieter water areas.

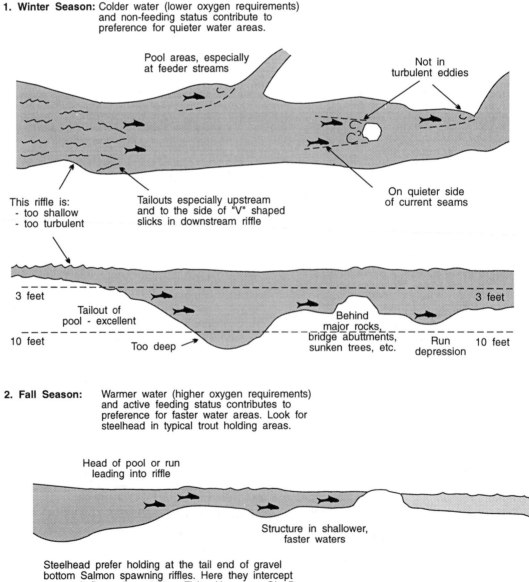

Pool areas, especially at feeder streams

Not in turbulent eddies

On quieter side of current seams

This riffle is:
- too shallow
- too turbulent

Tailouts especially upstream and to the side of "V" shaped slicks in downstream riffle

3 feet

3 feet

Tailout of pool - excellent

Behind major rocks, bridge abuttments, sunken trees, etc.

Run depression

10 feet

Too deep

10 feet

2. Fall Season: Warmer water (higher oxygen requirements) and active feeding status contributes to preference for faster water areas. Look for steelhead in typical trout holding areas.

Head of pool or run leading into riffle

Structure in shallower, faster waters

Steelhead prefer holding at the tail end of gravel bottom Salmon spawning riffles. Here they intercept roe as it floats downstream. Fish with roe or Glo Bugs.

In runs the fish can be more spread out and holding in less obvious structure, behind smaller submerged rocks and in stream bottom depressions. These runs may have to be fished methodically in order to find fish.

Fish also concentrate at:

1. The mouth of rivers where the tidal swings affect the river level. Steelhead (and salmon) will enter the river with the high tides and hold here while acclimating to the change from salt to fresh water or, in low water conditions, wait for the river to rise.

2. At the junction of feeder, spawning streams. Typically there are deeper pools formed by streams entering the main river. Steelhead will concentrate here to rest and to wait for rain to fill the spawning streams.

Because of the vulnerability of fish holding at these junctions, there are some restrictions in the major spawning streams. See current DFG regulations for details.

3. Fish will stack in areas below dams that prevent or significantly hinder their upstream progress. Also the water conditions are consistently good in these areas because of the controlled releases of water such as:

- Below Iron Gate dam on the Klamath River off highway 5 north of Redding
- Below Van Arsdale dam on the Eel river, off highway 20, north of Ukiah
- Near Lewiston and Douglas City on the Trinity River off highway 36

Structure, Fall Season Adults:

Steelhead are feeding, are more active, and require more oxygenated water in the fall. They will hold more in typical rainbow trout structure. They will be at the head of pools and at the downstream end of the deeper riffles.

Structure, Half Pounders:

Immature "half pounders" frequent the lower river stretches in the fall and early winter months. They are actively feeding and prefer riffles and shallow runs.

When

Winter (Wet) Season: October to February. January and February are typically the best months. Winter fish are considerably larger but are not actively feeding. When you can see your lure in 2 to 3 feet of water, start fishing.

Steelhead Fishing Calendar

■————————■ = Prime Seasons
■- - - - - - - ■ = Secondary Seasons

Month:	September	October	November	December	January	February	March

Klamath fall run, mouth to Orleans, Somes Bar

Klamath fall run, upriver to Iron Gate dam

Klamath winter run

Trinity, Weitchpec to Cedar Flat

Upper Trinity, Big Bar to Lewiston

Smith, especially between hwy. 101 and 199 bridges

Russian River

Eel River

Feather River, fall run

Feather River, winter run

Fall (dry) Season: September until first rains, normally late October or November. The Klamath and Trinity have a fall run of "half pounders", smaller fish from 1/2 to 3 pounds. These fish are active, feeding fish and are easier to catch and provide more action than the larger sized winter run fish. The bite is best in the early morning or at twilight. Fly fishing for the smaller fish is popular. Pale morning dun and callibaetis hatches start in early and late November.

| **Bait/Lures** | Bait: Roe, nightcrawler, tuna ball, crayfish tail. In tidal areas: Cut mackerel, anchovy. |

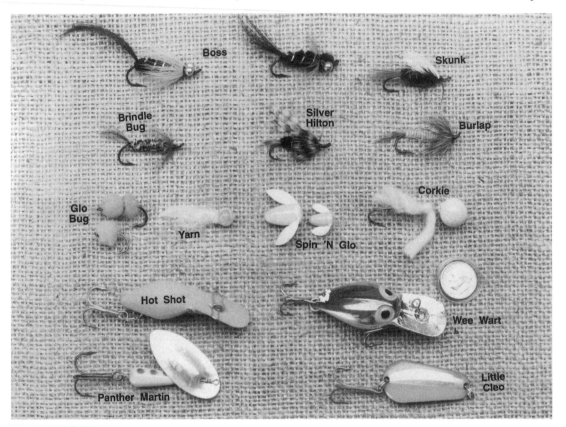

In the winter season especially in dirty water and/or low light, shady conditions, use size #5 or #4 spinner lures with bright, shiny french style blades. Colors: florescent orange, red, yellow, or chartreuse.

In the fall season especially in clear water, bright light conditions use smaller #2 to #3 spinner lures still with dull, dark french style blades. Colors: florescent kelly green, darker reds, yellow, black.

Rig

Because of the "feel" required to detect a steelhead pickup, rods with flexible tips, especially graphite rods are preferred.

Backtrolling, Drifting, Lure Casting

	Lgth	Line	Lure/Wt.	Power / Action
Rod	7 - 9	10 - 16	1/4 - 2 oz.	Light to Medium Moderate to Fast
	Type	**Size**		**Examples**
Reel	Conv Spin	200 yds of 12#		Conv: Penn Squidder, Daiwa SL20SH; Ambassadeur 5000, 6000 Spin: Daiwa 2600; Shimano Baitrunner 3500

Flyfishing

Rod	Lgth	Line	Wt.	Examples
	8 - 10	2 - 6	8 - 11 graphite	Fenwick FF85, FF108, FF95; Sage Graphite II Model 990 RP; Comparable Loomis rods
Reel	Capacity			
	150 yds dacron + 70 yds of 20# mono + 30 ft. of shooting Hi Speed, Hi-D fly line			

Flyfishing Half Pounders

Rod	Lgth	Wt.	Examples
	8 - 10	4 - 6 graphite	Lamiglas G1298-4, G1298-5

Rig the fly reel with 150 yds. of dacron backing + 70 yds. of 20# mono + a 30' shooting head, Hi-speed, Hi-D, fly line.

For half pounders use a floating or sinking tip fly line and a 6# tippet.

1. Bait Drift Rig: load with roe, nightcrawler, etc.

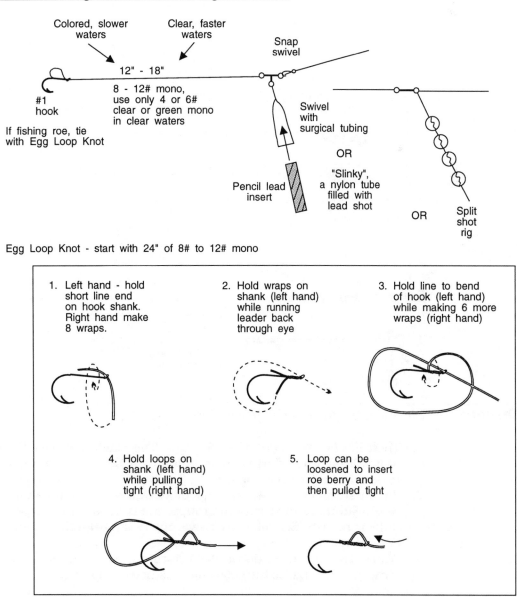

2. Floating Lure Rigs

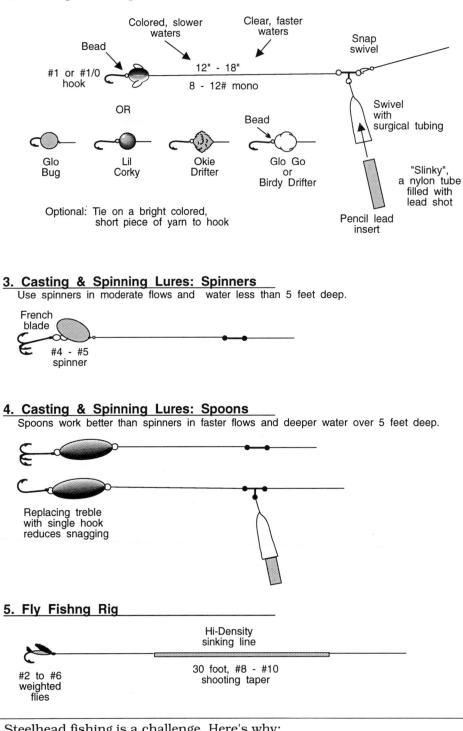

Colored, slower waters

Clear, faster waters

Snap swivel

Bead

#1 or #1/0 hook

12" - 18"

8 - 12# mono

Swivel with surgical tubing

OR

Bead

Glo Bug

Lil Corky

Okie Drifter

Glo Go or Birdy Drifter

"Slinky", a nylon tube filled with lead shot

Pencil lead insert

Optional: Tie on a bright colored, short piece of yarn to hook

3. Casting & Spinning Lures: Spinners
Use spinners in moderate flows and water less than 5 feet deep.

French blade

#4 - #5 spinner

4. Casting & Spinning Lures: Spoons
Spoons work better than spinners in faster flows and deeper water over 5 feet deep.

Replacing treble with single hook reduces snagging

5. Fly Fishng Rig

Hi-Density sinking line

#2 to #6 weighted flies

30 foot, #8 - #10 shooting taper

Technique   Steelhead fishing is a challenge. Here's why:

1. There is a large amount of fishing area. The Klamath is over 190 miles long. Every mile of it will hold fish during some time in the season. Other major rivers, the Eel and Russian are also quite long.

2. Winter storms can make streams or stream sections unfishable for up to 3 weeks.

3. Steelhead move upstream in groups. Areas separating these migrating schools hold little or no fish. Schools may move upstream 4-6 miles in one day. Most traveling is done at night.

4. Winter run steelhead do not feed during their upstream voyage. This reluctance to strike means precise lure placement is needed for success.

5. Even if the steelhead are currently known to be in a particular stretch of the river, they still will only be found in very limited holding areas (see Where: Structure). Unless you are very familiar with a section of the river or are very experienced at reading steelhead water, there is a good chance you will be fishing dead areas.

6. Steelhead bites can be hard to detect. Especially when fishing bait, a steelhead pickup can be very hard to recognize. Experience and close attention are needed. Shorter casts of 20 to 30 feet allow more line feel and bite detection than longer casts.

7. Because of the necessity for placing the lure/bait near the stream bottom, snags and lost tackle are common.

8. Steelhead in clear or low water are easily spooked.

So how do we deal with this challenge?

Fishing Strategy:

1. Get current reliable informa-
    tion by calling information
    numbers. See the Steelhead
    Information and Stream
    Clearing Speed maps. Ask
    "Where are the fish?" Steel-
    head move up the river in
    clusters. Ask "What are the
    water conditions?" Look for
    clearing water with 2 to 3
    foot visibility.

    •   Some stream areas clear
        considerably faster than
        others. It can vary from
        1 - 2 days to 3 weeks.

    •   The upper sections of riv-
        ers clear quicker than
        the lower sections.

    Guide Jack Ellis released this bright metalhead on the Klamath River

    •   Smaller feeder streams
        and their junction with the major rivers are fishable earlier.

    •   What's the weather report? If its raining hard now or expected soon, don't go.

2. If you are new to steelheading, I very highly recommend hiring a guide. Learn as much as you can during this guiding trip. This could save you man-years of effort.

3. In an area with recently reported fish and good water condition;
    •   Fish known steelhead areas. See Hotspots Map, Structure diagram.
    •   Limit your time fishing unproductive waters. Consistently good anglers stay on the move until they find fish concentrations. If fishing lures, if no action, move on after covering the area with casts. If fishing bait, which is a slower process, if no action move on in 30 to 45 minutes. **It is critical to keep moving until successful.**

4. It is helpful to intimately learn a certain stretch of water. If you have fished a known steelhead area before and have gained knowledge of its fish holding structure, and the reports say fish are in the area and the water is right, fish it again, learn more, catch more steelhead!

5. **If the water is clear and especially if the river level is low, it is critical to use stealth in your approach, technique and tackle.** Stay as low as you can when ap-proaching the stream. Stay as far back from the fish holding area as possible while still being close enough to accurately and quietly place your cast. Cast carefully to minimize the splash. Cast sideways to a point some distance from the fish holding spot and work the lure back to the fish. Place your cast so the line doesn't pass over the fish. Only use 4 pound or 6 pound clear or green mono line or leader.

Fishing Techniques:

1. Backtrolling plugs or roe. This technique is very similar to backtrolling for salmon. The major difference is the use of double ender drift boats. This technique requires a full time boat handler.

   Work the structure area slowly and thoroughly covering the width of the suspected holding area, and very slowly slipping downstream. It can take an 8 hour day to properly fish a 5 mile stretch of water.

2. Drifting plugs or bait. This technique can be used from the bank, wading, or from an anchored boat. If the current is strong enough to move a drift rig and the bottom is relatively smooth and free of sunken timber and other snags, use a drift fishing rig and:

   - Work the near water first.
   - Make a quartering cast upstream of the structure/holding area.
   - Maintain enough line tension during the drift so that you can feel the occasional tapping when the weight hits the bottom and you don't interfere with the downstream drift of the lure/bait.
   - If a slower current area causes the lure to stop, reel in slowly only until the current again picks up the rig.

   Use "tailing" when necessary to extend a drift to downstream holding areas. Tailing is a controlled release of line. With a spinning reel this is done by reeling backwards slowly. With a conventional casting reel, freespool and thumb control does the job.

   Some runs will require systematic coverage (nearest water first). This is especially true if there are no obvious holding structures and this is new water to you. Be careful when retrieving your rig not to disturb unfished holding areas. Fish closer areas first.

   Drifted nightcrawlers are effective all throughout the season. During salmon season, use salmon eggs, roe or glo-bugs in areas below spawning salmon.

3. Drifting spoons or spinners. If the holding water is not deep, or the current is to slow for a drift rig, or the area would cause too much snagging with a drift rig, then use a spinner, spoon, or wobbler. This technique can be used from the bank, wading, or from an anchored boat.

   Don't cast and retrieve. Drift these lures, allowing the current to move them through the same critical fish-holding structures. Maintain a slight line tension on the lure during the drift to enhance correct lure action and reduce snagging. **The lure must be just off the bottom**. Vary lure weight and style to keep it on the bottom or use the pencil lead drift-fishing rig. Use a swivel to minimize line twisting.

   Lighter spinners are best suited for moderate flows and water less than 5 feet deep. Some spinners work well in slow water flows. Heavier spoons work better in faster flows and in water deeper than 5 feet.

4. Fly Fishing. Fly fishing can be a very effective technique. Clearer waters are required for flies to be visible. Most fly fishing is done in the fall for half pounders. Fly fishing tackle is also used for backtrolling. No casting is required. The rig is simply let out behind the boat the same as with conventional rigs.

The Law   Special restrictions and closures are common. Consult current DFG regulations. Steelhead are included within the "trout" regulations. A Steelhead Trout Catch Report Registration Card is required for documenting any fish over 16 inches.

Records	State: 27 lbs. 4 oz.; Smith River; Dec. 1976
	IGFA: 42 lbs. 2 oz., Alaska, 1970
Access	See Streamtime Maps, Cotati, CA (707) 664-8604 for the Russian, Eel, Klamath, and Smith rivers. These maps accurately describe river access areas and drift boat launch/take-out spots.
See Also	Salmon, rainbow trout

Steelhead & Salmon Rivers, Best Seasons
The first heavy rain is usually in late September

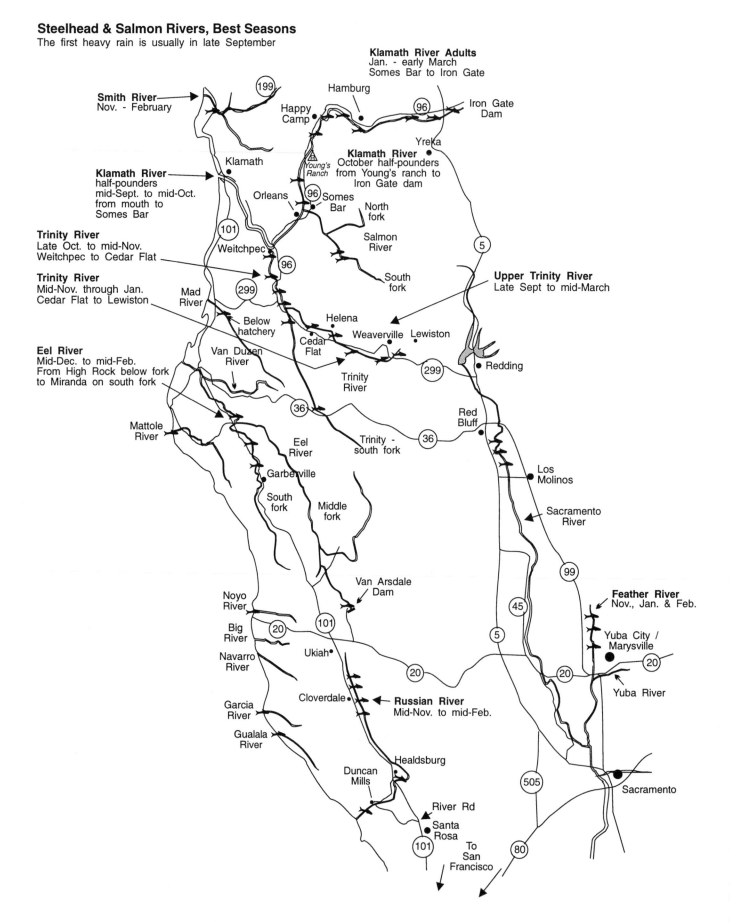

Klamath River Adults
Jan. - early March
Somes Bar to Iron Gate

Smith River
Nov. - February

Klamath River
October half-pounders
from Young's ranch to
Iron Gate dam

Klamath River
half-pounders mid-Sept. to mid-Oct. from mouth to Somes Bar

Trinity River
Late Oct. to mid-Nov.
Weitchpec to Cedar Flat

Trinity River
Mid-Nov. through Jan.
Cedar Flat to Lewiston

Upper Trinity River
Late Sept to mid-March

Eel River
Mid-Dec. to mid-Feb.
From High Rock below fork
to Miranda on south fork

Feather River
Nov., Jan. & Feb.

Russian River
Mid-Nov. to mid-Feb.

Steelhead Rivers, Clearing Speeds
The first heavy rain is usually in late September
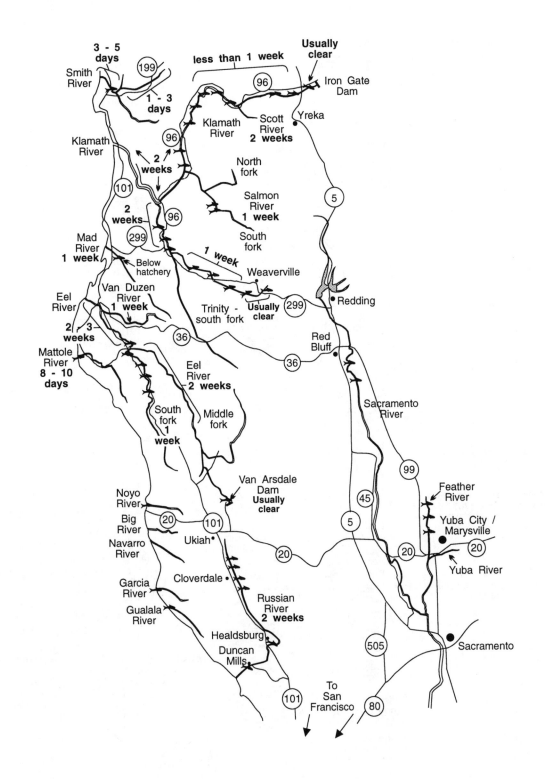
= good fishing and easy access

Steelhead Guides and Information

These info sources below will also recommend good local guides

= good fishing and easy access

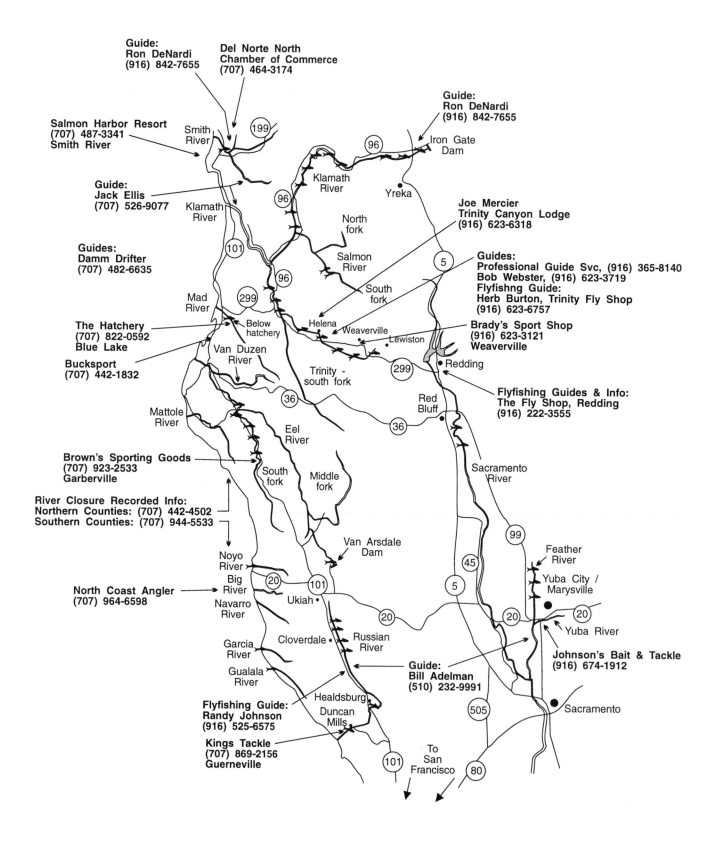

Guide:
Ron DeNardi
(916) 842-7655

Del Norte North
Chamber of Commerce
(707) 464-3174

Guide:
Ron DeNardi
(916) 842-7655

199

96

Iron Gate
Dam

Salmon Harbor Resort
(707) 487-3341
Smith River

Smith
River

Klamath
River

Yreka

Joe Mercier
Trinity Canyon Lodge
(916) 623-6318

Guide:
Jack Ellis
(707) 526-9077

96

North
fork

101

Klamath
River

Salmon
River

5

Guides:
Professional Guide Svc, (916) 365-8140
Bob Webster, (916) 623-3719
Flyfishng Guide:
Herb Burton, Trinity Fly Shop
(916) 623-6757

Guides:
Damm Drifter
(707) 482-6635

96

South
fork

Mad
River

299

The Hatchery
(707) 822-0592
Blue Lake

Below
hatchery

Helena

Weaverville

Lewiston

Brady's Sport Shop
(916) 623-3121
Weaverville

Bucksport
(707) 442-1832

Van Duzen
River

Trinity -
south fork

299

Redding

Mattole
River

Trinity -
south fork

36

Red
Bluff

Flyfishing Guides & Info:
The Fly Shop, Redding
(916) 222-3555

Brown's Sporting Goods
(707) 923-2533
Garberville

Eel
River

36

Sacramento
River

South
fork

Middle
fork

River Closure Recorded Info:
Northern Counties: (707) 442-4502
Southern Counties: (707) 944-5533

99

Van Arsdale
Dam

Feather
River

North Coast Angler
(707) 964-6598

Noyo
River

Big
River

20

45

5

Yuba City /
Marysville

Navarro
River

101

Ukiah

20

20

Yuba River

20

Garcia
River

Cloverdale

Russian
River

Johnson's Bait & Tackle
(916) 674-1912

Gualala
River

Guide:
Bill Adelman
(510) 232-9991

505

Sacramento

Flyfishing Guide:
Randy Johnson
(916) 525-6575

Healdsburg
Duncan
Mills

Kings Tackle
(707) 869-2156
Guerneville

101

To
San
Francisco

80

Steelhead, Lodging and Camping

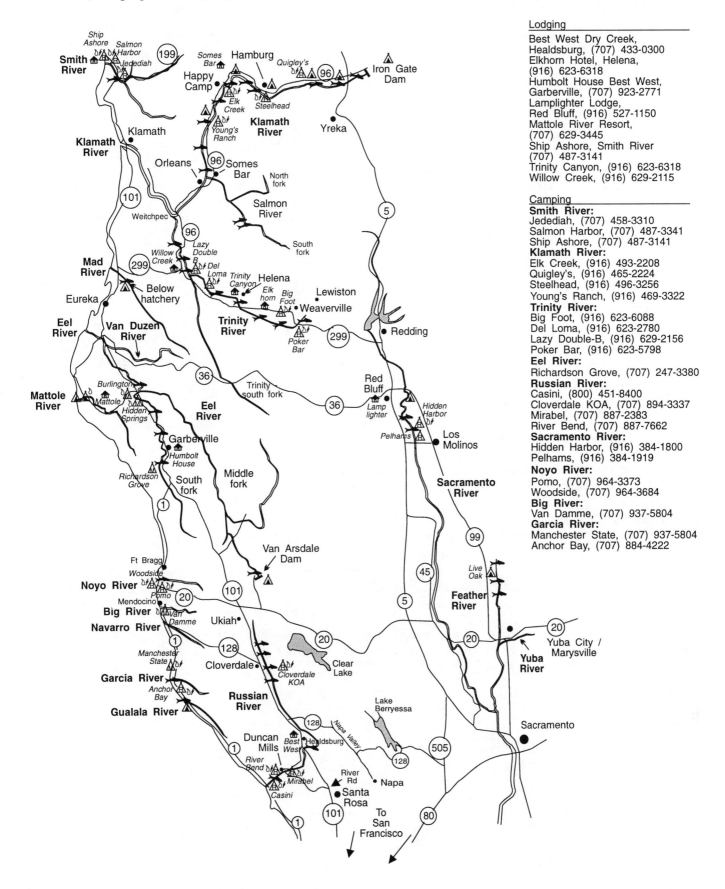

Lodging

Best West Dry Creek,
Healdsburg, (707) 433-0300
Elkhorn Hotel, Helena,
(916) 623-6318
Humbolt House Best West,
Garberville, (707) 923-2771
Lamplighter Lodge,
Red Bluff, (916) 527-1150
Mattole River Resort,
(707) 629-3445
Ship Ashore, Smith River
(707) 487-3141
Trinity Canyon, (916) 623-6318
Willow Creek, (916) 629-2115

Camping

Smith River:
Jedediah, (707) 458-3310
Salmon Harbor, (707) 487-3341
Ship Ashore, (707) 487-3141
Klamath River:
Elk Creek, (916) 493-2208
Quigley's, (916) 465-2224
Steelhead, (916) 496-3256
Young's Ranch, (916) 469-3322
Trinity River:
Big Foot, (916) 623-6088
Del Loma, (916) 623-2780
Lazy Double-B, (916) 629-2156
Poker Bar, (916) 623-5798
Eel River:
Richardson Grove, (707) 247-3380
Russian River:
Casini, (800) 451-8400
Cloverdale KOA, (707) 894-3337
Mirabel, (707) 887-2383
River Bend, (707) 887-7662
Sacramento River:
Hidden Harbor, (916) 384-1800
Pelhams, (916) 384-1919
Noyo River:
Pomo, (707) 964-3373
Woodside, (707) 964-3684
Big River:
Van Damme, (707) 937-5804
Garcia River:
Manchester State, (707) 937-5804
Anchor Bay, (707) 884-4222

STURGEON

Where/When February to March in the Sacramento/San Joaquin Delta soon after rains have muddied the bay. April to June on the Sacramento River between Colusa and Princeton on ghost shrimp at night.

Structure Sturgeon feed on the bottom:

- Along shallow dropoffs in 15 to 20 foot deep water.
- In areas where water slows in moving to deeper water at the shoulders of deeper water channels.
- Along rip lines where one side is still and flat, the other side is moving and choppy. Fish the moving water side of the rip.

The best bites are:

- When the delta is flushed by medium-to-heavy winter rains.
- During big (winter) tidal swings with 5 or more feet difference between the high and low tides.

Bob's Bait, Isleton

Janel Twiford hooked, landed and released this 200 lb. sturgeon caught on grass shrimp

Sturgeon are sensitive to fishing pressure. Anglers have more success during weekdays and other uncrowded periods.

Bait/Lures Use grass shrimp, mudshrimp, or ghost shrimp. Put 4 to 6 on the hook at once. Thread them on the hook, tail first, with the point coming out slightly from the head. Mudsuckers are not as good as shrimp.

	Lgth	Line	Lure/Wt.	Action	Examples
Rod	6 - 7 1/2	20 - 50		Med	Fenwick 196, 270, 870 Comparable Calstar, Seeker & Daiwa rods
	Type	**Size**	**Speed**		**Examples**
Reel	Conv	300 yds 25#	2:1 6:1		Penn 500; Newell 300 series; Shimano TLD 15; Daiwa 300H

Rig

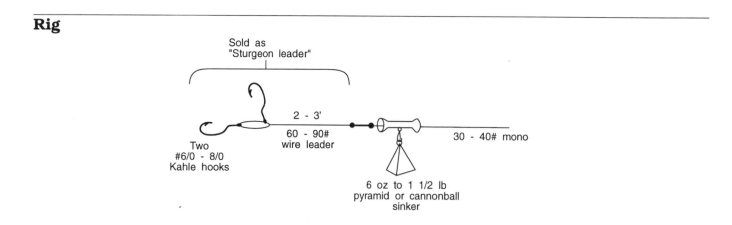

Sold as
"Sturgeon leader"

2 - 3'
60 - 90#
wire leader

30 - 40# mono

Two
#6/0 - 8/0
Kahle hooks

6 oz to 1 1/2 lb
pyramid or cannonball
sinker

Technique	Cast out 15 yards from the boat. Leave weight on the bottom—it must be flat on the bottom. Use pyramid or cannonball sinkers, flat sinkers plane off the bottom from strong tidal flows. Set the rod down and watch the tip. The bite is a pumping action. Set the hook when the rod tip is down.

Sturgeon will drop a bait as soon as they feel resistance. A balance bar can be used to improve success. A length of notched wood is laid across the boat stern. After casting out, the rod is balanced on the notched bar such that the slightest tug on the bait will move the rod down. The alert angler must then quickly pick up the rod at the same time moving the tip in the direction of the pulling fish. When the fish pulls on the bait again—set the hook.

The Law	All year, one per day between 46 and 72 inches total length.
	No sturgeon may be taken from the North Coast District waters.

Records	State: 468 lbs., July 1981, Carquinez Straits
	IGFA: " " "
	Commercial: 1800 lbs., Fraser River, B.C., Canada.

See Also	Striped Bass

Sturgeon Fishing Spots: Delta Area

CAUTION!   Not to be used for navigation.

Fishing Info:
Martinez Bait & Tackle, (510) 229-9420
The Bait Shop, Pittsburg, (510) 458-4904
The Trap, Rio Vista, (707) 374-5554

Party Boats:
Party Boats out of Crockett:
Morning Starr & So. Pacific,
(707) 745-1431, (800) 464-1431
Sturgeon King, (800) 850-5464
Party Boat out of Martinez:
Nobilis, (510) 757-2946,
(800) 773-6997

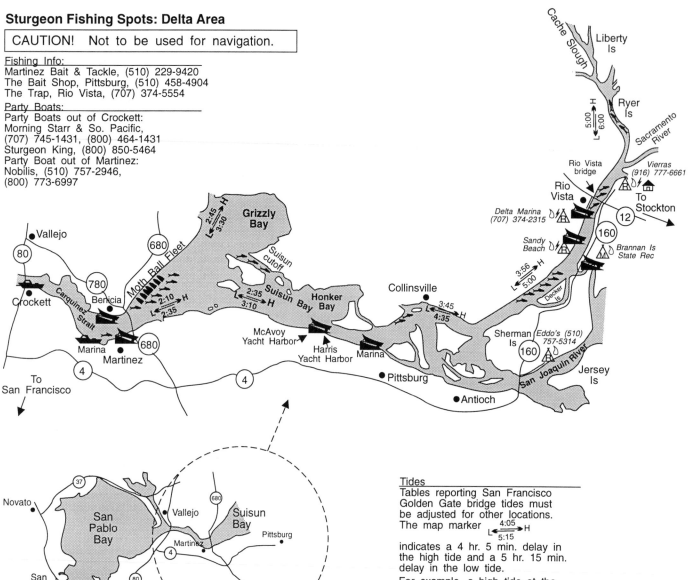

Tides

Tables reporting San Francisco Golden Gate bridge tides must be adjusted for other locations. The map marker

indicates a 4 hr. 5 min. delay in the high tide and a 5 hr. 15 min. delay in the low tide.

For example, a high tide at the Golden Gate at 1:30 PM would mean a high tide at Rio Vista at 5:35 PM.

TROUT: GENERAL

Trout location is dictated by the location of aerated, 58 to 64° water temperatures. Use a fish finder and a temperature guage to find these areas.

November to mid-March: Fishing can be good at lower elevation lakes, below 5,000 feet, following trout plants. Dirty water runoffs from winter storms will stop trout action until water clears. **Fish shortly after plants near where they are planted.**

Ice Out (late March to mid-April in the Sierras): Inland and mountain lakes at elevations over 5,500 feet will probably get snow and ice. When the ice just breaks off the surface, the trout will be looking for warmer water. The sunny northern, protected coves will warm first and attract fish. Fish are hungry from their winter fast but are moving slowly because of the cold water. On deep lakes, until the surface water turns over, subsurface temperatures may be warmer than the surface. The warmest, preferred water, may be 5 to 10 feet deep. During this time big browns are hungry and especially vulnerable to anglers, especially during low visibility periods—dusk and dawn, overcast and inclement weather. Cold waters require slow action lures or bait techniques. Troll very slowly with lures or nightcrawlers. Bait dunkers should occasionally and very slowly retreive their rig toward shore. The finger jig technique can work well in cold water.

Lower elevation lakes are generally clear from earlier, storm runoffs. Water temperatures are ideal and fishing can be excellent. **Fish slowly. Fish feeder stream areas. Slow troll 1 to 2 colors.**

Early Spring: (late April through May) Temperatures in a large part of the lake are ideal. This is the best season for shore anglers. In early spring rainbow trout will spawn in inlet rivers and are vulnerable to anglers. Fish spread throughout lake at various structure including shallow water dropoff lines and weed bank dropoffs. Low land lakes and coastal lakes will experience spring-like water temperatures throughout the winter months lasting from November or December through to the following spring. **Fish feeder stream areas. Fish shallow water dropoffs or outside edges of weed beds.**

Late Spring: (early June) Trout in lakes below 7,000 feet are starting to look for cool water spots. Trout are found actively feeding in the shallows only in the early mornings and at twilight. They will be at cool water creek inlets during most of the day. They will also be near the dam outlet. Some lakes formed by spillwater releases from higher elevation impoundments may also have extended late spring conditions. Examples are Lewiston Lake below Trinity Lake and McSwain Lake below McClure Reservoir. Mountain and alpine lakes above 7,000 feet will experience late spring conditions well into or even throughout the entire summer season. Alpine lakes at 9,000 feet and higher will not be clear of ice and snow until early June. **Fish early mornings and dusk. Fish creek inlets. Fish dam outlets.**

Summer: (mid-June through mid-Octoer): The only cool water is deep. Remaining planted trout are concentrated in deeper water especially at the dam close to the water outlet. Deep water techniques, leadcore and downrigger trolling can be productive. Summer outflows of water from dams may create good fishing in spillwaters. **Troll the thermocline. Troll dam outlets.**

Fall: (September and October): Mackinaw trout spawn over deep water islands. Big mackinaw are vulnerable to trolled plugs. Brown trout stage at river inlets to spawn upstream and are vulnerable to anglers especially during low-light (dusk/dawn/overcast) or inclement weather periods. In Inyo and Mono county, the season ends Oct. 31. Stocking stops early October. Therefore by the end of the season there is a reduced stock of rainbows. **Fish the lake surface the hour past sunset. Fish bad weather near inlets for trophy browns.**

Fall Turnover: (mid-October through November or December) brings fish to the surface and spreads them throughout lake. These are mostly leftover planters so there are not many fish but they are hungry. Brown trout can be vulnerable to long line near-surface trolling especially during low-light mornings and evenings. Lake turnover times vary significantly based on elevation, volume and depth of the particular lake. **Fish near surface early mornings and dusk.**

BROOK TROUT

Where	Brook trout are found in hundreds of mountain streams and lakes above 6000 feet. Brookies don't require running water to spawn so are often found in clear, quiet pools. Pools formed by beaver dams in mountain streams are ideal. A few notable lakes and streams are:

• Gold Lake near Quincy (see rainbow trout map)
• Parker Creek north of June Lake Loop (see Rainbow Trout map)
• Walker Creek north of June Lake Loop (see Rainbow Trout map)
• Higher lakes of the Mammoth Lakes chain
• Lake Genevieve and Dorothy Lake above Convict Lake

When   Brook trout spawn in the fall and are more active and hungry then.
Lake Kirman is known for its trophy size brookies. There is about a 3 mile walk to the lake. You'll need a float tube to reach the better fishing around the weedline.

Bait/Lures   Red worm on small bronze hook. Small spinners like a yellow Panther Martin. Try a scud imitation in the early AM and a Woolly Bugger during the day and at dusk.

Rig   Use ultra-light to light spinning or flyfishing tackle with 2-4# mono.

Fly Fishing

	Lgth	Wt.	Examples
Rod	7 - 9	2	Sage GFL279LL

The Law   Brook trout are included in the "trout" regulations. Even though the general rule is a 5 trout daily bag limit, many special restrictions apply. Most lakes in the "North Coast" and "Sierra" Districts (north coast, Redding area, Lake Tahoe area, and Bishop area) allow an additional 10 brook trout under 8 inches. See current DFG regulations.

Lake Kirman regs: Season, Last Saturday in April through Oct. 31. Mininum size, 16".

Records   State: 9 lbs. 12 oz.; Silver Lake; September 1932
IGFA: 14 lbs. 8 oz., Canada, 1916

See Also   If you are in the Bridgeport area you might want to sample these unusual fisheries:

1. Artic grayling are in Lobdell Lake and Desert Creek.
2. There is a special fall season for the big brooder cutthroat trout in Heenan Lake located a short distance up highway 395.
3. Hugh brown trout are in Twin Lakes and trophy browns inhabit the flyfishing waters of the East Walker River.

Brook Trout Lakes & Streams, Bridgeport

Season: Lakes & Streams from last Saturday in April through October.
Limit 5/day + 10 brook trout under 8". No night fishing.
Lakes best from opening to mid-June and mornings and dusk in June, July.
Lakes above 7000' best from late June through October.

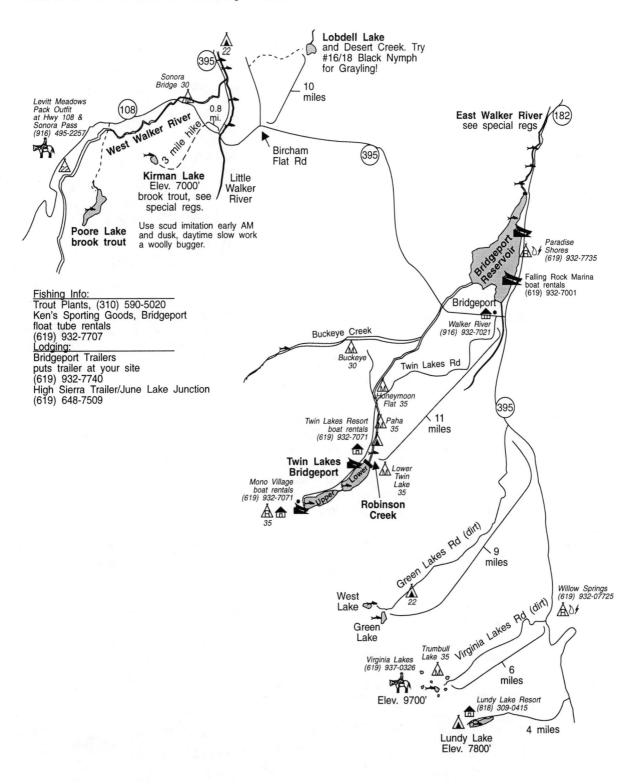

Lobdell Lake
and Desert Creek. Try
#16/18 Black Nymph
for Grayling!

10 miles

East Walker River
see special regs

182

22

395

Sonora
Bridge 30

Levitt Meadows
Pack Outfit
at Hwy 108 &
Sonora Pass
(916) 495-2257

108

0.8 mi.

West Walker River

3 mile hike

Bircham
Flat Rd

395

Paradise
Shores
(619) 932-7735

Kirman Lake
Elev. 7000'
brook trout, see
special regs.

Little
Walker
River

Bridgeport
Reservoir

Falling Rock Marina
boat rentals
(619) 932-7001

**Poore Lake
brook trout**

Use scud imitation early AM
and dusk, daytime slow work
a woolly bugger.

Bridgeport

Walker River
(916) 932-7021

Fishing Info:
Trout Plants, (310) 590-5020
Ken's Sporting Goods, Bridgeport
float tube rentals
(619) 932-7707
Lodging:
Bridgeport Trailers
puts trailer at your site
(619) 932-7740
High Sierra Trailer/June Lake Junction
(619) 648-7509

Buckeye Creek

Buckeye
30

Twin Lakes Rd

Honeymoon
Flat 35

Twin Lakes Resort
boat rentals
(619) 932-7071

Paha
35

11
miles

395

**Twin Lakes
Bridgeport**

Mono Village
boat rentals
(619) 932-7071

Lower

Upper

Lower
Twin
Lake
35

**Robinson
Creek**

35

Green Lakes Rd (dirt)

9
miles

West
Lake

22

Willow Springs
(619) 932-07725

Green
Lake

Virginia Lakes Rd (dirt)

Trumbull
Lake 35

Virginia Lakes
(619) 937-0326

6
miles

Elev. 9700'

Lundy Lake Resort
(818) 309-0415

4 miles

Lundy Lake
Elev. 7800'

BROWN TROUT

Where

Many lakes and streams have brown trout. They are caught using the techniques and rigs described in the Rainbow Trout section. Very few waters have the giant browns described in this section. These fish demand special techniques.

Structure

Lakes Brown trout prefer 50 to 60 degree water. Inlet stream areas are cool water areas and prime fall season spots. Fish the dark side of rocks, shady banks, shorelines and shoreline points. Almost all big browns are caught in water less than 15 feet deep.

Streams Fish pockets in white water rapids, during low-water conditions, that would be difficult to reach at higher stream levels. In the fall, browns will begin their spawn by heading into the streams entering into the lake.

If you see someone wearing a cap that says "Sierra Brownbaggers" you are in the right place. This is an exclusive club requiring the owner to have caught 2 brown trout over 10 pounds.

Alan Cole picked this 10 lb. 5 oz. brown trout from lower Twin Lake on opening day

When

Especially the opening and closing seasons from early April, Mid-September through October. Pleasant Valley Reservoir is open all year but the best season is from December through March. Fishing can be good at night. Inyo County, which includes Pleasant Valley Reservoir, allows night fishing. First and last hour of daylight are prime for browns. Many big fish are caught during bad weather with windy, broken surface conditions and wave-washed shorelines and cloudy, low light conditions

Bait/Lures

The type and size of lure varies considerably depending on weather you are seeking a small, stream brown versus a giant Bridgeport brown trout. See the Rainbow Trout section for bait and lures for average sized fish.

Lures for big fish: Trout imitations: #13 to #18 Rapala, 6" Rebel. Shad imitations: Shad Rap, Storm ThinFin.

Rig

See Rainbow Trout section for bait and lure rigs for average sized fish.

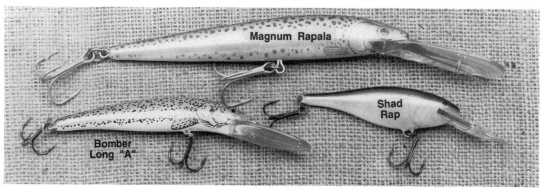

Techniques   Average sized fish can be caught using all the techniques listed in the Rainbow Trout section. Brown trout are more wary than rainbows. **You must use stealth techniques to be successful.**

Big Fish

Trolling for big browns:

- Troll with the lure well back of the boat—40 to 50+ yards (120 to 150+ feet). Use a side planer for added stealth. Big browns are easily spooked.
- Use 6 - 8# test quality mono.
- Troll slowly with lure 5 feet off the bottom in water 10 to 20 feet deep.
- Vary the trolling pattern and speed. Yank on the rod to add lure action.
- In the first hour of daylight use a floating Rapala, after that use a magnum (sinking, countdown) Rapala.
- Use #13 to #18 Rapalas or Rebels (5"-7") in rainbow or silver & black patterns or,

Casting Shad Raps in lakes with shad or Sacramento perch forage.

- Cast beyond the suspected holding structure and work back by reeling in a few feet to pull lure beneath the surface 2+ feet.
- Let the lure suspend temporarily.
- Twitch or reel in a short distance.
- Repeat.

The Law   Generally 5 in Lakes but there are many exceptions. See current DFG regulations under "Trout & Salmon".

See Also   Rainbow Trout

Trophy Brown Trout Spots, Eastern Sierra Region

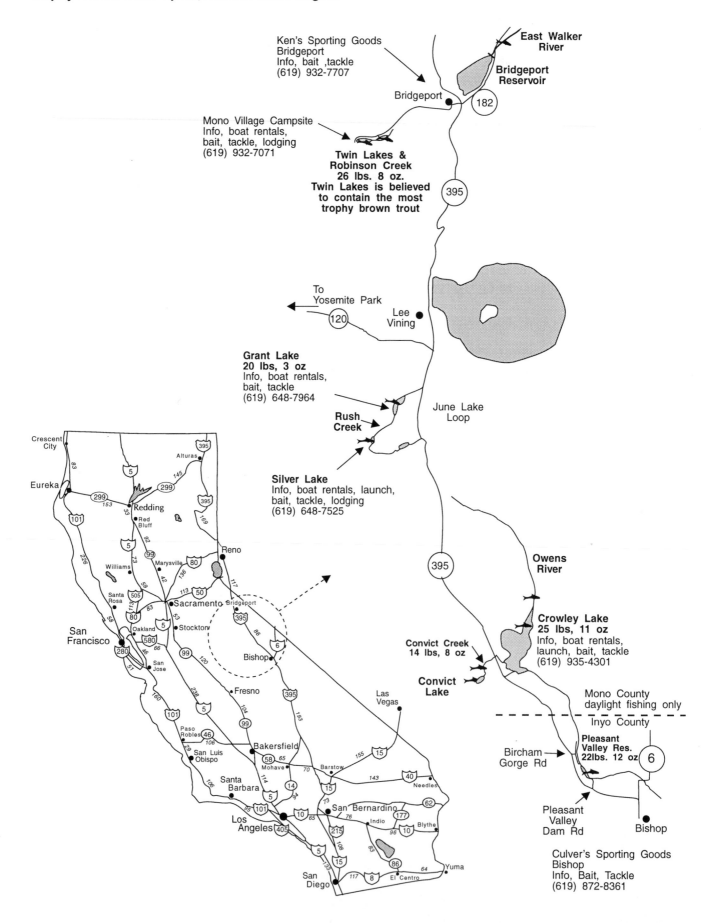

Ken's Sporting Goods
Bridgeport
Info, bait ,tackle
(619) 932-7707

East Walker
River

Bridgeport
Reservoir

Bridgeport

182

Mono Village Campsite
Info, boat rentals,
bait, tackle, lodging
(619) 932-7071

Twin Lakes &
Robinson Creek
26 lbs. 8 oz.
Twin Lakes is believed
to contain the most
trophy brown trout

395

To
Yosemite Park

120

Lee
Vining

Grant Lake
20 lbs, 3 oz
Info, boat rentals,
bait, tackle
(619) 648-7964

Rush
Creek

June Lake
Loop

Silver Lake
Info, boat rentals, launch,
bait, tackle, lodging
(619) 648-7525

Crescent
City

Alturas

5

395

145

Eureka

299

299

153

Redding

395

169

Red
Bluff

5

92

99

33

Reno

Williams

Marysville

80

117

42

136

Santa
Rosa

505

113

50

113

Sacramento

Bridgeport

83

53

395

San
Francisco

580

Oakland

5

Stockton

86

6

280

66

65

Bishop

San
Jose

51

99

120

Fresno

395

160

101

238

5

193

Paso
Robles

46

106

99

Las
Vegas

104

Bakersfield

Owens
River

395

Crowley Lake
25 lbs, 11 oz
Info, boat rentals,
launch, bait, tackle
(619) 935-4301

Convict Creek
14 lbs, 8 oz

Convict
Lake

Mono County
daylight fishing only

Inyo County

San Luis
Obispo

39

58

65

Mohave

70

Barstow

155

15

Santa
Barbara

114

143

40

106

14

15

Needles

605

94

San Bernardino

62

101

73

177

5

10

65

76

Indio

Blythe

Los
Angeles

405

215

96

10

Pleasant
Valley Res.
22lbs. 12 oz

6

Bircham
Gorge Rd

Pleasant
Valley
Dam Rd

Bishop

5

108

83

15

86

San
Diego

117

8

El Centro

64

Yuma

Culver's Sporting Goods
Bishop
Info, Bait, Tackle
(619) 872-8361

CUTTHROAT TROUT

Where	Walker Lake, Nevada, 10 miles north of Hawthorne, 1 hour drive from Lee Vining, 1 1/2 hours from Bishop. Pyramid Lake, Nevada. 33 miles from Reno. Best fly fishing areas are "The Nets", Blockhouse, Popcorn, and Dago Bay. Heenan Lake, Calif.
When	Shore fishing is good in October and early November. Boat trolling the dropoffs is most effective from December through early February. Shore fishing peaks in the early spring, from late February through March, when big cutthroats move into shallow water to spawn. The best fly fishing areas are The Nets, Blockhouse, Popcorn and Dago Bay. During the spawn, cutthroats hug the bottom. Storm fronts turn off fishing action for 2+ days. The Pyramid Lake season is from October 1 through June 30. The Walker Lake season is open all year. Heenan Lake is open Friday, Sat. and Sun. from the Friday before Labor Day through the last Sunday in October..
Bait/Lures	Powerbait K8 & K10 Kwikfish, V20 Flatfish & larger Tor-P-Do Wobblers (1/2 - 3/4 oz.), Apex spoons Colors: Frog pattern, chartreuse with red dots, black with red dots. Also green & black, green & white, red & white.
Rig	See Rainbow Trout Bait and Lure. See Rainbow Trout Downrigger.
Technique	Troll lures very slowly. Use a downrigger with a second sliding, dropper lure to troll at deeper levels. For calm conditions with metered fish less than 150 feet deep, try 3/4 ounce blue, purple or black marabou jigs fished 5 to 15 turns off the bottom. Shoreline fly fishing with white, black, or black & red Wooly Worms or Wooly Buggers can be effective especially in spring, but also early season in October and early November. Use a fast-sinking line and a 5-6 foot leader. Neoprene waders will keep you warm and allow you to wade to the drop offs where fish hold when not spawning in the shallows.
The Law	Pyramid Lake allows only artificial lures and flies. The daily bag limit is 2 fish. The maximum possession limit is two daily limits. You can only keep fish between 16 and 19 inches and only one fish over 24 inches. Boating and fishing permits are required. Walker Lake has no size limit, 5 fish daily bag and possession. Bait is allowed. Heenan Lake allows only barbless artificials. All fish must be released.
Records	Walker Lake record: 19 lbs, 1968. At Pyramid Lake a 22 lb. fish was caught in 1989. IGFA: 41 lbs., Pyramid Lake, Nev., 1925
See Also	Pyramid Lake also has Sacramento perch.

Cutthroat Trout: Pyramid and Walker Lake, Nevada

CAUTION!   Not to be used for navigation.

NEVADA:
Pyramid Fishing Info:
Fish Connection, (702) 782-4734
Gilley Fishing Store, (702) 358-6113
Marina, (702) 476-1156
Guides and Info:
Pyramid-Tahoe Charters, (702) 852-3474
Pyramid Store, (702) 476-0555
Walker Lake Info
Gun & Tackle Shop, Hawthorne
(702) 945-3266
Walker Lake Lodging & Guides
El Capitan Lodge & Casino
Hawthorne, (702) 945-3321
Trout Derby$
Sponsored by El Capitan Lodge
big fish Oct to early May
CALIFORNIA:
Heenan Lake
Season: Only Fri, Sat, & Sun
from Frid. before Labor Day
through last Sun in Oct.
Info: Ken's Sporting Goods
Bridgeport, (619) 932-7707

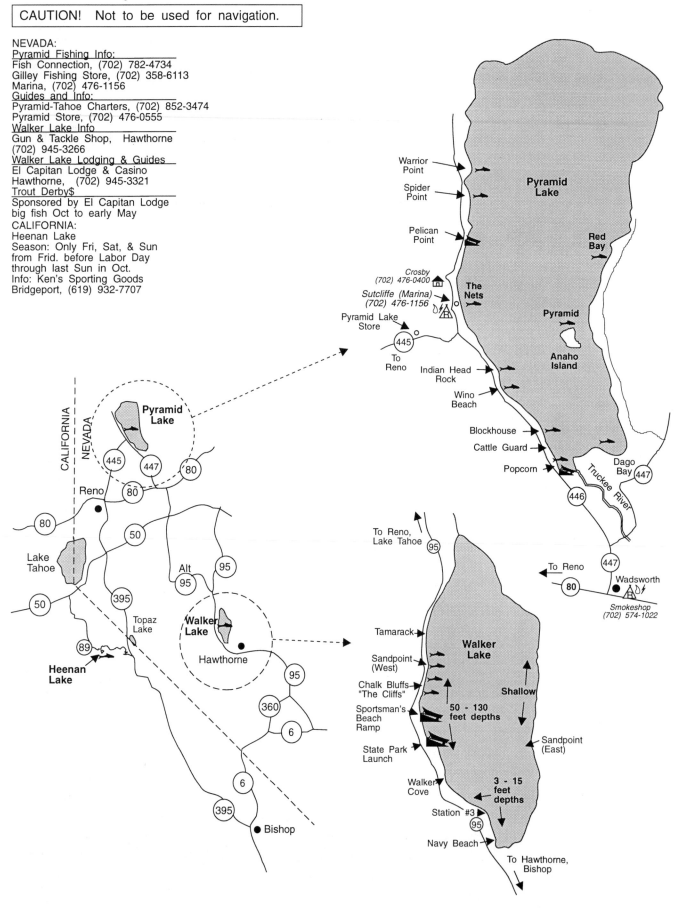

GOLDEN TROUT

Where   Golden trout are only found in lakes above 9000 feet. See maps.

When   Early July and mid-September are considered best for trophy goldens. Pan-sized trout fishing is good throughout the ice and snow free season, from July to early October. See maps for "fishing seasons". Surface fishing turns on at dusk.

Bait/Lures   Flies: No. 14 or 16 dry flies. Use larger, no. 10 to 12 size flies when targeting trophy sized fish. Hare's Ear Nymph, Scud, Brown Leech, Caddis pupa, Elk Hair Caddis.
Also: Sierra Bright Dot, Mosquito, Doc's Twin Lake Special, Pheasant Tail, Charlie Crockett
Lures: Small (1/16-1/8 oz.) gold or yellow lures, Super Duper, Dardevle, Panther Martin, Mepps or Kastmaster.

Rig   Fly fishing rig or ultra-light spinning.

Dress fly
with floatant

3'
2 - 4# mono   Small
casting bobber

Technique   The best technique for pan-sized fish is to use a fly and bubble rig, with the fly on a 6 foot length of 2-4# mono leader. Generally the best times to fish are early evening and very early morning hours when the lake surface comes alive with the dimples of trout feeding. Simply cast out the fly-and-bubble rig and retrieve very slowly. Carry a good floatant for applying to the fly. At times the fish will only hit a fly that is riding high on the surface.

For **big fish**, low-light early mornings and twilight periods are best. Fish drop-offs near creek inlets. Approach and fish these areas with maximum stealth. Stay low. Avoid overhead casting movements. Place flies and lures quietly.

Records   State: 9 lbs. 14 oz.; Virgina Lake; August 1952
IGFA: 11 lbs., Wyoming, 1948.

Golden Trout, Cottonwood Lakes

Season: July 1 through Oct. 31. Barbless, artificials only. Lakes 5 fish daily and bag except see No Fishing lakes on map. See Cottonwood Creek special regs.

Facilities Info:
Chamber of Commerce, Lone Pine,
(619) 876-4444
Camping:
Hiking permits, Mt. Whitney Ranger Dist, (619) 876-6200
Use Cirque Peak topo map

To Mt. Whitney

To Bishop, 58 miles

Lone Pine

Portal Rd

Best Western Frontier (619) 876-5571

no water

Diaz Lake
Open all year for planted rainbow trout

Horseshoe Meadow Rd

395

To Los Angeles 209 miles

20 miles to trailhead

No Fishing

Cottonwood Lakes 5 & 6

Muir Lake

Cottonwood Creek trail 6 1/2 miles to South Fork Lakes

High Lake

3
4
2 1

Long Lake

Cirque Lake

South Fork Lakes

no water

Cottonwood (619) 878-2015

Crescent City
Alturas
Eureka
Redding
Red Bluff
Reno
Marysville
Williams
Santa Rosa
Sacramento
Bridgeport
Oakland
Stockton
San Francisco
San Jose
Bishop
Fresno
Las Vegas
Paso Robles
Bakersfield
San Luis Obispo
Mohave
Barstow
Needles
Santa Barbara
San Bernardino
Los Angeles
Indio
Blythe
San Diego
El Centro
Yuma

Golden Trout Lakes, Golden Trout Wilderness

Use Mount Tom & Mt. Hilgard topo maps

Season: Last Saturday in April to Nov. 15. However high elevation lakes aren't ice free until July and bad weather escalates after mid-September.

Fishing Info:
Mac's Sporting Goods, Bishop, (619) 872-9201
Culver's Sporting Goods, Bishop, (619) 872-8361

Camping Info:
US Forest Service, Bishop, (619) 873-4207

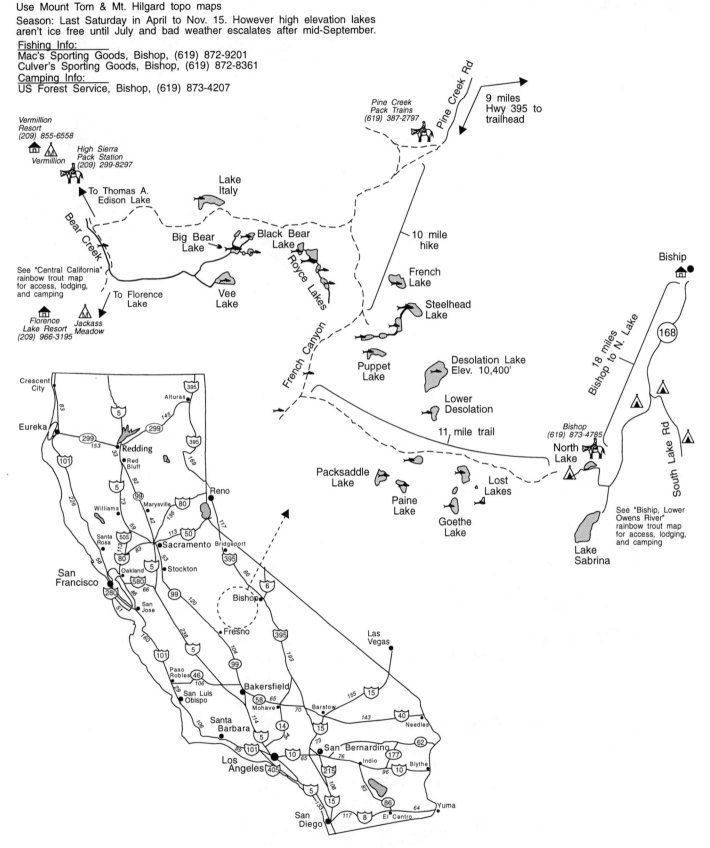

Vermillion Resort (209) 855-6558

Vermillion

High Sierra Pack Station (209) 299-8297

To Thomas A. Edison Lake

Bear Creek

See "Central California" rainbow trout map for access, lodging, and camping

To Florence Lake

Florence Lake Resort (209) 966-3195

Jackass Meadow

Lake Italy

Big Bear Lake

Black Bear Lake

Royce Lakes

Vee Lake

French Canyon

Pine Creek Pack Trains (619) 387-2797

Pine Creek Rd

9 miles Hwy 395 to trailhead

10 mile hike

French Lake

Steelhead Lake

Puppet Lake

Desolation Lake Elev. 10,400'

Lower Desolation

11 mile trail

Packsaddle Lake

Paine Lake

Goethe Lake

Lost Lakes

Biship

North Lake

Bishop (619) 873-4785

Bishop 18 miles Bishop to N. Lake

168

South Lake Rd

See "Biship, Lower Owens River" rainbow trout map for access, lodging, and camping

Lake Sabrina

Crescent City
Eureka
Redding
Red Bluff
Alturas
Reno
Marysville
Williams
Santa Rosa
Sacramento
Bridgeport
Oakland
Stockton
San Francisco
San Jose
Bishop
Fresno
Las Vegas
Paso Robles
San Luis Obispo
Bakersfield
Mohave
Barstow
Santa Barbara
Needles
San Bernardino
Indio
Blythe
Los Angeles
Yuma
San Diego
El Centro

MAKINAW TROUT (Lake Trout)

Where

Structure Mackinaw trout hug the bottom in deep water, usually holding just off the bottom near cliffs, rocky ledges, points, large boulders or underwater mounds and high spots. They prefer water temperature from the upper 40's to the lower 50's.

Larger fish are most often found at depths from 100 down to 300 feet. The preferred depth will vary with the season and water temperature. Smaller fish will frequent shallower water. Larger fish tend to be loners most of the year but will mix with the smaller fish and become more vulnerable to trolled lures in the fall from late August and early September.

Guide Bruce Hernandez reeled in this trophy mackinaw trout from the depths of Lake Tahoe, within sight of the casinos.

When

Lake Tahoe is best in the winter months through early May. Fishing can be good in late August and early September during the spawn. Donner Lake is best in February and March near the north shore, the old highway and around "the islands" off the south shore. Jenkinson Reservoir (off Hwy 50 near Placerville) mackinaws turn on in late Autust.

The early morning hours from first light to about 9 or 10 AM are most productive. Late day hours, 5 PM and later, can also be good.

Bait/Lures

Bait: Redsides, shiners, paiute sculpins, tahoe suckers, tui chubs. All these minnows are native to Lake Tahoe minnows. Mackinaw prefer paiute sculpins.
Trolling lures: J-plugs, T55 Flatfish, Rebel or Rapala plugs, rubber minnows. Colors: Blue & chrome, chrome, green.
Jigging lures: 3 to 4 oz. spoons. Examples: Krocodile, Kastmaster, Hopkins, Buzz Bomb, Apex, Bomber slab spoon with or without a bucktail. Colors: White, yellow, chrome.

Rig

For trolling, use a medium weight 6 1/2 to 7 1/2 foot rod rated for 15 to 20# mono. Pick a level wind reel with capacity for 200 yards of 20# mono.

1. Slow Trolling off Downrigger

8# - 10#
mono

Minnow
or lure

2 - 3'

10 - 15'

Jensen Dodger:
#000 to #00 for bait,
small spoons
#0 to #1 for plugs

20 - 30' off bottom
in 100 - 250' deep water

2. Live Bait Drifting

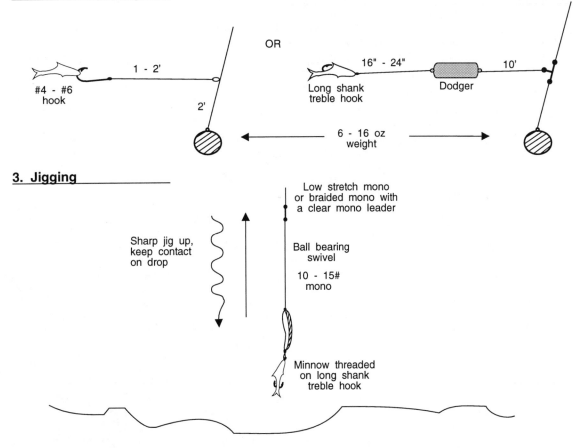

3. Jigging

Technique	**A quality, high resolution depth finder with the power to reach to 300 feet is a must.**

Downrigger Trolling Don't start trolling until you locate bottom structure and fish. Slow troll or use a controlled drift along the edge of dropoffs and over underwater high spots or mounds. If you get a strike, or fish, retroll the area. Makinaw are great followers. You need to alter the action of the trolled lure to motivate them to strike. Try pumping the rod, temporarily changing the trolling speed or direction, raise or lower the downrigger weight a short distance.

Jigging Freespool to the bottom and reel up 3 to 5 feet. Start jigging with sharp, quick upward swings of your rod. On the drop, keep light contact with the lure so you can feel the lure weight. Mackinaw almost always enhale the lure on the drop. You won't feel the bite. You must concentrate to feel the weight come off the line. Reel in rapidly and set the hook.

The Law   Makinaw trout are included in the "trout" regulations along with salmon and trout of all species in determining daily bag limits. See the map for seasons and limits.

Records   State: 37 lbs. 6 oz.; Lake Tahoe; January 1974
IGFA: 65 lbs., Canada, 1970

See Also   Kokanee Salmon, Rainbow Trout, Brown Trout

Makinaw Trout, Lake Tahoe, Donner Lake, Fallen Leaf

> **CAUTION!** Not to be used for navigation.

Season: all year
Lake Tahoe: Limit 5 trout but only 2 mackinaw.
See special regs. for tributary areas.
Donner and Fallen Leaf: Limit 5/day, 10 in possession
Guides:
North Lake Tahoe:
  Mickey Daniels, Tahoe City,
  (800) 877-1462
  Larry Schuelke, Tahoe City,
  (916) 525-5360
South Lake Tahoe:
  Bruce Hernandez, (916) 577-2246
  Rick Muller, (916) 544-4358
  Larry Tomer, (916) 577-4135
Donner Lake Guides:
  Chris Turner, (916) 587-9302
  Ted Samford, (916) 389-2748
Boat Rentals / Launching:
Meeks Bay Resort, (916) 525-7242
Anchorage Marina, (916) 541-1777
Sierra Boat Co., (916) 546-2552
Tahoe Keys Marina, (916) 541-2155
Zephyr Cove Marina, (702) 588-3833
Lodging
Best Western (916) 587-4525

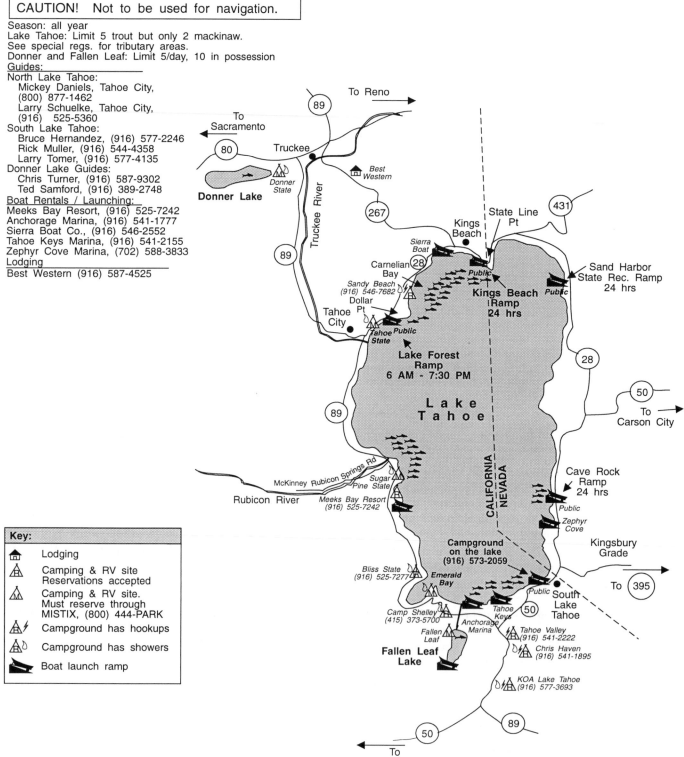

Key:

🏠 Lodging

🏕 Camping & RV site
    Reservations accepted

🏕 Camping & RV site.
    Must reserve through
    MISTIX, (800) 444-PARK

🏕⚡ Campground has hookups

🏕💧 Campground has showers

⛵ Boat launch ramp

RAINBOW TROUT

Rainbow trout are stocked in hundreds of lakes and streams throughout California. The maps included in this guide are for a select few lakes and streams which offer the best trout fishing in that area.

There are countless ways of fishing for trout. The following recommended techniques may not be the best technique for a particular lake, or time. However, these are proven, consistent ways of catching trout. I would suggest that you become familiar and adept at these techniques before inventing your own.

1. Lake fishing:
   Cool weather months .... Page 137-139
   Warm weather months .... Page 140-142
2. Stream fishing... Page 142-145
3. Lake & stream maps.. Page 146-169

LAKES, COOL WEATHER MONTHS

When/Where   For northern California lower elevation lakes, the cool weather trout season is mid-to-late September through May. Higher elevation lakes have extended cool water conditions in the summer but may be iced over in mid-winter. In southern California good cool-water trout action usually starts in late October or early November and lasts through early May.

Structure

Winter Months: The fish will be near the surface. Fish this structure from October through April and in summer months during early morning & twilight hours.

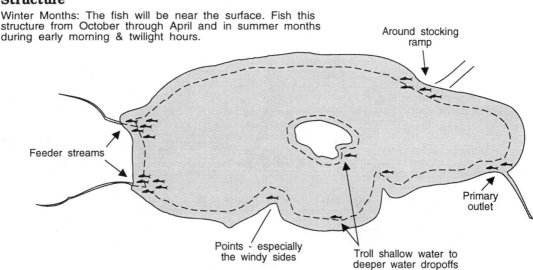

Around stocking ramp

Feeder streams

Primary outlet

Points - especially the windy sides

Troll shallow water to deeper water dropoffs

Bait/Lures   Bait: Power Bait, floating cheese, nightcrawlers, salmon eggs, marshmallows, crickets.

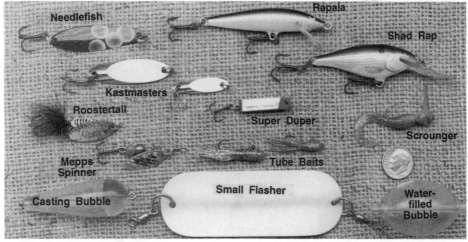

Needlefish

Rapala

Shad Rap

Kastmasters

Roostertail

Super Duper

Scrounger

Mepps Spinner

Tube Baits

Casting Bubble

Small Flasher

Water-filled Bubble

Rig   Ultra-light to Medium weight spinning outfit

Trout Bait and Lure

Rod	Lgth	Line	Lure/Wt.	Power / Action	
	5 - 7	4 - 8	1/16 - 1/4 oz.	Ultra Light Slow to Moderate	
	Type	**Size**			
Reel	Conv Spin	150 yds of 4#			

Trout Special Bait & Finger Jig

Rod	Lgth	Line	Lure/Wt.	Power / Action	Examples
	7 1/2- 10	4 - 8	1/16 - 1/4 oz.	Ultra Light to Light Soft	Long parabolic soft action rods Kencore PAC73DL; Daiwa noodle rods EL10--10, 105, 12
	Type	**Size**			
Reel	Conv Spin	150 yds of 4#			

1. Bottom   Bait Fishing

#14 - #16 treble hook
covered by Power
Bait, floating cheese,
marshmellow, or combo

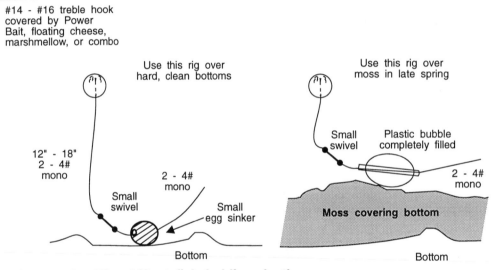

2. Nightcrawler Rig: drift at fish holding depth

Break nightcrawler in
half and thread over
hook and split-shot

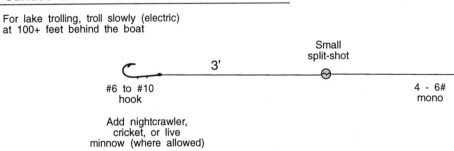

3. Surface Lake Slow Troll or Stream Drift

For lake trolling, troll slowly (electric)
at 100+ feet behind the boat

4. Lake Surface Bubble & Fly

Troll slowly with an electric motor with bubble
40 - 50 yards behind the boat. This technique
is especially effective during twilight insect hatches.

Small
swivel

6' - 7'

2# mono

4 - 6#
mono

Fly: Woolly Worm,
Woolly Bugger, etc.

Plastic bubble
2/3 water filled

5. Lake - Near Surface

a. Bobber Rig

- Cast out and slowly
  retrieve while,
- Twitching the rod tip
  slightly to give bobber
  action

Small
casting bobber

3'

2 - 4# mono

Finger (tube) Jig
1/64 oz

b. Fly Line Rig

- Cast out and let sink. Retrieve slowly while either,
- Lifting the rod tip   slightly to give lure
  action, and/or
- Extending the right hand   index finger to intercept
  line on the retrieve, giving   the lure a twitch on each
  spinning reel revolution

Finger (tube) Jig
1/32 oz

6. River Drift Rig

#6 baitholder
hook with
nightcrawler
or cricket

2 - 3'

10# mono

OR

Kwikfish (K4, K5),
Flatfish (F4, F5),
Wee Wart, Hot Shot.
Crayfish pattern or gold

8 - 10"

6#
mono

Split
shot

OR

Steelhead drifting
weight or "Slinky"

Technique

1. Bait Fishing The most popular shoreline technique involves using a floating cheese bait (Berkeley's power bait or Zeke's), or marshmallows. **The success of this technique is highly dependent on using a very light line.** By default use 2 pound test clear mono. The trout must first not be alarmed by a heavy mono line. Secondly the fish must feel minimum resistance when it picks up the bait and starts moving away. Therefore, use the lightest weight line, split-shot, and hook you can get away with.

Slowly moving the bait on a regular basis, can increase success. Watch for other shoreline anglers catching fish. Try to determine how deep, far from shore they are fishing. Are they fishing just off the bottom or are they fishing below a bobber? Trout usually move in schools so if you catch a fish, bait up quickly and cast back into the same spot.

In California, almost all the trout out there are from the DFG stocking program. The newspaper lists, in the weekly outdoor section, what lakes and streams, by county, will be stocked. The maps in this section also give the trout plant information phone numbers. Find out where the stocking truck unloads and fish that area. The trout will eventually spread out throughout the lake, but it takes some time.

2. Surface Trolling Slow troll or retreive just fast enough to get the proper action from your lure—the blade spin on a Roostertail or the body action of a Rapala. **The biggest mistake in casting or trolling a lure is working too fast.**

For surface and shallow depths during early morning hours, deeper waters during midday. Lures: Kastmasters either gold or silver, Roostertails, Super Dupers, #7 floating Rapalas, Needlefish, Triple Teaser, Sep's Pro Secret.

- Troll slowly off structure, see diagram.
- Set trolling speed by holding your lure over the side and varying the motor speed until the natural lure action is maximized. Spinners should spin regularly and constantly, spoons should wobble, not spin.
- Vary the speed of the troll.
- Troll in "S" pattern, gently weaving the boat back and forth.
- Occasionally pull on the rods to give the lure more action.
- Troll at different depths—use a "troll-eze" device, Lake Troll, adjustable weights rig, leadcore line or a downrigger.

3. Shoreline lure fishing is effective in early morning hours and at dusk. Lures: Roostertail; finger jigs in smoke, smoke sparkle, smoke rainbow, rainbow sparkle; or a small Scrounger in white or smoke colors.

- Keep moving to find fish and look for dark, shady spots and dropoffs. Fish on the windy side of points, near water/creek inlets and try different depths.
- Generally avoid days following full moon nights.
- Keep the bait/lure moving.
- When retrieving small lures with a spinning outfit, stick your index finger out to intercept the line on each reel revolution. This gives the lure an extra action. Twitching the rod tip slightly can also give desired lure action.

4. Bubble & fly fishing:

- Works best in the early morning and late dusk periods. It may be important to keep the fly on the surface by applying floatant.
- Get in a position with the wind at your back. The wind blows the insect hatch off the land points and over the water. The fish will migrate to these shore areas at sunset.
- Retrieve the fly **very slowly** to minimize the bubble wake. Twitch the rod tip irregularly to give action to the fly.
- Strike as soon as the fish takes the fly.

LAKES, WARM WEATHER MONTHS

When	Generally from mid-June through early September. See maps for more detail.

Where   **Structure**

Summer Months: The fish will be deep.
Fish this structure from July through early September.

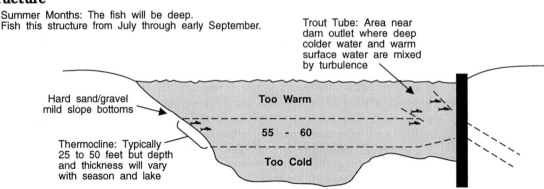

Trout Tube: Area near dam outlet where deep colder water and warm surface water are mixed by turbulence

Hard sand/gravel mild slope bottoms

Too Warm

55 - 60

Thermocline: Typically 25 to 50 feet but depth and thickness will vary with season and lake

Too Cold

How to find the thermocline:

- The easiest way is to use your fish finder to locate the consistent holding depth of metered fish suspended off the bottom usually between 25 to 60 feet down. Shallower readings will probably be bait fish, near bottom readings at greater depths will probably be rough fish or,
- Better fish finders will locate the thermocline as a hazy gray line at constant depth, usually between 25 and 60 feet, when the instrument sensitivity is turned up or,
- Find a deeper part of the lake and lower a temperature probe to detect where the temperature drops rapidly in a short range or,
- Locate the right depth by altering either the length of line out, with lead core, or the weight used until a fish is caught, then switch other rigs to the right setup.

Rig   Light to medium weight conventional reel for trolling.

Trout Downrigger

Rod	Lgth	Line	Lure/Wt.	Power / Action	
	7 - 9	8 - 20	1/4 - 2 oz.	Medium Slow to Moderate	
Reel	Type	Size	Examples		
	Conv Spin	150 yds 4#	Conv: Ambassadeur 5500, Penn Pd3886, 3880; Daiwa EL784GI; Fenwick MFS86C Spin: Shimano TDR2802, MFS86-S		

Trout Leadcore

Rod	Lgth	Line	Power / Action
	6 - 6 1/2	18 leadcore	Medium Moderate to Fast
Reel	Type	Size	Examples
	Conv	100 - 200 yds 18# leadcore	Penn 209, 309

Lake - Below Surface Trolling Options

Precise depth trolling is critical. Downriggers are much more precise than other deep trolling methods. Lead core line works well for shallower depths to 10 or 15 feet.

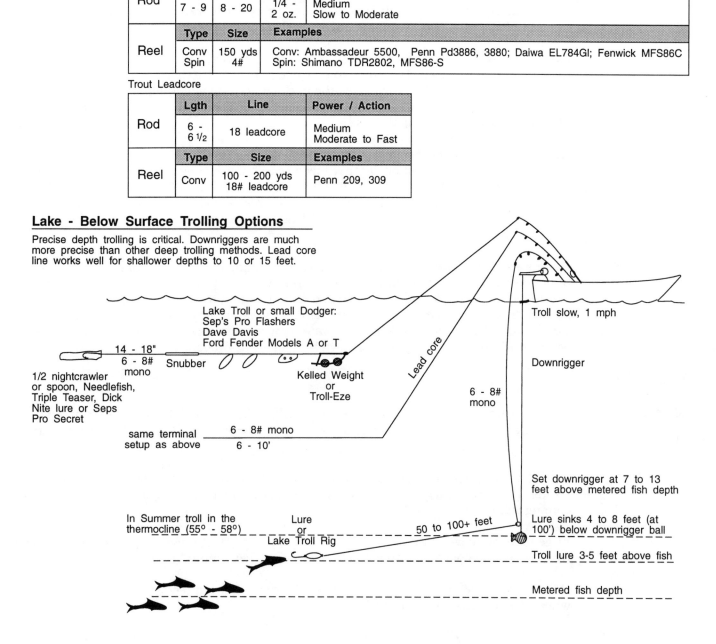

Bait/Lures	See listing under Cool Weather Months.

Technique	General warm weather strategies:

- During the first and last 2 hours of daylight feeder stream areas, especially those draining north facing slopes, are productive.
- After the first 2 hours, move to intermediated depth areas off points and weedlines.
- During mid-day hours, confine efforts to deeper water trolling techniques. It is vital to locate the fish holding depth, normally the thermocline, and carefully locate lure or bait trolling at that depth. See "Structure: How to locate the thermocline".

Trolling:

Lead core line Lead core line is marked with different line colors every 10 yards. Fishing reports often indicate the number of "colors" to troll. For every color of line out, the lure depth increases by about 5 feet. Use a 30 foot leader of 8# mono tied to 18 lb. leadcore with a nail knot. Determine the proper trolling speed by holding the lure at a shallow depth and increasing speed until the action is right. Lead core lines and heavy rigs take most of the fight and fun out of trout catching—see Downriggers.

Downriggers Downriggers with depth counters combined with a good fish finder are the ideal rig for fishing deep. The lure can be trolled at a precise depth for maximum success with minimum effort. They also allow the use of a light rig which makes the catching fun. Note that a downrigger will slow the boat some so for the ideal lure action run the boat a little faster before dropping the lure.

Adjustable weight rig The Luhr-Jensen Troll-eze can be used with various weights when searching for the right trolling depth. Start a search pattern by letting out a known length of line by reeling backwards "x" counts on the reel handle—try 30 to 40 turns first. Depths can be tested by letting out more line or by adding weight. This same technique can be used without the Troll-eze by using simple lead weights off a snap swivel. It is necessary to use light 4 to 6# mono for this technique to work.

Deep-water bait fishing Summer trout will be holding in upper 50's and lower 60's water temperature, normally found on the bottom in water depths of 25 to 60 feet. To be successful you need to pinpoint the correct depth by taking thermometer readings. Once the correct depth is determined, preferred fishing areas are any areas where a current may exist—areas where the wind keeps the water moving, aerators, reservoir inlets where fresh water is flowing. Look for gravel or hard bottom areas on gently sloping banks.

STREAMS

When	Early morning and twilight hours are usually the best time to fish a trout stream. Fish are generally active and feeding during these times. Some of the best insect "hatches" occur in the early evening.

In cold winter areas, trout tend to be less wary and more aggressively hungry in the early spring. This feeding aggression picks up again in the fall as the fish start to prepare for the coming winter.

In general rainbow trout spawn in the early spring. This spawning puts mature, large trout in sections of feeder streams close to where they empty into lakes.

Brown trout spawn in streams in the fall. Fish for them in feeder stream sections near where the streams empty into lakes.

Where   Studies have shown that stream trout do 90% of their feeding on or near the bottom of the stream. Therefore, I recommend that unless you see the fish actively feeding off the surface, fish the bottom of the stream with lures, bait, or weighted flies.

Trout Stream Structure

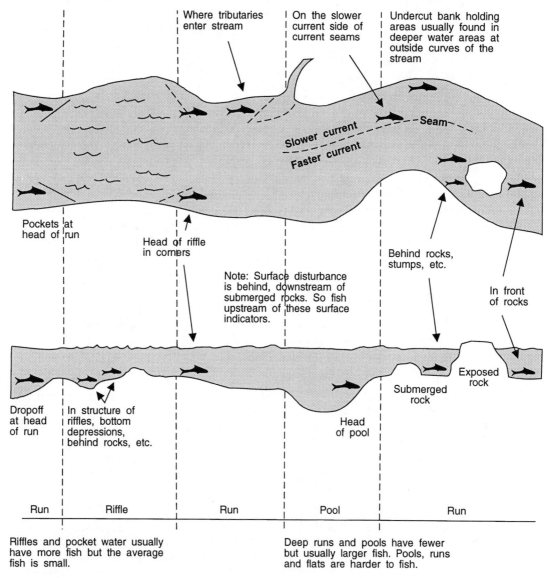

Riffles and pocket water usually have more fish but the average fish is small.

Deep runs and pools have fewer but usually larger fish. Pools, runs and flats are harder to fish.

Trout prefer cool water temperatures around 55-65 degrees. In cold weather, they will seek out the warmest stream waters. In the warm mid-summer months, they will seek the coolest waters. Use the following guidelines for selecting likely stream sections to try.

1. Streams that drain open slopes warm faster.
2. Streams that drain slopes facing south warm faster.
3. Low altitude streams warm faster.
4. Wide canyon streams warm faster than deep and narrow canyon streams.

Baits/Lures   See Lure Pictures in Lakes Section

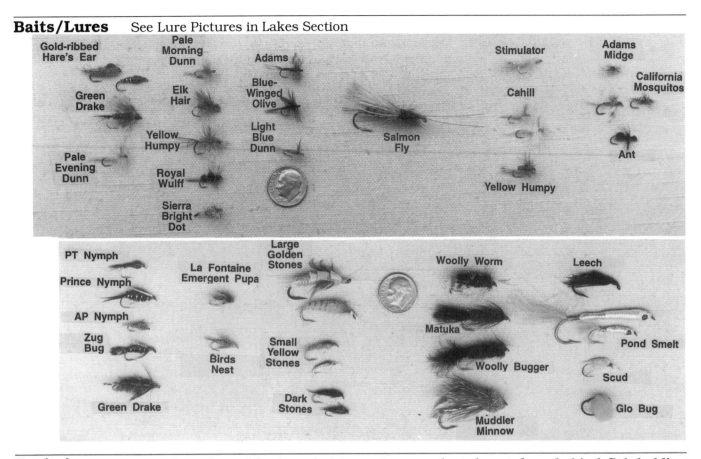

Technique

Trout have limited backward vision, so **approach and cast from behind fish-holding structure**. When approaching prime trout structure, **it is critical to keep a low profile for your body and your casting motion** especially in clear water areas like flats and pools. It is also critical that your bait or lure drifts close to the bottom occasionally ticking it but still drifting with the current. You may have to add splitshot to get your bait down. You must place your cast so that your lure or bait will have already sunk to the bottom before it drifts into the prime fish holding structure.

If fishing baits, cast the bait upstream and allow it to drift into the prime trout holding areas while maintaining controlled line slack. Pools immediately upstream from fast moving water are trout rest areas. Fish these pools and the riffles at the end of the pool. See the Trout Stream Structure diagram for more fish holding spots.

If fishing lures, make a quartering cast upstream and immediately start to **retreive only fast enough so the current and your retreive get some action from the lure, to slowly turn the blade of the spinner, no faster!**. An occasional flick of the rod tip can add a life-like darting action to the lure. When the lure drifts directly behind you in the stream, slowly retrieve the lure with the occasional darting movements of a frightened minnow. Also fish this technique with a split-shot against the head of a fly, for example a 2" Muddler Minnow fly, and for fishing finger jigs.

Typical Northern California Hatch Sequence

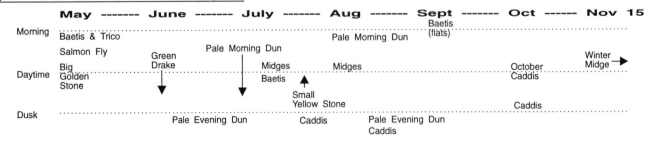

Fly Selection Guide

Dry Fly Imitations:

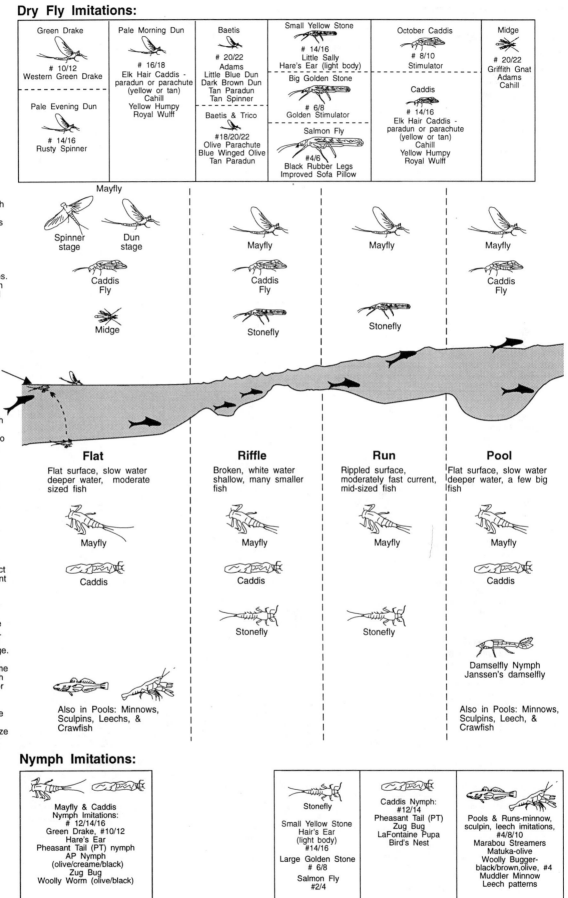

Green Drake	Pale Morning Dun	Baetis	Small Yellow Stone	October Caddis	Midge
# 10/12 Western Green Drake	# 16/18 Elk Hair Caddis - paradun or parachute (yellow or tan) Cahill Yellow Humpy Royal Wulff	# 20/22 Adams Little Blue Dun Dark Brown Dun Tan Paradun Tan Spinner	# 14/16 Little Sally Hare's Ear (light body)	# 8/10 Stimulator	# 20/22 Griffith Gnat Adams Cahill
Pale Evening Dun		Baetis & Trico	Big Golden Stone	Caddis	
# 14/16 Rusty Spinner		#18/20/22 Olive Parachute Blue Winged Olive Tan Paradun	# 6/8 Golden Stimulator / Salmon Fly #4/6 Black Rubber Legs Improved Sofa Pillow	# 14/16 Elk Hair Caddis - paradun or parachute (yellow or tan) Cahill Yellow Humpy Royal Wulff	

Dry Flies:
Adult Stage

The chart shows which type of trout forage frequent different parts of a stream.

Don't fish dry flies unless you see fish actually breaking the surface for floating flies. See hatch calendar on facing page for typical northern California hatches and hatch periods.

Mayfly — Spinner stage, Dun stage · Caddis Fly · Midge

Mayfly · Caddis Fly · Stonefly

Mayfly · Stonefly

Mayfly · Caddis Fly

Wet Flies:
Emerger Stage

Even during a hatch, most trout will still be feeding below the surface film on the emerging insects. Fish will show their backs and tails as they rise to the film. Fish a wet fly with a dead drift and rising lift technique. Imitations: Caddis - LaFontaine Emerging Pupa; Mayfly - Callibaetis Cripple.

Flat
Flat surface, slow water deeper water, moderate sized fish

Mayfly · Caddis

Riffle
Broken, white water shallow, many smaller fish

Mayfly · Caddis · Stonefly

Run
Rippled surface, moderately fast current, mid-sized fish

Mayfly · Caddis · Stonefly

Pool
Flat surface, slow water deeper water, a few big fish

Mayfly · Caddis · Damselfly Nymph Janssen's damselfly

Nymphs:
Larval Stage

The chart shows insect nymphs which frequent certain parts of a stream.

Ninety percent of a trout's feeding is done on or near the bottom. Nymphs are the most common bottom forage. Therefore you should spend 90% of your time fishing the bottom with nymphs, streamers, or lures.

Pickup a rock from the stream bottom and match the nymphs' size and color.

Also in Pools: Minnows, Sculpins, Leechs, & Crawfish

Also in Pools: Minnows, Sculpins, Leech, & Crawfish

Nymph Imitations:

Mayfly & Caddis Nymph Imitations: # 12/14/16 Green Drake, #10/12 Hare's Ear Pheasant Tail (PT) nymph AP Nymph (olive/creame/black) Zug Bug Woolly Worm (olive/black)	Stonefly Small Yellow Stone Hair's Ear (light body) #14/16 Large Golden Stone # 6/8 Salmon Fly #2/4	Caddis Nymph: #12/14 Pheasant Tail (PT) Zug Bug LaFontaine Pupa Bird's Nest	Pools & Runs-minnow, sculpin, leech imitations, #4/8/10 Marabou Streamers Matuka-olive Woolly Bugger- black/brown,olive, #4 Muddler Minnow Leech patterns

Rainbow Trout Map Index

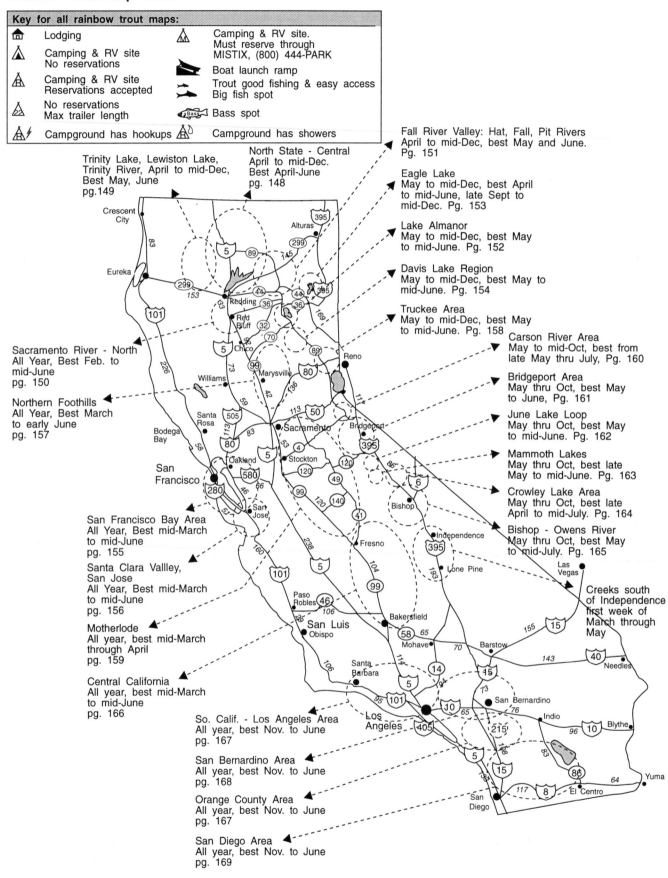

Key for all rainbow trout maps:

Lodging

Camping & RV site
No reservations

Camping & RV site
Reservations accepted

No reservations
Max trailer length

Campground has hookups

Camping & RV site.
Must reserve through
MISTIX, (800) 444-PARK

Boat launch ramp

Trout good fishing & easy access
Big fish spot

Bass spot

Campground has showers

Trinity Lake, Lewiston Lake,
Trinity River, April to mid-Dec,
Best May, June
pg.149

North State - Central
April to mid-Dec.
Best April-June
pg. 148

Fall River Valley: Hat, Fall, Pit Rivers
April to mid-Dec, best May and June.
Pg. 151

Eagle Lake
May to mid-Dec, best April
to mid-June, late Sept to
mid-Dec. Pg. 153

Lake Almanor
May to mid-Dec, best May
to mid-June. Pg. 152

Davis Lake Region
May to mid-Dec, best May to
mid-June. Pg. 154

Truckee Area
May to mid-Dec, best May
to mid-June. Pg. 158

Sacramento River - North
All Year, Best Feb. to
mid-June
pg. 150

Northern Foothills
All Year, Best March
to early June
pg. 157

Carson River Area
May to mid-Oct, best from
late May thru July, Pg. 160

Bridgeport Area
May thru Oct, best May
to June, Pg. 161

June Lake Loop
May thru Oct, best May
to mid-June. Pg. 162

Mammoth Lakes
May thru Oct, best late
May to mid-June. Pg. 163

Crowley Lake Area
May thru Oct, best late
April to mid-July. Pg. 164

Bishop - Owens River
May thru Oct, best May
to mid-July. Pg. 165

San Francisco Bay Area
All Year, Best mid-March
to mid-June
pg. 155

Santa Clara Vallley,
San Jose
All Year, Best mid-March
to mid-June
pg. 156

Motherlode
All year, best mid-March
through April
pg. 159

Central California
All year, best mid-March
to mid-June
pg. 166

Creeks south
of Independence
first week of
March through
May

So. Calif. - Los Angeles Area
All year, best Nov. to June
pg. 167

San Bernardino Area
All year, best Nov. to June
pg. 168

Orange County Area
All year, best Nov. to June
pg. 167

San Diego Area
All year, best Nov. to June
pg. 169

Index to Premier Fly Fishing Trout Streams

* Excellent maps for streams denoted by "*" can be ordered from The Fly Shop, Redding, 800-669-FISH (3474) or from Streamtime Maps, (707) 664-8604

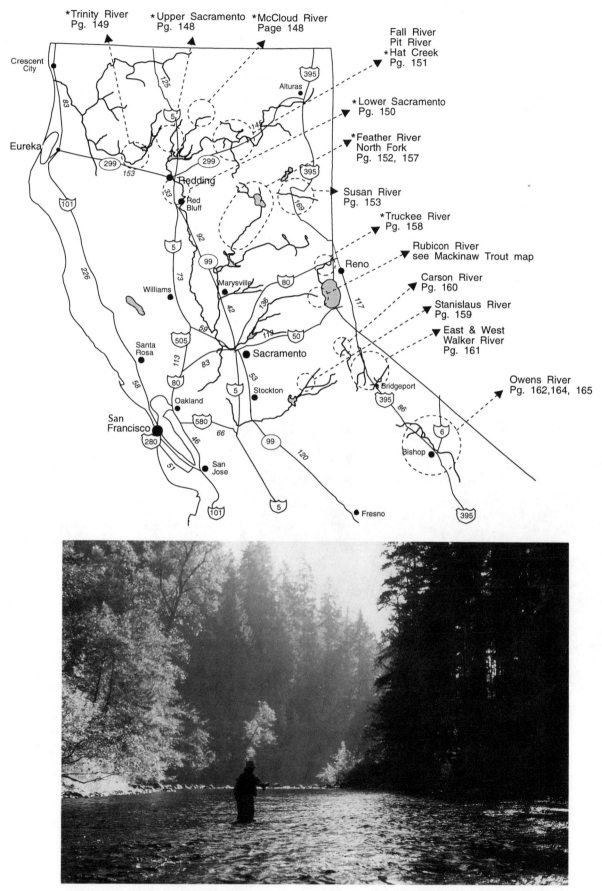

Trout Lakes & Streams: North State Central

Season: Streams open from last Saturday April to November 15. Lakes are open all year.
Limit: 5 / day plus 10 brook trout < 8". Daylight fishing only for trout and salmon. See special regs. for Klamath and McCloud Rivers.
Lakes best from April opening to mid-June. Deep troll the thermocline from mid-June.
Rivers best from opening through June except during heavy runoffs caused by early season warm weather.
Upper Sacramento River best in afternoon and early evening. Good in evening only June and July.
Special Forage: Upper Klamath has crawdads. Use crawfish colored crankbaits.
Lake Shasta late November turnover brings trout to surface feed on shad.

Fish Info & Guides:
Trout Plants, (916) 225-2146
• Ron DeNardi for the Klamath River, (916) 842-7655
• Ted Fay Fly Shop, Dunsmuir (916) 235-2969
• The Fly Shop, Redding (916) 222-3555
• Frank Holminski, Mt. Shasta (916) 926-6648
Camping:
Lake Shasta
U.S.F.S., Redding
(916) 275-1587
Facilities Info:
• Shasta Cascade Wonderland Redding, (916) 275-5555
• Redding Area Chamber of Commerce (916) 225-4433
• Shasta Lake Info Ctr. (916) 275-1587

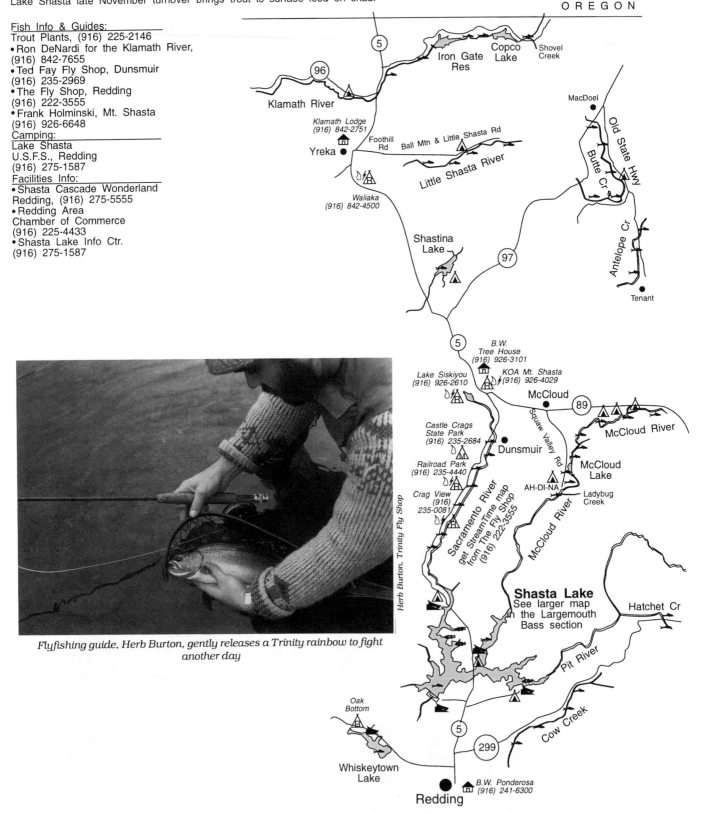

Flyfishing guide, Herb Burton, gently releases a Trinity rainbow to fight another day

Trout Lakes & Streams: Trinity Lake, Lewiston Lake, Trinity River

Season: Lakes open all year. Streams open from last Saturday in April to Nov. 15.
Limit: 5 / day + 10 brook trout under 8". Daylight fishing only for trout and salmon.
See special regs. for Trinity River. Lakes best between mid-April and mid-June
Deep troll from mid-June. Trinity Lake turnover in late September.
Streams best near mouths between opening through June, evenings in June & July.
Lewiston Lake has good fishing year around.
Trinity River steelhead Sept. to mid-March.
Trinity River salmon fishing from September through November.
Special forage: Trinity River lamprey eels, use eel imitation streamers.
Trinity Lake bass limit 2 from March 1 through May 31, 5 the rest of year.

Fishing Info & Guides:
Trout Plants, (916) 225-2146
• Trinity Fly Shop, Lewiston
(916) 623-6757
• Lakeview Terrace Resort
Lewiston Lake, (916) 778-3803
• The Fly Shop, Redding
(916) 222-3555
• Brady" Sport Shop, Weaverville
(916) 623-3121
• Don Johnson, Lewiston Lake
(916) 778-3091

Camping:
U.S.F.S., Weaverville
(916) 623-2121, (916) 275-1587

Facilities Info:
• Shasta Cascade Wonderland
Redding, (916) 275-5555
• Trinity Lake Area
Chamber of Commerce
(916) 623-6101

Central Lewiston, Trinity River
From Old Lewiston Bridge north to 250 feet
below Lewiston Dam, artificial barbless flies only.
See other special regulations.

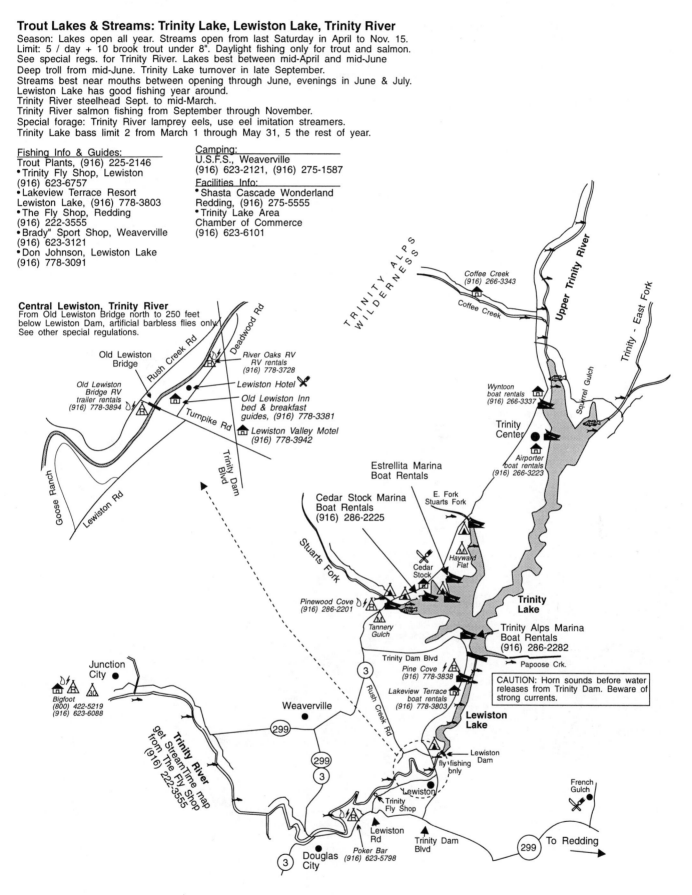

Trout Lakes & Stream: Lower Sacramento
Redding to Red Bluff

From Sept. 1 through Feb. 28, no rainbow trout or steelhead over 22 inches.
Best from February to mid-June. May be washed out by high flows in mid-to-late March or April.
Special Forage: Salmon roe during summer and fall salmon runs. Use Glo Bug imitator.

> CAUTION!   River contains many hazardous riffles & rapids
> Do NOT use this map for navigation!

Fishing Info:
The Fly Shop, Redding, (916) 222-3555
Guides:
Tom Stanton, (916) 628-5176
Bob Wigham, (916) 222-8058
Hank Mautz, (916) 365-1447

	Jan	Feb	Mar	April	May	June	July	Aug	Sept	Oct	Nov	Dec
Hatch:	Caddis ■━━━━━━━━━ High Water ━━━━(try worms/crickets)━━━━ Midge (evenings) ■━━━━━■ Yellow Stone ■━━━━━━ Some May Flies ■											
Flies:	Daytime: #14 or #16 Caddis Pupa, LaFontaine Emerger, Zug Bug Glo Bugs or salmon eggs during salmon run Evening: Elk Hair dry											
Lures:	Gold Hotshot #50 or Kwikfish, Wee Wart Rebel F76 crayfish pattern, Spinners: Panther Martin, Roostertail Plugs or drifted worms work best after March-April caddis hatch											

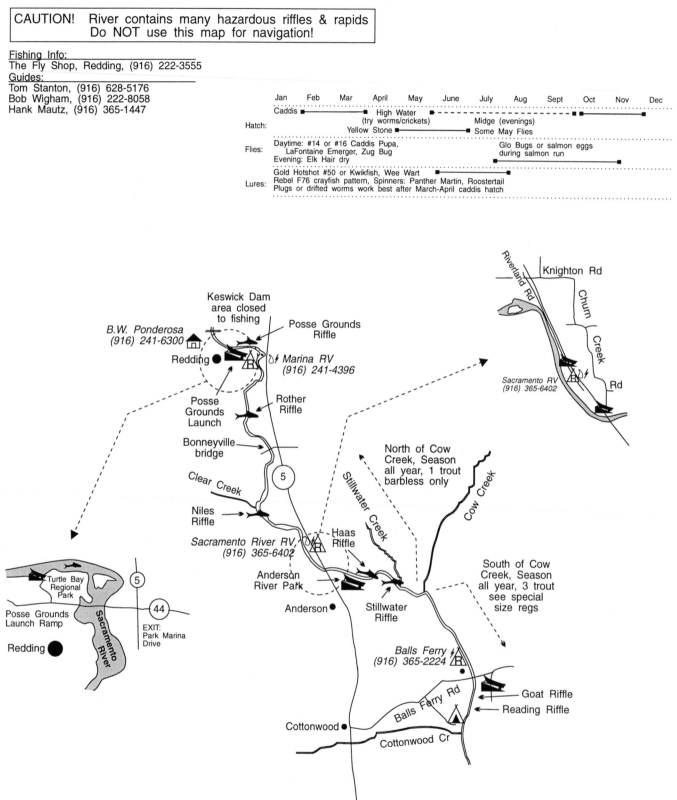

Riverland Rd
Knighton Rd
Churn Creek
Sacramento RV (916) 365-6402
Rd

Keswick Dam area closed to fishing
Posse Grounds Riffle
B.W. Ponderosa (916) 241-6300
Redding
Marina RV (916) 241-4396
Posse Grounds Launch
Rother Riffle
Bonneyville bridge
Clear Creek
Niles Riffle
Sacramento River RV (916) 365-6402
Haas Riffle
Anderson River Park
Anderson
Stillwater Creek
North of Cow Creek, Season all year, 1 trout barbless only
Cow Creek
South of Cow Creek, Season all year, 3 trout see special size regs
Stillwater Riffle
Balls Ferry (916) 365-2224
Goat Riffle
Reading Riffle
Balls Ferry Rd
Cottonwood
Cottonwood Cr

Turtle Bay Regional Park
Posse Grounds Launch Ramp
Redding
Sacramento River
5
44
EXIT: Park Marina Drive

Trout Lakes And Streams: Pit & Fall Rivers, Hat Creek

Season: Lakes & streams from last Saturday in April to Nov. 15.
Limit: Lakes - 5 / day, Streams - 2 / day. See special size, limit, and gear restrictions for rivers in this area.
Lakes best from opening to mid-June.
Streams best from opening through June and evenings in summer.

Fishing Info:
Trout plants, (916) 225-2146
Vaughn's Fly Shop
Burney, (916) 335-2381
Shasta Angler, Fall River Mills
(916) 336-6600
Lodging, Guides, Boats:
Clearwater Trout Tours, Cassel
(916) 335-3530, Guide & Boat
The Fly Shop, Redding
(916) 222-3555
Camping Info:
Burney Commerce, (916) 335-2111
Fall River Commerce, (916) 336-5840

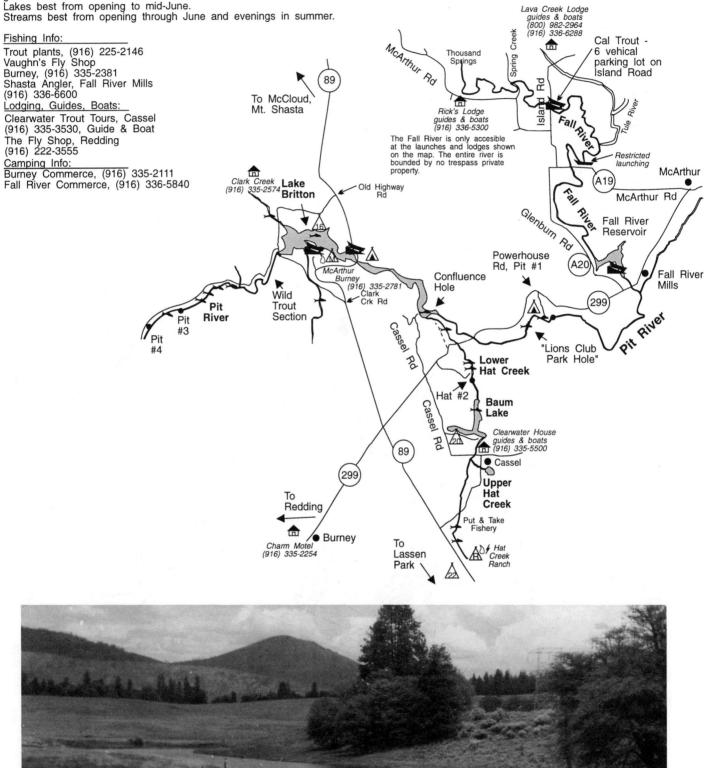

Lava Creek Lodge
guides & boats
(800) 982-2964
(916) 336-6288

Cal Trout -
6 vehical
parking lot on
Island Road

McArthur Rd

Thousand
Springs

Spring Creek

Island Rd

Fall River

Tule River

Rick's Lodge
guides & boats
(916) 336-5300

Restricted
launching

The Fall River is only accesible at the launches and lodges shown on the map. The entire river is bounded by no trespass private property.

McArthur

A19

Fall River

McArthur Rd

Glenburn Rd

Fall River
Reservoir

A20

Fall River
Mills

299

Pit River

To McCloud,
Mt. Shasta

89

Clark Creek
(916) 335-2574

Lake
Britton

Old Highway
Rd

16

McArthur
Burney
(916) 335-2781

Clark
Crk Rd

Wild
Trout
Section

Pit
River

Pit
#3

Pit
#4

Cassel Rd

Confluence
Hole

Powerhouse
Rd, Pit #1

"Lions Club
Park Hole"

Lower
Hat Creek

Hat #2

Baum
Lake

20

Clearwater House
guides & boats
(916) 335-5500

Cassel

Upper
Hat
Creek

Cassel Rd

89

299

To
Redding

Charm Motel
(916) 335-2254

Burney

To
Lassen
Park

22

Put & Take
Fishery

Hat
Creek
Ranch

Trout Lakes and Streams, Lake Almanor Area
The lake gets windy around mid-day.

Season: Lakes all year, streams from
last Sat. in April to Nov. 15. Limit: 5 / day.
Almanor tributaries and Butt Creek open
from Sat. before memorial day to Nov. 15.
Best trout / lake salmon mid-April to mid-June.
Best smallmouth bass, April to early June.
Special Forage: Pond smelt - use #4 - #6
white / silver streamers, or white Gitzit
imitations

Fishing Info:
Trout Plants, (916) 351-0832
Lassen View Resort
boat rentals, (916) 596-3437
Sportsman's Den, (916) 283-2733

Boat Rentals:
McDonald, (916) 259-2959
Guide:
Roger Keeling
(916) 258-2283
Camping:
Lassen View, (916) 596-3437
Lodging:

Chester Manor Motel, (916) 258-2441
Dorado Inn, (916) 284-7790
Knotty Pine Resort, (916) 596-3348
Lassen View Resort, (916) 596-3437
Plumas Pines Resort, (916) 259-4343
Timber House Lodge, (916) 258-3175

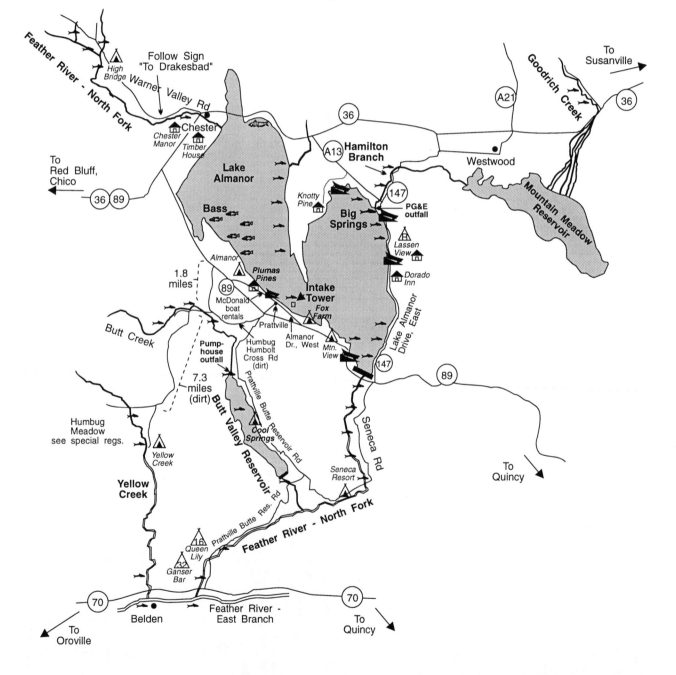

Eagle Lake

Season: Memorial Day to December 31. Limit: 3 / day.
Best in cool months, from opening to mid-June and late September to mid-December.
Bite occurs before dawn and early a.m. almost all year. During warm water months, late June to late September, fish are concentrated near underwater springs. * = major spring areas on map. Boat concentrations will be over springs. During cool water months, fish are in the shallows just out from weed bank edges.

Fishing Info:
Eagle Lake Marina, (916) 825-3454
Boat Rentals, bait, tackle
Eagle Lake General Store, Spaulding
(916) 825-2191
Guides:
D.O.N. Guide Svc, (916) 825-3229
Camping:
Eagle Lake RV, (916) 825-3133
Camping Info: (916) 257-2151
Lodging:
Lakeview Inn, (916) 825-3223
boat rentals
Best Western Trailside,
Susanville, (916) 257-4123

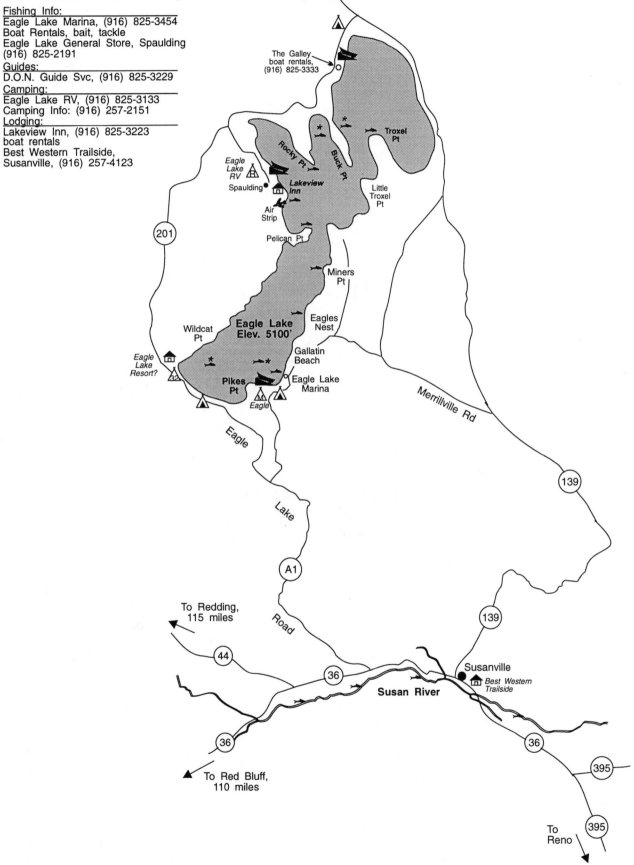

Trout Lakes & Streams, Davis Lake Region

Season: Lakes open all year, Davis and Frenchman are ice free from mid-May through Nov. Gold Lakes are ice free in early June.
Streams open from last Sat. in April to Nov. 15. Limit: 5 / day.
Best from early May to mid-June, mornings and dusk in July & August.
Deep troll starting mid-June.

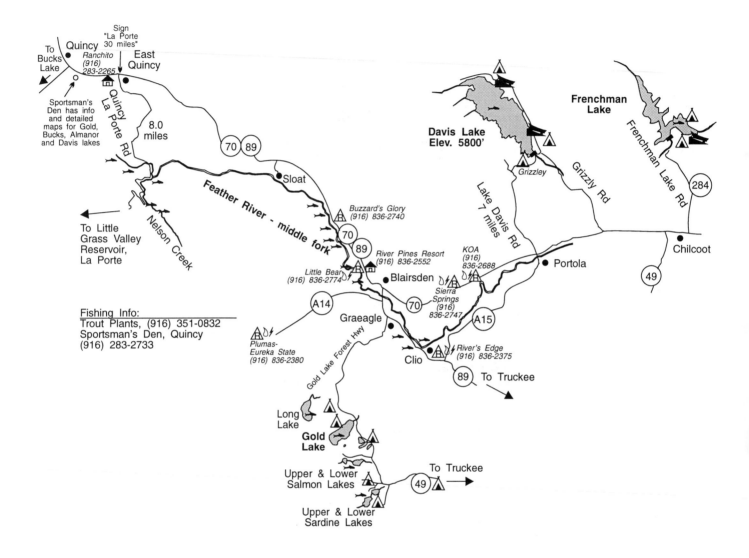

Trout Lakes & Streams: San Francisco Bay Area

Season: All year. Limit: 5 / day.
Best from mid-March with clearing water to late May.
Daytime fishing only for trout except at Berryessa.
Troll deep starting in June at Berryessa, San Pablo.
Lake Merced planted all year.
Fly Fishing School:
Orvis San Francisco, (415) 392-1600

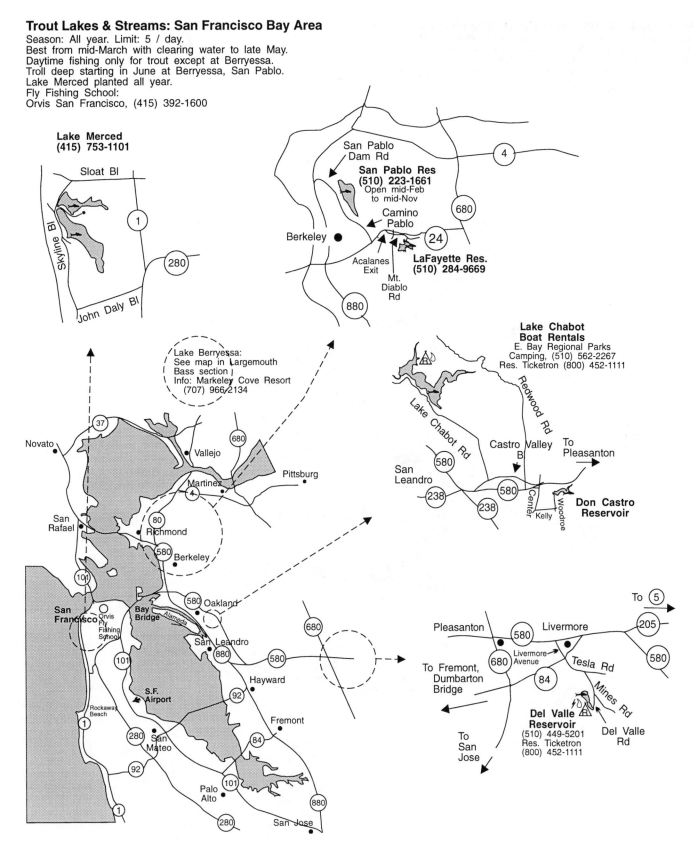

Lake Merced
(415) 753-1101

Sloat Bl

Skyline Bl

John Daly Bl

1

280

San Pablo
Dam Rd

San Pablo Res
(510) 223-1661
Open mid-Feb
to mid-Nov

4

680

Camino
Pablo

Berkeley

24

Acalanes
Exit

Mt.
Diablo
Rd

LaFayette Res.
(510) 284-9669

880

Lake Berryessa:
See map in Largemouth
Bass section
Info: Markeley Cove Resort
(707) 966-2134

Lake Chabot
Boat Rentals
E. Bay Regional Parks
Camping, (510) 562-2267
Res. Ticketron (800) 452-1111

Lake Chabot Rd

Redwood Rd

Castro Valley
B

To
Pleasanton

San
Leandro

580

580

238

238

Center

Kelly

Woodroe

Don Castro
Reservoir

Novato

37

680

Vallejo

Pittsburg

Martinez

4

San
Rafael

80

Richmond

580

Berkeley

101

580   Oakland

680

San
Francisco

Orvis
Fly
Fishing
School

Bay
Bridge

Alameda

San Leandro

880

580

Hayward

92

S.F.
Airport

Rockaway
Beach

101

Fremont

84

1

280   San
Mateo

92

Palo
Alto

101

280

San Jose

880

To   5

Pleasanton   580   Livermore

205

580

680   Livermore
Avenue

Tesla Rd

84

Mines Rd

To Fremont,
Dumbarton
Bridge

Del Valle
Reservoir
(510) 449-5201
Res. Ticketron
(800) 452-1111

Del Valle
Rd

To
San
Jose

Trout Lakes & Streams: Santa Clara Valley, San Jose
Season: Lakes all year. Streams last Sat. in April to mid-Nov.
Best from mid-March with clearing water to late May.
Troll deep starting in June. Limit: 5 / day
Anderson and Coyote Res. may be unfishable in drought years.
Fishing Info:
Coyote Discount Bait & Tackle
(408) 463-0711

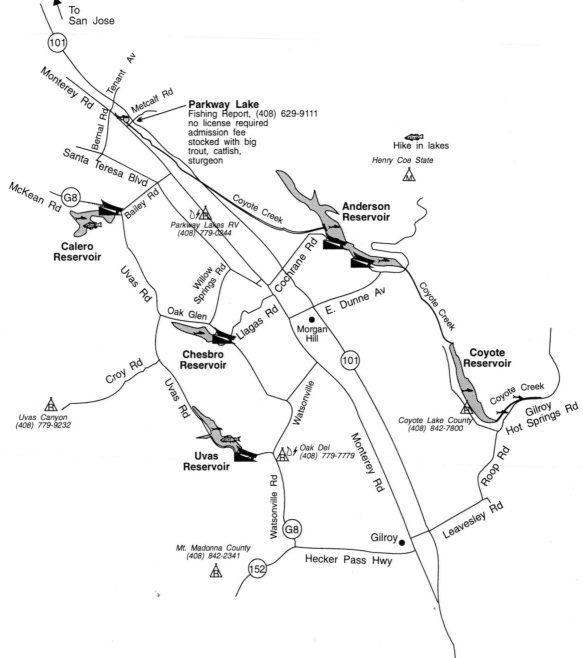

To
San Jose

101

Monterey Rd

Tenant Av

Bernal Rd

Metcalf Rd

Parkway Lake
Fishing Report, (408) 629-9111
no license required
admission fee
stocked with big
trout, catfish,
sturgeon

Santa Teresa Blvd

Hike in lakes

Henry Coe State

McKean Rd   G8

Bailey Rd

Parkway Lakes RV
(408) 779-0244

Coyote Creek

**Anderson
Reservoir**

**Calero
Reservoir**

Uvas Rd

Willow Springs Rd

Cochrane Rd

E. Dunne Av

Coyote Creek

Oak Glen

Llagas Rd

Morgan
Hill

**Coyote
Reservoir**

Croy Rd

**Chesbro
Reservoir**

101

Watsonville

Coyote Creek

Uvas Canyon
(408) 779-9232

Uvas Rd

Coyote Lake County
(408) 842-7800

Gilroy
Hot Springs Rd

**Uvas
Reservoir**

Oak Del
(408) 779-7779

Monterey Rd

Roop Rd

Watsonville Rd

Leavesley Rd

G8

Gilroy

Mt. Madonna County
(408) 842-2341

152   Hecker Pass Hwy

Trout Lakes & Streams: Northern Foothills

Season: Lakes & streams all year. Limit: 5 trout / day, 2 salmon.
Trout & salmon daytime only north of hwy 80 except Oroville,
Collins and Camp Far West lakes. See special regs. for below
Oroville Dam.
Best early March with clearing waters to early June. Troll deep
near dams after mid-June.

Lake Oroville
Fishing Info:
Feather River B&T, (916) 534-0605
Fly Fishing School & Guides
Powell Fly Fishing, (916) 345-3396
Facilities Info:
State Rec. Area, (916) 538-2200
Boat Rentals:
Limesaddle Marina
Fishing & Houseboats
(916) 877-2414
Bidwell Marina
Fishing & Houseboats
(800) 637-1767
(916) 589-3165

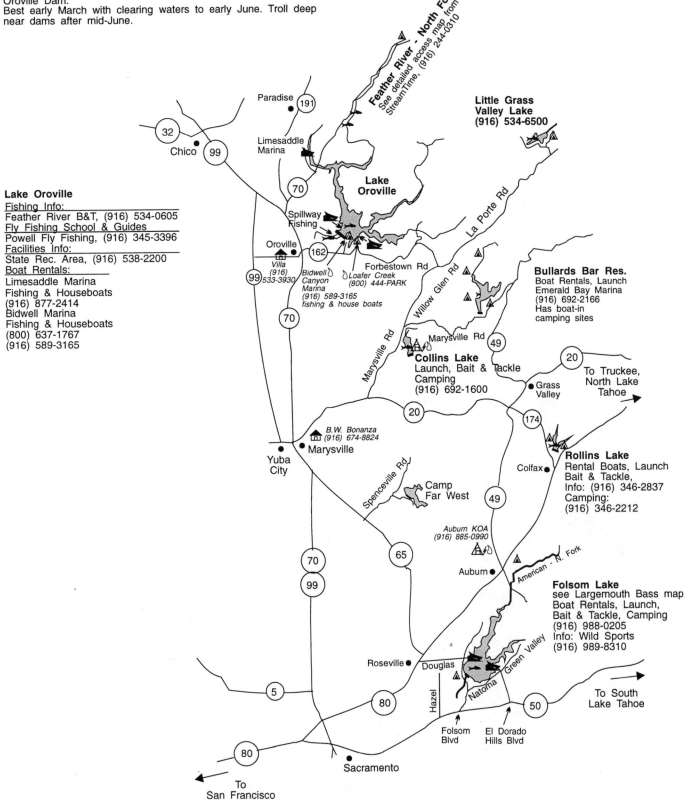

Feather River - North Fork
See detailed access map from
StreamTime, (916) 244-0310

Paradise (191)

(32)

Chico (99)

Limesaddle
Marina

Little Grass
Valley Lake
(916) 534-6500

Lake
Oroville

(70)

Spillway
Fishing

La Porte Rd

Oroville
Villa
(916)
533-3930

(99) (162)

Bidwell
Canyon
Marina
(916) 589-3165
fishing & house boats

Loafer Creek
(800) 444-PARK

Forbestown Rd

Willow Glen Rd

Bullards Bar Res.
Boat Rentals, Launch
Emerald Bay Marina
(916) 692-2166
Has boat-in
camping sites

(70)

Marysville Rd

Marysville Rd (49)

Collins Lake
Launch, Bait & Tackle
Camping
(916) 692-1600

(20)

Grass
Valley

(20)

To Truckee,
North Lake
Tahoe

(174)

B.W. Bonanza
(916) 674-8824
Marysville

Colfax

Rollins Lake
Rental Boats, Launch
Bait & Tackle,
Info: (916) 346-2837
Camping:
(916) 346-2212

Yuba
City

Spenceville Rd

Camp
Far West

(49)

Auburn KOA
(916) 885-0990

American - N. Fork

(70)

(99)

(65)

Auburn

Folsom Lake
see Largemouth Bass map
Boat Rentals, Launch,
Bait & Tackle, Camping
(916) 988-0205
Info: Wild Sports
(916) 989-8310

Roseville

Douglas

Green Valley

Natoma

Hazel

(5)

(80)

(50)

To South
Lake Tahoe

Folsom
Blvd

El Dorado
Hills Blvd

(80)

Sacramento

To
San Francisco

Trout Lakes and Streams: Truckee Area

Season: Lakes all year, Streams from last Saturday in April to Nov. 15. The Nevada Truckee is open all year. Limit: 5/day. Lakes best from early May to mid-June. Streamtime makes an excellent access map - order from The Fly Shop, (916) 222-3555.

Fishing Info:
Trout Plants, (916) 351-0832
Tourist Liquors, Truckee
(916) 587-3081
For Nevada Truckee:
The Gilly, (702) 358-6113

Guides:
Ted Samford, (916) 389-2748
Dennis Pierce, (916) 426-3362
Flyfishing Guides:
Randy Johnson, Truckee
(916) 525-6575
Frank Pisciotta, Truckee
(916) 587-7333
Reno Fly Shop, Reno
(702) 825-FISH

Calif. School of Flyfishing
Truckee, (916) 587-7005
Facilities Info:
Truckee Rec. Dept,
(916) 587-3558
Camping Info:
Boca, (916) 265-4531
Martis, (916) 639-2342
Prosser, (916) 265-4531
Stampede, (916) 582-0120

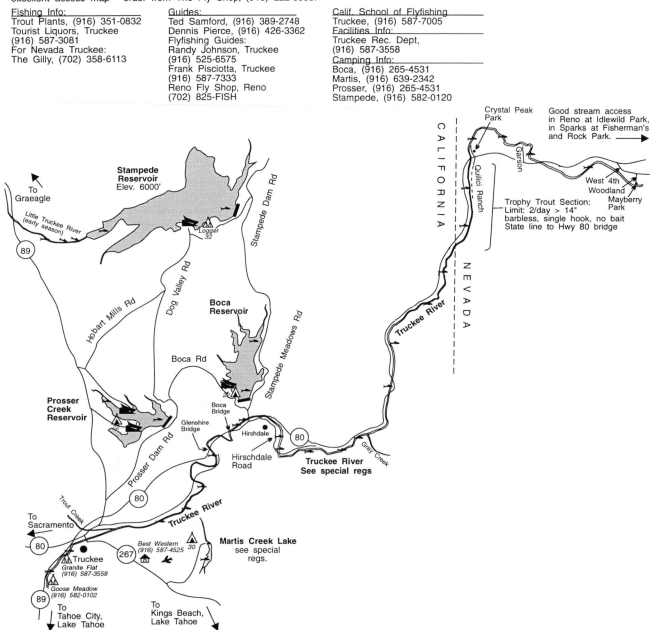

Trout Lakes & Streams: Motherload

Season: All year. Limit: 5 / day.
Best from mid-March with clearing
water to late April. May to September
troll deep. McSwain stays cool until July.
Phone Area Code is 209

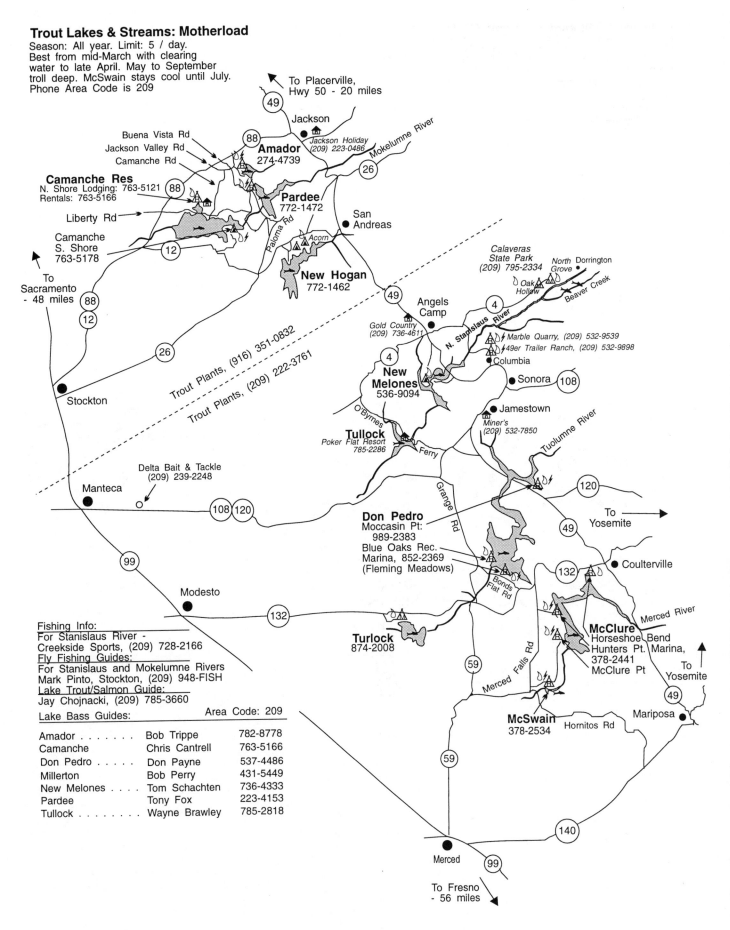

Fishing Info:
For Stanislaus River -
Creekside Sports, (209) 728-2166
Fly Fishing Guides:
For Stanislaus and Mokelumne Rivers
Mark Pinto, Stockton, (209) 948-FISH
Lake Trout/Salmon Guide:
Jay Chojnacki, (209) 785-3660

Lake Bass Guides: Area Code: 209

Amador	. . . . . .	Bob Trippe	782-8778
Camanche		Chris Cantrell	763-5166
Don Pedro	. . . .	Don Payne	537-4486
Millerton		Bob Perry	431-5449
New Melones	. . . .	Tom Schachten	736-4333
Pardee		Tony Fox	223-4153
Tullock	. . . .	Wayne Brawley	785-2818

Trout Lakes & Streams: Carson River Area

Markleeville, Carson River, Heenan Lake, Topaz Lake
Season: Topaz Lake - Jan. 1 through Sept. 30.
Other lakes all year, Streams from last Saturday in April to Nov. 15
Limit: 5/day. Best from late May through July.
Fishing Info:
Trout Plants, (916) 351-0832
Monty Wolf's Trading Post
Markleeville, (916) 694-2201
Guide: Sorenson's Resort
(916) 694-2203

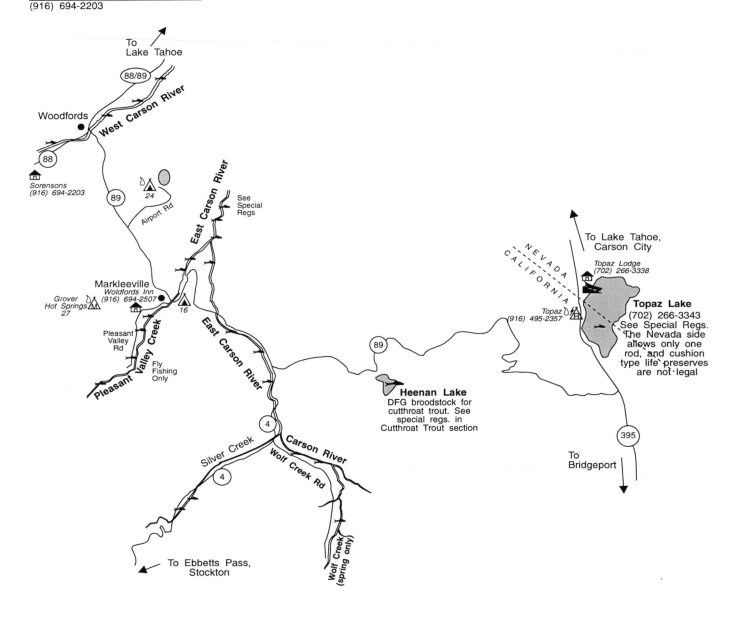

Trout Lakes & Streams: Bridgeport

Season: Lakes & Streams from last Saturday in April through October.
Limit 5/day + 10 brook trout under 8". No night fishing.
Lakes best from opening to mid-June and mornings and dusk in June, July.
Lakes above 7000' best from late June through October.

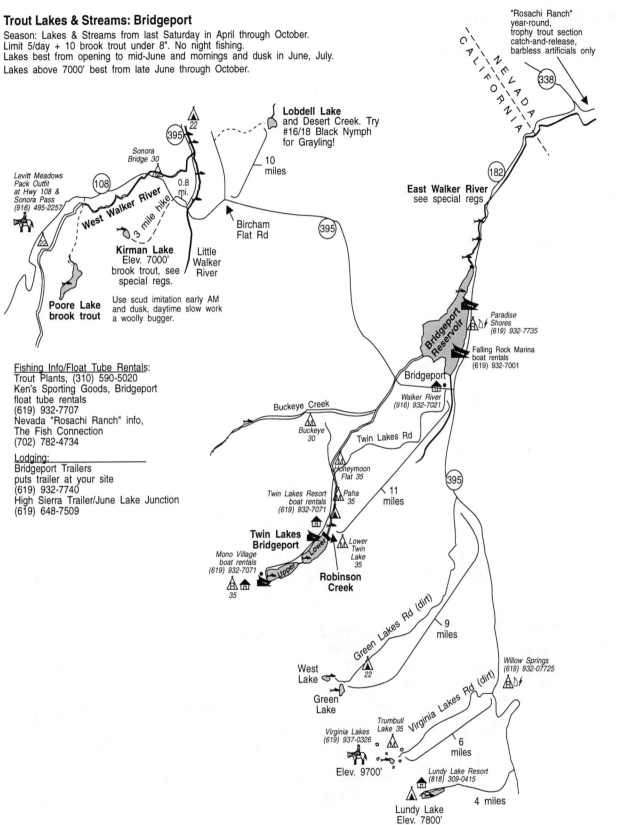

"Rosachi Ranch"
year-round,
trophy trout section
catch-and-release,
barbless artificials only

Lobdell Lake
and Desert Creek. Try
#16/18 Black Nymph
for Grayling!

10 miles

East Walker River
see special regs

Sonora Bridge 30

Levitt Meadows
Pack Outfit
at Hwy 108 &
Sonora Pass
(916) 495-2257

West Walker River

0.8 mi.

3 mile hike

Bircham Flat Rd

Kirman Lake
Elev. 7000'
brook trout, see
special regs.

Little Walker River

Poore Lake
brook trout

Use scud imitation early AM
and dusk, daytime slow work
a woolly bugger.

Bridgeport Reservoir

Paradise Shores
(619) 932-7735

Falling Rock Marina
boat rentals
(619) 932-7001

Bridgeport

Walker River
(916) 932-7021

Fishing Info/Float Tube Rentals:
Trout Plants, (310) 590-5020
Ken's Sporting Goods, Bridgeport
float tube rentals
(619) 932-7707
Nevada "Rosachi Ranch" info,
The Fish Connection
(702) 782-4734

Lodging:
Bridgeport Trailers
puts trailer at your site
(619) 932-7740
High Sierra Trailer/June Lake Junction
(619) 648-7509

Buckeye Creek

Buckeye 30

Twin Lakes Rd

Honeymoon Flat 35

Twin Lakes Resort
boat rentals
(619) 932-7071

Paha 35

11 miles

Twin Lakes
Bridgeport

Lower Twin Lake 35

Mono Village
boat rentals
(619) 932-7071

Lower

Upper

35

Robinson Creek

Green Lakes Rd (dirt)

9 miles

Willow Springs
(619) 932-07725

West Lake

22

Green Lake

Virginia Lakes Rd (dirt)

Trumbull Lake 35

Virginia Lakes
(619) 937-0326

6 miles

Elev. 9700'

Lundy Lake Resort
(818) 309-0415

Lundy Lake
Elev. 7800'

4 miles

Trout Lakes & Streams: June Lake Loop

Season: Last Saturday in April through October. Limit: 5/day + 10 brook trout less than 8"
No night fishing
Best from May to mid-June, mornings & dusk from June to early October.

Fishng Info:
Plants, (310) 590-5020
Ernie's Tackle, June Lake
(619) 648-7756
Facilities Info:
Chamber of Commerce,
(619) 648-7584
Camping:
Pine Cliff, (619) 648-7558
High Sierra Trailer Rental
Puts trailer at your site
(619) 648-7509
Tioga Vacation Rental
(619) 647-6488
Lodging:
Alpers Ranch, (619) 648-7334
Arcularius Ranch, (619) 648-7807
Boulder Lodge, (619) 648-7533
June Lake Motel, (800) 648-7547
Silver Lake Resort, (619) 648-7525
Pack Trips:
Frontier Pack Train
(619) 648-7701

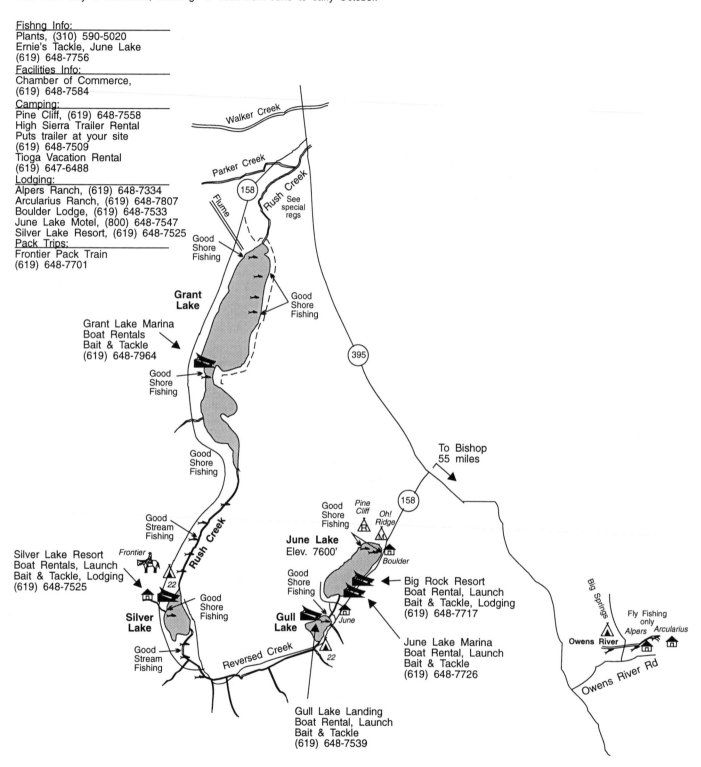

Walker Creek

Parker Creek

158

Rush Creek

Flume

See special regs

Good Shore Fishing

Grant Lake

Grant Lake Marina
Boat Rentals
Bait & Tackle
(619) 648-7964

Good Shore Fishing

Good Shore Fishing

Good Shore Fishing

395

To Bishop
55 miles

158

Good Shore Fishing

Pine Cliff

Oh! Ridge

June Lake
Elev. 7600'

Boulder

Big Rock Resort
Boat Rental, Launch
Bait & Tackle, Lodging
(619) 648-7717

Good Shore Fishing

June

June Lake Marina
Boat Rental, Launch
Bait & Tackle
(619) 648-7726

Good Stream Fishing

Rush Creek

Frontier

Silver Lake Resort
Boat Rentals, Launch
Bait & Tackle, Lodging
(619) 648-7525

22

Silver Lake

Good Shore Fishing

Gull Lake

Good Stream Fishing

Reversed Creek

22

Gull Lake Landing
Boat Rental, Launch
Bait & Tackle
(619) 648-7539

Big Springs

Fly Fishing only
Alpers   Arcularius

Owens River

Owens River Rd

Trout Lakes & Streams, Mammoth Lakes

Season: Last Saturday in April through October. Ice Free: late May through October
Limit: 5/day + 10 brook trout under 8". No night fishing.
Best from late May to mid-June, early mornings and dusk from June to early October.

Fishing Info, Fly Fishing Guides &
Float Tube Rentals
Plants, (310) 590-5020
Sierra Bright Dot, (619) 934-5514
Kittredge's, (619) 934-7566
float tube rentals
Rick's Sport Center, float tube &
wader rentals, (619) 934-3416
David Moss, (619) 934-4168
Jim Pettigrew (619) 934-4897
Gary Hooper (619) 934-8625
Kevin Peterson (619) 934-8253
Lodging:
Mammoth Reservations,
(800) 462-5571,
(800) 462-5585
Facilities Info:
Visitors Bureau,
(800) 367-6572,
(619) 934-8006
Camping:
• Mammoth Ranger District
(619) 934-2505
• Inyo Forest District
(619) 924-5500
• High Sierra Trailer Rentals
puts trailer at your site
(619) 648-7509
• Sierra Vacation Trailer,
(619) 935-4263
• Tioga Vacation Trailer,
(619) 647-6488

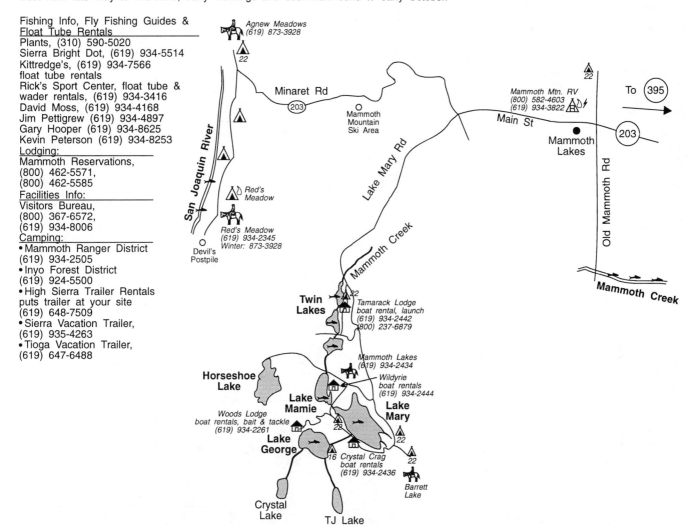

Trout Lakes & Streams: Crowley Lake & Upper Owens

CAUTION! Not to be used for navigation.
Crowley Lake has high winds starting mid-day.

Season/Limit: Last Saturday of April through July 31, 5/day, 10 possession.
Aug. 1 through Oct. 31, 2 trout, min. size 18". See other regs for tributaries.
Other lakes: 5 / day + 10 brook trout < 8".
Best from opener to mid-July.
Special forage: Sacramento perch fry. limitations are #8 matuka, small minnow
lures (1-1 1/2" Rapala), woolly buggers, Stan's perch fly
<u>Fishing Info/Float Tube Rentals</u>
Trout plants, (310) 590-5020
• Brocks,Bishop (619) 872-3581
   float tube rentals
• Crowley Lake, (619) 935-4301
• Culver's Sporting Goods
   Bishop, (619) 872-8361
<u>Fly Fishing Guides:</u>
• Jeff Parker, (619) 935-4879
   Rock Creek area specialist
• The Trout Fitter, (619) 924-3676
   Crowley Lake specialist
• Hot Creek Ranch, (619) 935-4214
<u>Camping:</u>
Sierra Vacation Trailer,
puts trailer at your site
(619) 935-4263

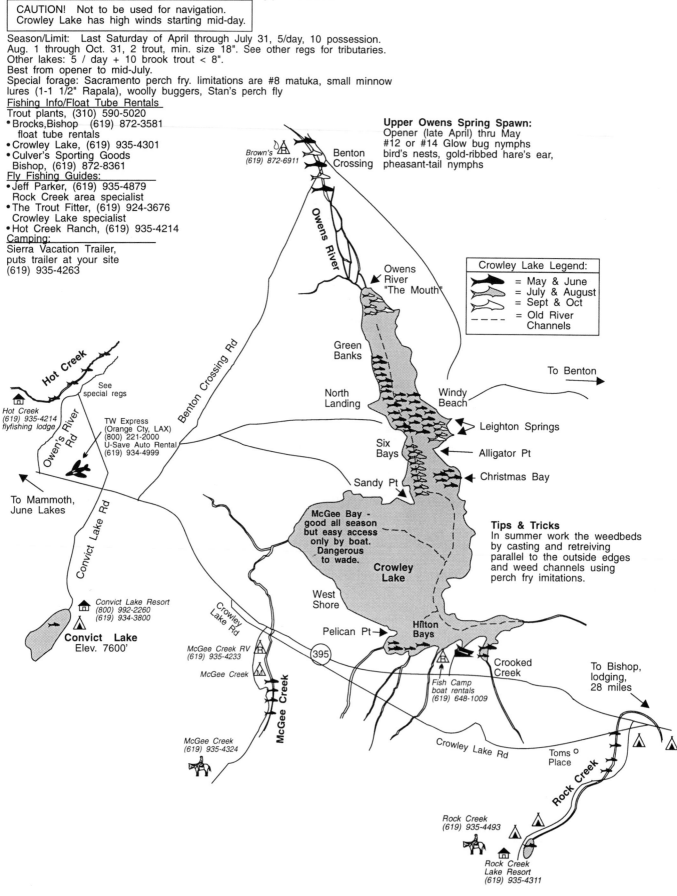

Upper Owens Spring Spawn:
Opener (late April) thru May
#12 or #14 Glow bug nymphs
bird's nests, gold-ribbed hare's ear,
pheasant-tail nymphs

Brown's
(619) 872-6911

Benton
Crossing

Owens River

Owens
River
"The Mouth"

Crowley Lake Legend:
= May & June
= July & August
= Sept & Oct
- - - = Old River
        Channels

Green
Banks

North
Landing

To Benton

Windy
Beach

Leighton Springs

Six
Bays

Alligator Pt

Sandy Pt

Christmas Bay

Hot Creek

See
special regs

Hot Creek
(619) 935-4214
flyfishing lodge

Owen's River Rd

TW Express
(Orange Cty, LAX)
(800) 221-2000
U-Save Auto Rental
(619) 934-4999

Benton Crossing Rd

McGee Bay -
good all season
but easy access
only by boat.
Dangerous
to wade.

**Crowley
Lake**

Tips & Tricks
In summer work the weedbeds
by casting and retrieving
parallel to the outside edges
and weed channels using
perch fry imitations.

To Mammoth,
June Lakes

Convict Lake Rd

West
Shore

Convict Lake Resort
(800) 992-2260
(619) 934-3800

Convict   Lake
Elev. 7600'

Crowley Lake Rd

Pelican Pt

Hilton
Bays

Crooked
Creek

To Bishop,
lodging,
28 miles

McGee Creek RV
(619) 935-4233

McGee Creek

Fish Camp
boat rentals
(619) 648-1009

395

McGee Creek

McGee Creek
(619) 935-4324

Crowley Lake Rd

Toms
Place

Rock Creek

Rock Creek
(619) 935-4493

Rock Creek
Lake Resort
(619) 935-4311

Trout Lakes & Streams: Bishop Area and Lower Owens River

Bishop Area and Owens River
Season: Last Saturday in April through October. Pleasant Valley Reservoir open all year.
Limit: 5 / day + 10 brook trout less than 8". See map and DFG book for special regs.
Owens River and Pleasant Valley Res. best from opener to mid-July.
Lake Sabrina and other high elevation lakes best from mid-May to mid-July.

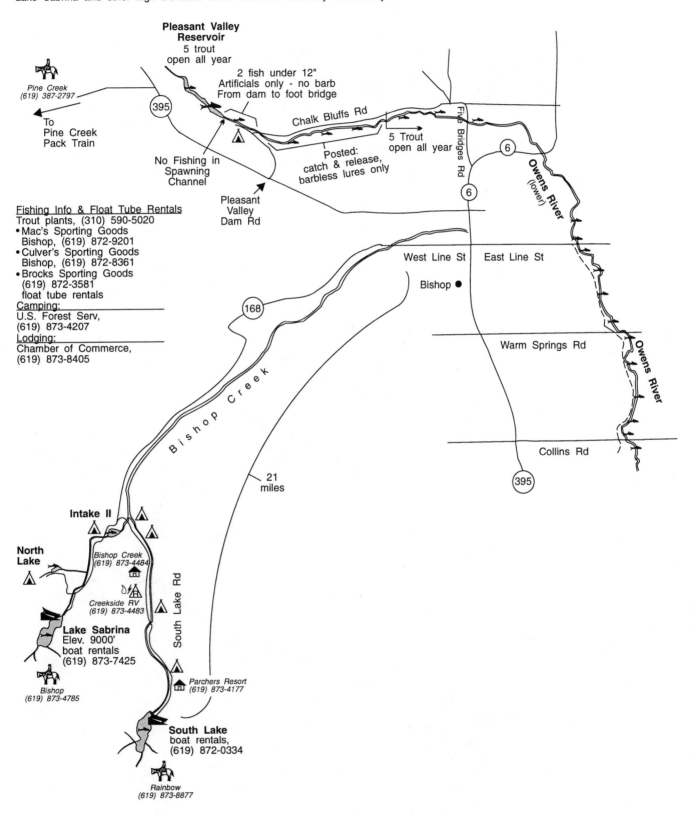

Pleasant Valley Reservoir
5 trout
open all year

2 fish under 12"
Artificials only - no barb
From dam to foot bridge

Chalk Bluffs Rd

Pine Creek
(619) 387-2797

To
Pine Creek
Pack Train

395

No Fishing in
Spawning
Channel

Pleasant
Valley
Dam Rd

Posted:
catch & release,
barbless lures only

5 Trout
open all year

Five Bridges Rd

6

6

Owens River
(lower)

Fishing Info & Float Tube Rentals
Trout plants, (310) 590-5020
• Mac's Sporting Goods
  Bishop, (619) 872-9201
• Culver's Sporting Goods
  Bishop, (619) 872-8361
• Brocks Sporting Goods
  (619) 872-3581
  float tube rentals
Camping:
U.S. Forest Serv,
(619) 873-4207
Lodging:
Chamber of Commerce,
(619) 873-8405

West Line St   East Line St

Bishop ●

168

Bishop Creek

Warm Springs Rd

Owens River

21
miles

Collins Rd

395

Intake II

North Lake

Bishop Creek
(619) 873-4484

Creekside RV
(619) 873-4483

South Lake Rd

Lake Sabrina
Elev. 9000'
boat rentals
(619) 873-7425

Bishop
(619) 873-4785

Parchers Resort
(619) 873-4177

South Lake
boat rentals,
(619) 872-0334

Rainbow
(619) 873-8877

Trout Lakes & Streams: Central California

Season: All year. Limit: 5 / day. See special Kern River regs.
Lakes below 5000' best from mid-March with clearing water through April. Deep troll from May on.
Higher lakes over 5000' iced over until mid-to-late March. Best from late March to
to mid-June. Deep troll from mid-June. All lakes, except Courtright, have boat rentals, bait & tackle
Trout plants, (209) 222-3761

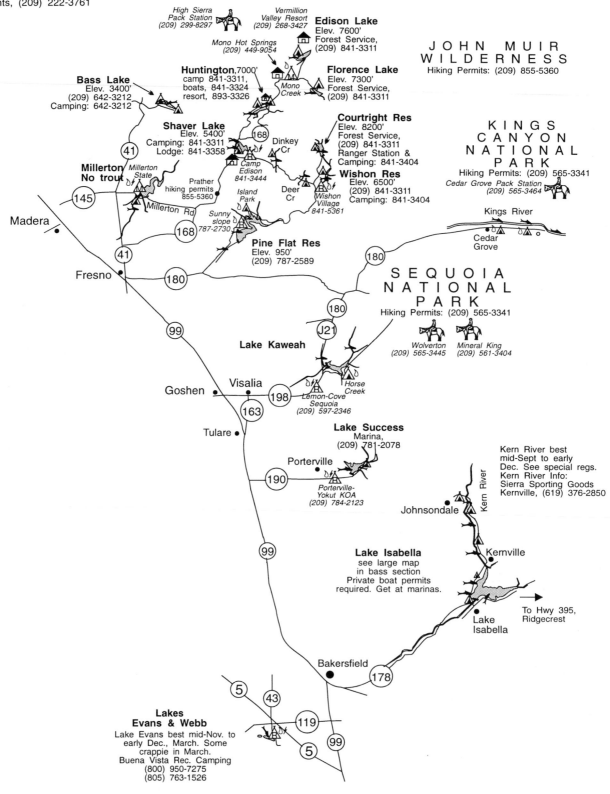

High Sierra
Pack Station
(209) 299-8297

Vermillion
Valley Resort
(209) 268-3427

Edison Lake
Elev. 7600'
Forest Service,
(209) 841-3311

Mono Hot Springs
(209) 449-9054

**J O H N   M U I R
W I L D E R N E S S**
Hiking Permits: (209) 855-5360

Bass Lake
Elev. 3400'
(209) 642-3212
Camping: 642-3212

Huntington, 7000'
camp 841-3311,
boats, 841-3324
resort, 893-3326

Mono Creek

Florence Lake
Elev. 7300'
Forest Service,
(209) 841-3311

Shaver Lake
Elev. 5400'
Camping: 841-3311
Lodge: 841-3358

Dinkey
Cr

Courtright Res
Elev. 8200'
Forest Service,
(209) 841-3311
Ranger Station &
Camping: 841-3404

**K I N G S
C A N Y O N
N A T I O N A L
P A R K**
Hiking Permits: (209) 565-3341
Cedar Grove Pack Station
(209) 565-3464

(41)

**Millerton
No trout**

Millerton
State

Camp
Edison
841-3444

Wishon Res
Elev. 6500'
(209) 841-3311
Camping: 841-3404

(145)

Prather
hiking permits
855-5360

Island
Park

Deer
Cr

Wishon
Village
841-5361

Kings River

Madera

Millerton Rd

Sunny
slope
787-2730

(168)

Pine Flat Res
Elev. 950'
(209) 787-2589

(180)

Cedar
Grove

(41)

(180)

Fresno

**S E Q U O I A
N A T I O N A L
P A R K**
Hiking Permits: (209) 565-3341

(99)

(180)

(J21)

Wolverton
(209) 565-3445

Mineral King
(209) 561-3404

Lake Kaweah

Goshen

Visalia

(198)

Horse
Creek

Lemon-Cove
Sequoia
(209) 597-2346

(163)

Tulare

Lake Success
Marina,
(209) 781-2078

Kern River best
mid-Sept to early
Dec. See special regs.
Kern River Info:
Sierra Sporting Goods
Kernville, (619) 376-2850

Porterville

(190)

Porterville-
Yokut KOA
(209) 784-2123

Johnsondale

(99)

Lake Isabella
see large map
in bass section
Private boat permits
required. Get at marinas.

Kernville

Bakersfield

(178)

To Hwy 395,
Ridgecrest

Lake
Isabella

(5)

(43)

(119)

**Lakes
Evans & Webb**
Lake Evans best mid-Nov. to
early Dec., March. Some
crappie in March.
Buena Vista Rec. Camping
(800) 950-7275
(805) 763-1526

(5)

(99)

Trout Lakes & Streams: So. California, Los Angeles Area

Los Angeles Area - North
Season: Open all year. Limit: 5 / day.
Best from November to mid-May. Deep troll by dam May through October.
Most lakes have more detailed maps in Largemouth Bass section.
All lakes have rental boats, bait & tackle.
<u>Fishing Info:</u>
Trout plants, (310) 590-5020

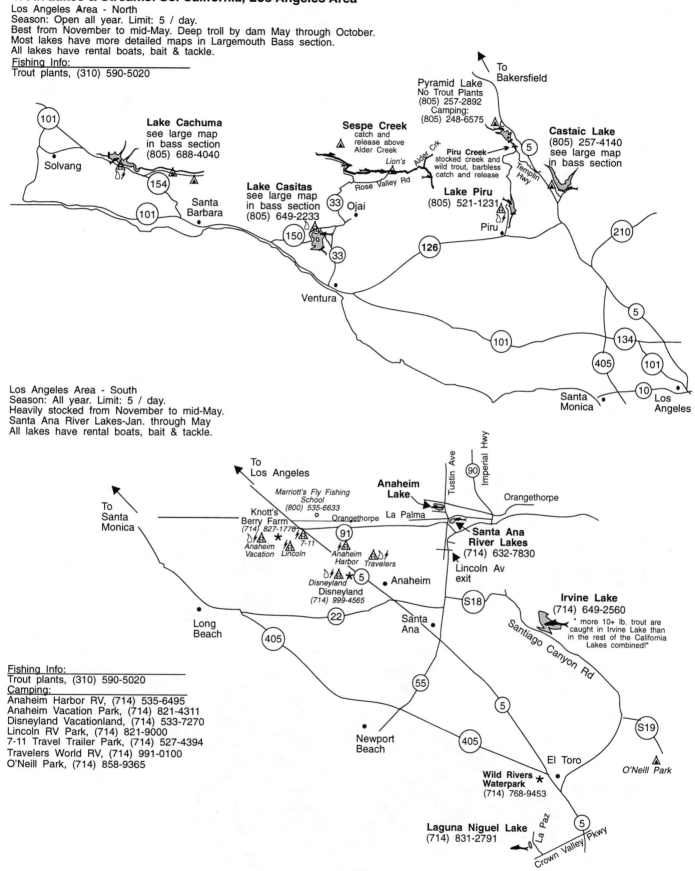

Pyramid Lake
No Trout Plants
(805) 257-2892
Camping:
(805) 248-6575

To Bakersfield

Castaic Lake
(805) 257-4140
see large map
in bass section

Lake Cachuma
see large map
in bass section
(805) 688-4040

Solvang

Santa Barbara

Sespe Creek
catch and
release above
Alder Creek

Lion's

Rose Valley Rd

Alder Crk

Piru Creek
stocked creek and
wild trout, barbless
catch and release

Templin Hwy

Lake Casitas
see large map
in bass section
(805) 649-2233

Ojai

Lake Piru
(805) 521-1231

Piru

Ventura

Los Angeles Area - South
Season: All year. Limit: 5 / day.
Heavily stocked from November to mid-May.
Santa Ana River Lakes-Jan. through May
All lakes have rental boats, bait & tackle.

Santa Monica

Los Angeles

To Los Angeles

Marriott's Fly Fishing School
(800) 535-6633

Knott's
Berry Farm
(714) 827-1776

To Santa Monica

Orangethorpe

7-11

Anaheim Vacation   *Lincoln*

Anaheim Harbor   *Travelers*

Tustin Ave

Imperial Hwy

Anaheim Lake

Orangethorpe

La Palma

Santa Ana River Lakes
(714) 632-7830

Lincoln Av exit

Disneyland
Disneyland
(714) 999-4565

Anaheim

Santa Ana

Irvine Lake
(714) 649-2560

" more 10+ lb. trout are caught in Irvine Lake than in the rest of the California Lakes combined!"

Santiago Canyon Rd

Long Beach

Newport Beach

El Toro

O'Neill Park

<u>Fishing Info:</u>
Trout plants, (310) 590-5020
<u>Camping:</u>
Anaheim Harbor RV, (714) 535-6495
Anaheim Vacation Park, (714) 821-4311
Disneyland Vacationland, (714) 533-7270
Lincoln RV Park, (714) 821-9000
7-11 Travel Trailer Park, (714) 527-4394
Travelers World RV, (714) 991-0100
O'Neill Park, (714) 858-9365

Wild Rivers Waterpark
(714) 768-9453

Laguna Niguel Lake
(714) 831-2791

La Paz

Crown Valley Pkwy

Trout Lakes & Streams: San Bernardino Area
Season: Except Big Bear, all year. Limit: 5 / day
Best from November through May,
Trout plants, (310) 590-5020

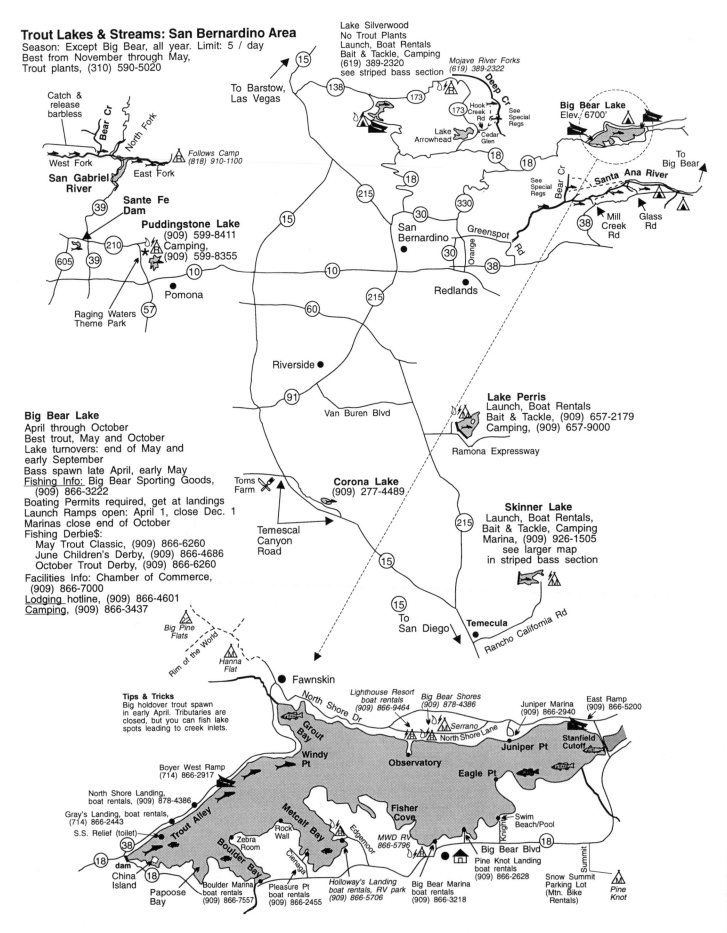

Catch & release barbless

Bear Cr

North Fork

West Fork

East Fork

Follows Camp
(818) 910-1100

San Gabriel River

Sante Fe Dam

Puddingstone Lake
(909) 599-8411
Camping,
(909) 599-8355

Pomona

Raging Waters Theme Park

Lake Silverwood
No Trout Plants
Launch, Boat Rentals
Bait & Tackle, Camping
(619) 389-2320
see striped bass section

Mojave River Forks
(619) 389-2322

Hook Creek Rd

Lake Arrowhead

Cedar Glen

See Special Regs

Big Bear Lake
Elev. 6700'

To Big Bear

Santa Ana River

See Special Regs

Bear Cr

Mill Creek Rd

Glass Rd

San Bernardino

Greenspot Rd

Orange

Redlands

To Barstow, Las Vegas

Big Bear Lake
April through October
Best trout, May and October
Lake turnovers: end of May and early September
Bass spawn late April, early May
Fishing Info: Big Bear Sporting Goods,
  (909) 866-3222
Boating Permits required, get at landings
Launch Ramps open: April 1, close Dec. 1
Marinas close end of October
Fishing Derbie$:
  May Trout Classic, (909) 866-6260
  June Children's Derby, (909) 866-4686
  October Trout Derby, (909) 866-6260
Facilities Info: Chamber of Commerce,
  (909) 866-7000
Lodging hotline, (909) 866-4601
Camping, (909) 866-3437

Riverside

Van Buren Blvd

Toms Farm

Temescal Canyon Road

Corona Lake
(909) 277-4489

Lake Perris
Launch, Boat Rentals
Bait & Tackle, (909) 657-2179
Camping, (909) 657-9000

Ramona Expressway

Skinner Lake
Launch, Boat Rentals,
Bait & Tackle, Camping
Marina, (909) 926-1505
see larger map
in striped bass section

To San Diego

Temecula

Rancho California Rd

Big Pine Flats

Rim of the World

Hanna Flat

Tips & Tricks
Big holdover trout spawn in early April. Tributaries are closed, but you can fish lake spots leading to creek inlets.

Fawnskin

North Shore Dr

Grout Bay

Lighthouse Resort boat rentals (909) 866-9464

Big Bear Shores (909) 878-4386

Serrano

North Shore Lane

Juniper Marina (909) 866-2940

East Ramp (909) 866-5200

Stanfield Cutoff

Windy Pt

Observatory

Juniper Pt

Boyer West Ramp (714) 866-2917

Eagle Pt

North Shore Landing, boat rentals, (909) 878-4386

Gray's Landing, boat rentals, (714) 866-2443

S.S. Relief (toilet)

Trout Alley

Metcalf Bay

Boulder Bay

Zebra Room

Rock Wall

Cienaga

Edgemoor

Fisher Cove

MWD RV 866-5796

Swim Beach/Pool

Knight

Big Bear Blvd

dam

China Island

Papoose Bay

Boulder Marina boat rentals (909) 866-7557

Pleasure Pt boat rentals (909) 866-2455

Holloway's Landing boat rentals, RV park (909) 866-5706

Big Bear Marina boat rentals (909) 866-3218

Pine Knot Landing boat rentals (909) 866-2628

Snow Summit Parking Lot (Mtn. Bike Rentals)

Summit

Pine Knot

Trout Lakes & Streams: San Diego Area

Season: All year. Limit: 5 / day. Heavily planted from December through May;
Cuyamaca Lake September through July; Santee Lakes, January through May.
San Diego County Lakes Info: (619) 465-3474
Sand Diego County Lakes Boat Rental: (619) 390-0222
Trout Plants, (310) 590-5020
See Largemouth Bass section for more detailed maps of Morena, San Vicente, and Wohlford lakes

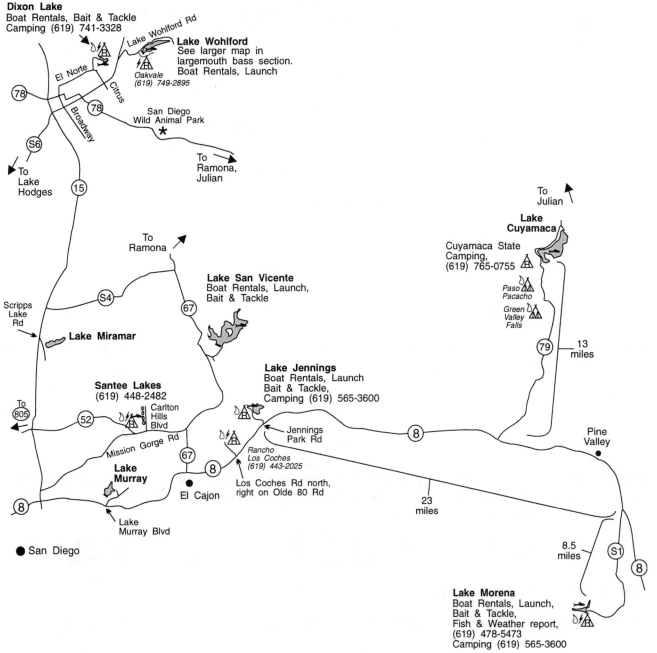

Dixon Lake
Boat Rentals, Bait & Tackle
Camping (619) 741-3328

Lake Wohlford Rd

Lake Wohlford
See larger map in
largemouth bass section.
Boat Rentals, Launch

Oakvale
(619) 749-2895

El Norte

Citrus

78

Broadway

78

S6

San Diego
Wild Animal Park
✳

To
Lake
Hodges

To
Ramona,
Julian

15

To
Ramona

To
Julian

**Lake
Cuyamaca**

Cuyamaca State
Camping,
(619) 765-0755

*Paso
Pacacho*

*Green
Valley
Falls*

S4

Lake San Vicente
Boat Rentals, Launch,
Bait & Tackle

67

79

13
miles

Scripps
Lake
Rd

Lake Miramar

Lake Jennings
Boat Rentals, Launch
Bait & Tackle,
Camping (619) 565-3600

Santee Lakes
(619) 448-2482

Carlton
Hills
Blvd

To
805

52

Mission Gorge Rd

Jennings
Park Rd

*Rancho
Los Coches
(619) 443-2025*

8

Pine
Valley

**Lake
Murray**

67

8

El Cajon

Los Coches Rd north,
right on Olde 80 Rd

23
miles

8

Lake
Murray Blvd

● San Diego

8.5
miles

S1

8

Lake Morena
Boat Rentals, Launch,
Bait & Tackle,
Fish & Weather report,
(619) 478-5473
Camping (619) 565-3600

Glossary

A

Alvey Reel A reel that resembles a large diameter fly reel, but which can be rotated on its axis to cast like a spinning reel, then returned to its original orientation for line retrieval like a conventional reel.

B

Backtrolling Running a boat motor just fast enough so that a river's current moves the boat slowly downstream.

Baitholder Hook A hook with short barbs along the outside shank to keep bait from slipping off.

Black Bass Generic bass name including largemouth, smallmouth and spotted bass.

Blueback Slang for silver, coho salmon.

Bright The silver color of a fresh river salmon. Spawning salmon gradually turn dark colored and the flesh turns soft and unappetising.

Bronzeback Nickname for smallmouth bass.

Bullhead A small rockfish called a staghorn sculpin. Usually used as bait for sturgeon in San Francisco Bay and the Sacramento Delta.

Bull Trout Nickname for Dolly Varden trout.

C

Caddisfly Nymph Nymph, wormlike stage is important bottom trout food. Some forms encase themselves with tubes of sand and small pebbles. The are most abundant in pools and runs. Fly Imitation: Hare's Ear, Elk Hair Caddis, Deer Hair Caddis.

Chum The action or the substance of a regular dispersion of live, dead, cut, or ground fish bait in order to attract and concentrate gamefish closer to the boat, dock, etc. and to work them into a feeding mood.

Coho Salmon Same as Silver Salmon.

Conventional Reel A reel where the spool shaft is perpendicular to the direction of the rod shaft.

D

Diamondback Nickname for sturgeon.

Dodger A rectangular metal blade that is usually highly reflective and is used as part of the terminal rigging as a fish attractant. The dodger is normally rigged within a couple of feet of the baited hook. Dodgers have a side-to-side swaying motion when trolled at optimum speed. Dodgers are usually smaller than flashers.

Drag (flyfishing) Unnatural drift of a fly caused by the fly line crossing an area of varying current speeds. If the closer current is slower, an upstream belly will form in the line causing the fly to drift unnaturally slow. If the closer current is faster, a belly will form downstream causing an unnaturally fast drift. Drag will spook a trout. Drag is prevented by mending.

Drag Drag is tension applied to unwinding line caused by the contact of drag disks or washers inside a reel. Drag washers made of the right materials and in good, smooth condition will allow a smooth, jerk-free drag.

Dun First winged adult stage of the May Fly. This is the brief stage between when the nymph stage emerger surfaces and flies to streamside for a final molt to the spinner stage.

E

Ebb Tide Outgoing tide, period from high tide to low tide.

Emerger The life stage of a stream bottom nymph when it rises to the water surface, shuffs of its nymphal case to become the adult form. Fly imitations of this transiant stage.

F

Flasher A fish attracting metal blade, quite similar to a dodger, that differs from a dodger in that it rotates (spins) at a regular speed when trolled at optimum speed. Flashers are usually longer than dodgers and has bent or cut ends.

Flat Slow moving water areas in a stream. Depth is generally between 1 to 4 feet. The slow water caused a flat surface and sub-surface plant growth.

Flood Tide Incoming tide. Period from low tide to high tide.

Freespool A term used with conventional reels that means disengaging the drag so that the line-filled spool turns freely.

Freestone Any stream with a rock streambed and displaying the streams riffle-run-pool structure. These are NOT meadow streams.

Fresh Run Salmon A salmon that hasn't been in the river long and thus is also bright.

Freshet A series of 2 to 3 heavy rains that fills and clears a river.

G

Gobey (Goby) A small fish of shallow bay areas and sloughs. They are commonly used for bait. A mudsucker is a goby.

Grilse A small, undersize king salmon.

H

Half Pounder Smaller, 1/2 to 3 pound, steelhead that are prevalent in the fall runs.

Hen A female steelhead.

J

Jack Also Jackspring. Small male salmon that re-enter streams a year or two earlier than normal. As a result they are quite small.

Jig This term is used for widely differing lures from pure metal jigs like striper or kokanee jigs, to much smaller leadhead jigs with plastic bodies and tails used for bass fishing to trolling lures used for albacore, bigeye, and marlin. It is also a verb which refers to the way a metal jig lure is fished.

K

Kahle Hook A type of hook with a wide throat and offset point.

L

Lake Troll A series of attractor blades on a mono line which is rigged on the line above the trolled lure or bait. The flashing blades are supposed to attract and bring fish in closer.

M

Mayfly Nymph The nymph form of the Mayfly takes different form depending on the species. Crawlers and clingers are common in riffles and runs. Fly Imitation: Olive Creeper, Zug Bug. Swimmers and burrowers are common in slower pools and flats. Fly Imitation: Pheasant Tail.

Meadow Stream Quiet running, meandering streams typically with flatter bottoms of sand or silt and having significant underwater plant growth. This is NOT a freestone stream.

Mending A flipping motion of the fly rod to cause an opposite bend in the fly line to correct or prevent a drag caused by the action of different current speeds on the fly line.

Metalhead A steelhead.

Mudpuppy A salamander commonly used for bait.

Mudsucker A small, shallow bay and slough fish, a goby, commonly used for bait.

P

Planer board Dual boards that pull a trolled line off to the side of the boat. They are useful for fishing shallow waters and boat-spooked fish.

Plastics Any of a group of soft plastic lures, normally incorporated with a leadhead jig for weight.

Plunge Pool Pool formed at the bottom of a waterfall.

Pool Holes in the streambed. The deepest parts of the stream. The flat surface waters reflect water depth.

Pocket Water In very fast flowing rapids areas, the pockets are small, quieter water areas formed by large rocks or short, more level water stretches.

Professional Overrun Facetious term used for a backlash tangle on a casting reel.

R

Redds Salmon spawning area.

Riffle Stretches of water, approximately 3 feet deep or less, with rapidly moving water over cobbled, rocky bottoms. This results in choppy, rippled surfaces.

Riprap Streamside banks lined with rock. These are man made and purposely provide bank erosion control and incidentally provide fish cover.

Roe Berry A glob of salmon eggs used for bait.

Run Stream area deeper and quieter than riffles, generally 3 to 6 feet deep. The water runs at a solid pace, but because of the depth, the surface is not choppy but has undulations reflecting subsurface structures.

S

Scud A freshwater shrimp living in the still water areas of streams and ponds—a preferred food of trout.

Seam The border between 2 currents of water, one moving faster than the other. This "line", usually oriented up-and-down stream, is a collecting spot for floating and subsurface insects. Trout hold in the slower current side of seams.

Shaker An undersize salmon (less than 22 inches).

Slider A second terminal rig attached to a downrigger trolled line with a snap. The rig will slide to the bend in the trolled line, about halfway to the bottom lure.

Slough Pronounced "slew". Extensive shallow waterways that interlace the Sacramento Delta area.

Smolt A young, immature salmon.

Snubber A piece of elastic surgical tubing with a swivel at both ends which is rigged in line and is supposed to reduce strike breakoffs on light-line trolling rigs.

Sonar Normally refers to a fish finding device that uses sonar.

Spent-Wing The dead or dying adult mayfly that float on the stream surface with wings flat to the surface.

Spinner Final winged, adult stage of the mayfly. The spinner mates and dies within a couple days. As the spinners lay their eggs in the stream, they fly in vertical loops just above the water or if fallen, spin on the surface. This usually happens on calm early evenings over riffled streams.

Spooled A sad condition where a powerful fish has pulled off all the line on your reel and is still heading for the horizon.

Spring Creek Any stream arising from a spring-head. This term is often erroneously used as a synonym for meadow stream.

Stacking Putting more than one lure on a single downrigger.

Standing End Longer line end of knot, etc. that leads to reel. Opposite of tag end.

Strike Indicator Typically a brightly colored piece of yarn tied to a fly fishing leader at approximately twice the water depth up from the fly. The indicator is a visual aid in detecting trout hits. Commercial strike indicators take different forms.

T

Tag End Short end of knot, opposite of standing end which leads to the reel.

Tailwaters River water areas immediately downstream of dams. The character of these waters is defined by the operations of the dam itself and how waters are released.

Thermocline A layer of cool oxygenated lake water that forms in the early summer. The depth and thickness of this layer increases with the summer heat. Trout stay in the thermocline from late-May to October or November. Colder, low oxygen water keeps fish from swimming deeper.

Troll See Lake Troll.

Tules Cattails.

Turnover In the spring and fall lakes turnover. As water layers either get warmer or cooler than 39 degrees it get lighter resulting in a mixing of the lakes cooler and warmer water layers. In the spring this change sparks a caddis hatch. In the fall it brings cool water and trout to the surface.

Tyee Slang name used to designate a big king salmon.

W

Wading Belt A belt for fly fishing waders. Besides helping hold up the waders, if sufficiently snug, the belt can make the waders somewhat water tight and a temporary floatation aid if the angler falls.

Wet Tip Fly lines where the forward portion sinks and the aft portion floats.

Worm King A soft plastic and lead jig lure with a single tail that closely resembles the Shakin Shad.

Appendix A: Sources of Current Fishing Information

Southern California Phone Info
Touch tone phone recordings: Sportsmans Info Exchange (213) or (310) or (818) 976-TUNA (8862)

San Diego Area: (619) 976-BITE

Magazines & Newspapers:

The Fish Sniffer is a bi-weekly newspaper. It concentrates on mid-to-northern California. It also covers Oregon and Baja. Northern Calif. Angler Publications Inc., P.O. Box 994, Elk Grove, CA 95759, (800) 748-6599 or (916) 685-2245.

Fishing & Hunting News is a bi-weekly newspaper. It is published in specific area editions including southern California, northern California and the Sacramento mid-state area. Outdoor Empire Publishing, 511 Eastlake Ave., E., Seattle, Washington 98109, (206) 624-3845.

Western Outdoor News (WON) is a weekly newspaper. It has southern California and northern California regional editions. Both editions cover Baja fishing. The address is 3197-E Airport Loop Drive, Costa Mesa, CA 92626, (714) 546-4370.

California Angler Magazine publishes 9 issues/yr. It covers saltwater and freshwater angling adventures across the Pacific rim. Most articles deal with areas in California or Baja. The address is P.O. Box 15261, N. Hollywood, CA 91615, (818) 760-8983.

Conservation Groups:

United Angler, Nothern California: (510) 525-3474, Southern California: (714) 891-5055. United Anglers is an excellent organization. They are active legally to protect natural resources. They were a key force in establishing the white seabass nurseries and in passing the anti-gillnet law.

Appendix B: Knots

The Surgeon's Knot System
The surgeon's knot works well with the new braided lines.

Surgeon's End Loop

1. Tie an overhand knot with double line.

    Thread hook or swivel first

2. Pull tight

3.

Surgeon's Loop for mid-line loops

1. Tie an overhand knot with double line.

    Thread hook or swivel first

2. Pull tight

3.

Palomar Knot for hook, lure, swivel connections
The Palomar Knot is just a surgeon's knot that you run through the hook eye before tying and loop over the hook before pulling tight.

1. Thread double line loop through eye of hook, swivel or lure.

2. Tie an overhand knot with double line.

3. Pull loop over hook and pull tight.

4.

Surgeon Knot for connecting main line to leader

1. Mainline

    Leader

    Make a 12" section of double line from the leader and main lines

2. Tie an overhand knot with the two overlaped lines

3. Pull tight and clip loose ends

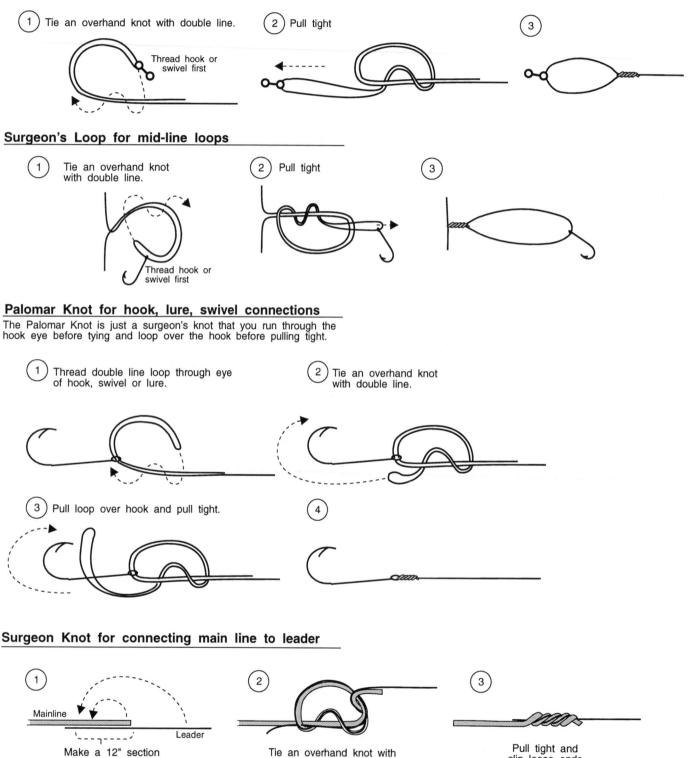

The Uni-knot System
The uni-knot works well with heavy lines.

Uni-Knot for hook, lure, swivel connections

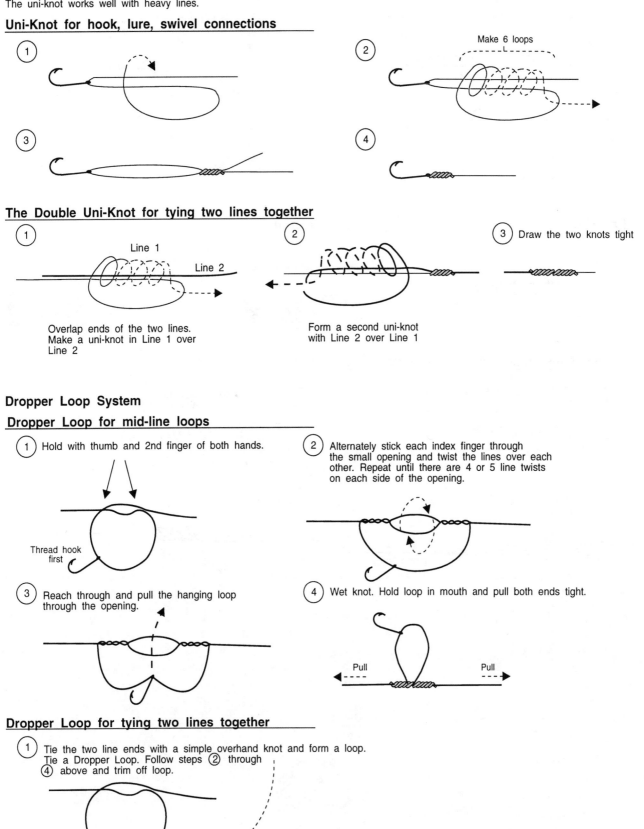

② Make 6 loops

The Double Uni-Knot for tying two lines together

① Line 1
Line 2

② Form a second uni-knot
with Line 2 over Line 1

③ Draw the two knots tight

Overlap ends of the two lines.
Make a uni-knot in Line 1 over
Line 2

Dropper Loop System

Dropper Loop for mid-line loops

① Hold with thumb and 2nd finger of both hands.

Thread hook
first

② Alternately stick each index finger through
the small opening and twist the lines over each
other. Repeat until there are 4 or 5 line twists
on each side of the opening.

③ Reach through and pull the hanging loop
through the opening.

④ Wet knot. Hold loop in mouth and pull both ends tight.

Pull   Pull

Dropper Loop for tying two lines together

① Tie the two line ends with a simple overhand knot and form a loop.
Tie a Dropper Loop. Follow steps ② through
④ above and trim off loop.

Improved Clinch Knot for hook, lure, swivel connections

(1) Make 5 loops around line

(2) Bring tag end back through first loop at the hook

(3) Run back through big loop, wet and pull tight

(4)

Nail Knot for connecting mono to leadcore or dacron

(1) Nail
leadcore or dacron
mono leader

(2) Wrap tag end of loop around both lines and nail 5 times.

(3) Run leader back through loops
Pull out nail and tighten

Jon Knot for connecting mono or dacron to leadcore

(1) Pull back sheath and cut off 3" of lead
leadcore line
3"

(2) Tie loose overhand knots in leadcore above empty sheath

(3) Work knots over empty sheath
mono line
1"   3"

(4) Pull tight

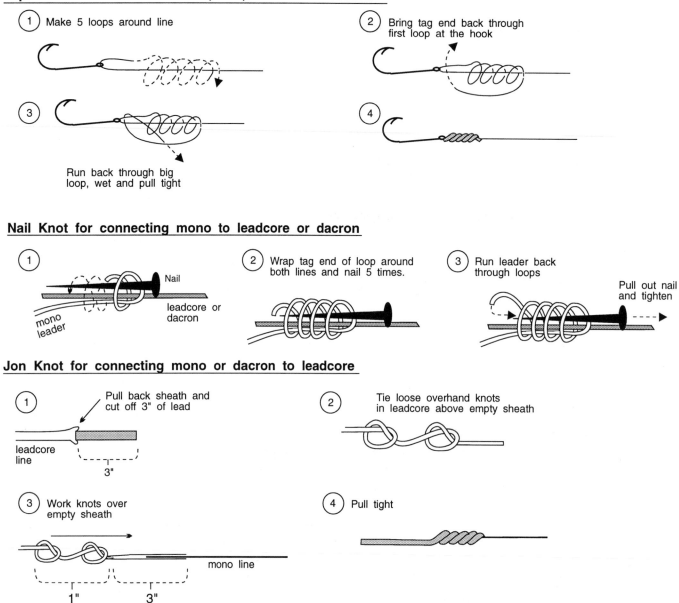

Fly Fishing Knots

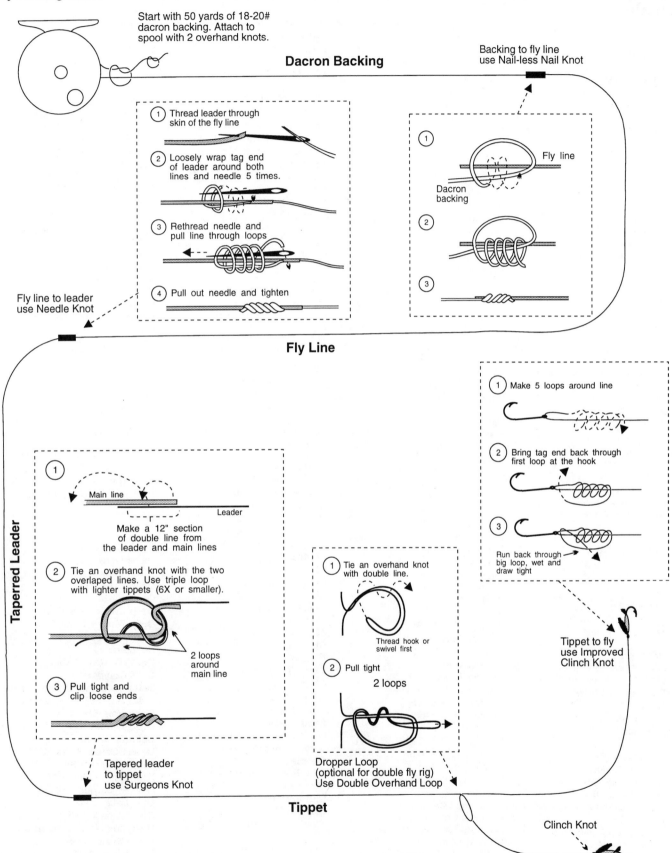

Index

Italic entries are RV, camping, and lodging entries.
Bold entries are primary maps.

Symbols

3 Mile Slough 68
7-11 167
49er Trailer Ranch 56, 159
99 Trailer 95, 105

A

Acorn 69, 159
Agnew Pack Station 163
AH-DI-NA 148
Airporter 149
Alamo River 84
All American Canal 81
Almanor 152
Alpers 162
Alpine Heights 59
Alpine 60
Alpine RV 59, 60
Amador 56, 76, 159
American River 95, 102, 105
Anaheim 167
Anaheim Harbor 167
Anaheim Lake 78, 167
Anaheim Vacation 167
Anchor Bay 119
Anchorage 53
Anderson 96, 150
Anderson Lake 156
Angels Camp 56, 159
Antelope Creek 148
Antlers Resort 52
Arcularius Ranch 162
Arizona
    Lake Mojave 72
    Lake Havasu 73
    Mittry Lake 81
Arrow Trailer 53
Auburn 157
Auburn KOA 157

B

B&W 68
B.W. Ponderosa 148
B.W. Tree House 148
Back Bouncing 92
Backtrolling 92, 114
Bacon Island 68
Bakersfield 58, 166
Balls Ferry 150
Balls Ferry RV 96
Bamboo Hollow 53
Barrett Cove 56
Barrett Lake 60
Barrett Lake Pack Station 163
Basalt 69
Bass. *See* Largemouth Bass
    largemouth 25
    smallmouth 12, 25
    spotted 25
    striped 62
    white 74
Bass Lake 166

Bass, Spotted 25, 27
Baum Lake 151
Beales Pt 55
Bear Creek 133, 168
Bear Mtn. RV 52
Beaver Creek 56, 159
Beaver Slough 68
Belden 152
Benbow 119
Benicia 122
Benton 164
Benton Crossing 164
Berkeley 155
Bert's 67
Best West Bonanza 157
Best West Ponderosa 148, 150
Best West Trailside 153
Best West Tree House 148
Bethel Island 68
Bidwell Canyon 157
Bidwell Canyon Marina 157
Big Bear Lake
    Golden Trout Wilderness 133
    San Bernardino 168
Big Bear Shores 168
Big Break 68
Big Foot 119, 149
Big Lagoon 9, 10
Big Pine Flats 168
Big River 116
Big Rock Resort 162
Big Springs 162
Bishop
    129, 130, 132, 133, 165
Bishop Creek 165
Bishop Creek Lodge 165
Black Bass-*See* Largemouth Bass
Black Bear Lake 133
Black Butte Reservoir 85, 107
Black Meadow 73
Bliss State 136
Blue Catfish 76–77
Blue Lakes 53
Blue Oaks 56
Blythe 79, 81
Boca 97
Boca Res. 158
Bombay Beach 84
Borrego Springs 84
Boulder Beach 72
Boulder Gulch 58
Boulder Lodge 162
Bradford Island 68
Brannan Island 68
Brannan State 68, 122
Bridge Bay 52
Bridgeport 97, 124–126, 161
Bridgeport Reservoir 125, 161
Brook Trout 124
Brown Trout 126–127
Browns 164
Buckeye 125, 161
Buckeye Creek 124, 125
Bullards Bar Res. 97, 101, 157
Bullhead City 72
Bullhead Community 72
Burlington 119
Burney 151
Burnt Ridge 101
Butt Creek 152

Butt Valley Reservoir 152
Butte Creek 148
Buzzards Glory 154

C

Cache Slough 7, 68
Cachuma 76
Cal Trout 151
Calaveras State 56, 159
Calero Res. 156
Calico Cat 53
Calipatria 84
Camanche N. Shore 56
Camanche Res. 56, 159
Camanche S. Shore 56, 159
Camp Far West 157
Carlton 59
Carmen Lake. *See* Lake
    Kirman
Carol's 68
Carpinteria 57
Carquinez Straits 121, 122
Carson City 100, 136
Carson River 160
Casini 119
Casitas Lake 76
Cassel 151
Castaic Lake 58, 62, 167
Castaic RV 58
Castle Crags State 148
Catfish
    blue 76
    channel 76
    flathead 79
    white 76
Cattail Cove 73
Cayote Creek 156
Cedar Flat 116
Cedar Grove 166
Cedar Grove Pack Station 166
Cedar Stock 149
Central Valley 52
Channel Catfish 76–77
Charm Motel 151
Chesbro Res. 156
Chester 152
Chester Manor 152
Chico 67, 107, 157
Chilcoot 154
Chinook RV 94
Chris Haven 136
Chula Vista 60
Cirque Lake 132
Clark Creek 151
Clear Creek 150
Clear Lake 25, **53**, 76, 85
Clear Lake State 53
Clearlake 53
Clearlake Oaks 53
Clearwater House 151
Clifton Court 68
Clio 154
Cloverdale 116
Cloverdale KOA 119
Coffee Creek 149
Colfax 157
Collins Lake 157
Collinsville 68, 122

Colorado River 76, 81
Columbia Cut 68
Colusa 67, 120
Colusa State 67
Comfort Inn 58
Connect Slough 68
Convict Creek 128
Convict Lake 124, 128, **164**
Convict Lake Resort 164
Cool Springs 152
Copco Lake 148
Copper Canyon 73
Corning 107
Corona Lake 76, 168
Corvina 82–83
Cottonwood 96, 150
Cottonwood Cove 72
Cottonwood Creek 150
Cottonwood Lakes 132
Cottonwood Pack Station 132
Coulterville 56, 159
Courtright Res. 166
Cow Creek 148, 150
Coyote County 156
Crag View 148
Crappie 85–87
Crazy Horse 73
Creek Side 53
Creekside RV 165
Crescent City 94
Crivelli's 94
Crockett 122
Crooked Creek 164
Crosby 130
Crowley Lake 88, 128, **164**
Crystal Crag 163
Crystal Lake 163
Cutthroat Trout 129

D

Dad's Camp 94
Davis Dam 72
Davis Lake 154
Dead Lake 10
Decker Island 68
Deep Creek 168
Deep Water Channel 68
Deer Creek 166
Del Loma 119
Del Valle Res. 155
Del's Camp 94
Delta—see Sacramento Delta
Delta Bait & Tackle 159
Delta Bay 68
Delta Marina 68, 122
Delta Resort 68
Desert Creek 124, 125
Desert Shores 84
Desolation Lake 133
Devil's Postpile 163
Diaz Lake 132
Dinky Creek 166
Disappointment Slough 68
Discovery Bay 68
Disneyland 167
Disneyland 167
Dixon Lake 61, 169
Don Castro 155

Don Pedro 56, 159
Donner Lake
       97, 100, 134, **136**
Donner State 136
Dorado Inn 152
Dorothy Lake 124
Dorrington 56, 159
   Dos Picos 61
Douglas City 109, 149
Downrigger 65, 135, 140, 142
Downriggers 99
Drakesbad 152
Driftwood RV 96
Dry Creek 102
Duck Island 68
Duncan Mills 116
Dunsmuir 148
Dutch Slough 68

E

Eagle 153
Eagle Lake 153
Eagle Lake Resort 153
Eagle Lake RV 153
East Quincy 154
East Walker River 124, 125,
       128, 161
Ebbetts Pass 160
Eddo's 68, 122
Edgewater 53
Edison Lake 133, 166
Eel River 93, 109, 116
El Cajon 59, 169
El Capitan Reservoir **59**, 85
El Centro 60
El Toro 167
Elk Creek 119
Elkhorn 119
Emerald Bay 136
Empire Cut 68
Escondido 61
Eureka 93, 94, 119
Evans Lake 166

F

Fair Oaks 55
Fall River 151
Fall River Mills 151
Fallen Leaf 136
Fallen Leaf Lake 97, 100, 136
False River 68
Fawnskin 168
Feather River
       12, 76, 93, 102,
       106, 116, 152, 157
Feather River KOA 154
Ferndale 53
Fish Camp 164
Fishermans Cut 68
Flathead Catfish 79–80
Fleming Meadows 56, 159
Florence Lake 133, 166
Florence Lake Resort 133
Flyfishing
   Fly Hatches 144, 150
   Guides
       Shad 105,106
   Steelhead 118
       Salmon   93
       Trout 54, 130, 148–149, 151
       157–160, 162–164

Knots see Appendix B
Lodges 151, 162, 164
Premier Trout Streams 147
Rigs
   Shad 103
       Steelhead 111, 112
       Brook Trout 124
   Schools 148, 155, 157, 158,
       165, 167
   Technique
       Steelhead 114
   Trout Flies 144–145
   Stream Structure 143, 145
Follows Camp 168
Folsom 55
Folsom Lake **55**, 157
Folsom lake 76
Fountain of Youth 84
Fox Farm 152
Franks Track 68
Freeport 95, 102, 105
Fremont 155
French Canyon 133
French Gulch 58, 149
French Lake 133
Frenchman Lake 154
Freshwater Lagoon 9, 10
Fresno 159, 166
Frontier Pack Station 162

G

Ganser Bar 152
Garberville 116
Garcia River 116
Georgiana Slough 68
Gerber 107
Gilroy 156
Glenhaven 53
Goethe Lake 133
Gold Country 56
Gold Lake 124, **154**
Golden Trout 131
Goodrich Creek 152
Goose Meadow 158
Goshen 166
Graeagle 154
Granite Flat 158
Grant Lake 128, **162**
Grant Line Canal **68**
Grass Valley 101
Grayling 124
Green Lake 124, 125, 161
Green Valley Falls 169
Gridley bridge 13
Grimes 67
Grizzley 154
*Grover Hot Spring*s 160
Gualala River 116
Gull Lake 162

H

Half Pounders 109, 110, 114
Hamburg 116
Hamilton Bend 67
Hamilton Branch 152
Hanna Flat 168
Happy Camp 116
Hap's Bait 68
Harrah's 72
Hat Creek 151
Hat Creek Ranch 151

Hatchet Creek 148
Havasu Landing 73
Hawthorne 130
Hayward 155
Hayward Flat 149
Healdsburg 53, 54, 102, 116
Healdsburg Best West 119
Heenan Lake 124, 129–130,
   160
Helena 116
Hemenway Harbor 72
Hemet 71
Henry Coe State 156
Henshaw 85
Herman & Helens 68
Hidden Harbor 96, 107, 119
Hidden Springs 119
High Bridge 152
High Lake 132
High Sierra Pack Station 133
Hirshdale 158
Hog Pen 68
Hog Slough 68
Holland Cut 68
Holland Tract 68
Holiday Harbor 52
Holloway's Landing 168
Honeymoon Flat 125, 161
Hoopa 102
Hoover Dam 72
Horseshoe Bend 56
Horseshoe Lake 163
Hot Creek 164
Hot Creek Ranch 164
Houseboats
   Lake Mead 72
   Lake Mohave 72
   Lake Havasu 73
   Oroville Reservoir 157
   Sacramento Delta 68
   Shasta Lake 52
Humbolt House 119
Hungry Gulch 58
Huntington Lake 166
Huntington Lake Resort 166
Hurricane Harbor Theme Park
   58

I

Imperial Dam 81
Independence 146
Indian Slough 68
Indio 84
Intake II 165
Inyokern 58
Iron Gate Dam 109, 116
Iron Gate Reservoir 148
Irvine Lake 76, **78**, 85, 167
Island Park 166
Islander RV 73
Isleton 68
Italian Slough 68

J

Jackass Meadow 133
Jackson 56, 159
Jackson Holiday 56
Jamestown 56, 159
Jamul 60
Jedediah 119

Jennings 59
Jersey Island 68
Jigging 98, 99, 134, 135
John Muir Wilderness 166
Jones Valley 52
Julian 61, 169
Junction City 149
June Lake 124, 162
June Lake Motel 162

K

Kamp Klamath 94
Kathrine's Landing 72
Kelseyville 53
Kern River 166
Kernville 58
Keswick Dam 150
Kings Beach 100, 136
Kings Canyon Park 166
Kings River 166
Kirman Lake 125, 161
Klamath 94, 108, 110
Klamath Cove 94
Klamath Glen 94
Klamath Lodge 148
Klamath River 94, 102, 109,
   116, 148
Knotty Pine 152
KOA Feather River 148
KOA Green Acres 107
KOA Lake Isabella 58
KOA Lake Tahoe 136
KOA Mt. Shasta 148
Kokanee Salmon 97–99
Konocti 53
Korth's 68

L

La Mesa 59
Ladybug Creek 148
LaFayette Res. 155
Laguna Dam 81
Lake Almanor 25, 89, **152**
Lake Arrowhead 168
Lake Berryessa 54, 85
Lake Berryessa Resort 54
Lake Britton 151
Lake Cachuma 57, 167
Lake Casitas 26, **57**, 167
Lake Castaic 26
Lake Chabot 155
Lake Cuyamaca 169
Lake Earl 10
Lake Genevieve 124
Lake George 163
Lake Havasu 73
Lake Havasu City 73
Lake Havasu Marina 73
Lake Henshaw 61
Lake Hodges **61**, 85
Lake Isabella **58**, 85, 166
Lake Isabella Motel 58
Lake Italy 133
Lake Jennings 169
Lake Kaweah 166
Lake Kirman 124
Lake Mamie 163
Lake Marina 53
Lake Mary 163
Lake McSwain 56, 159
Lake Mead 72

Lake Mendocino 66
Lake Merced 155
Lake Miramar 169
Lake Mohave 72
Lake Morena 169
Lake Murray 169
Lake Nacimiento 74
Lake Natoma 55
Lake Oroville 25, 157
Lake Perris 25, 76, **78**, 168
Lake Piru 167
Lake Sabrina 133, 165
Lake San Vicente 169
Lake Shasta 25, **52**, 89
Lake Shore Motel 58
Lake Silverwood
   51, **70**, 85, 168
Lake Siskiyou 148
Lake Skinner 62, 71, 168
Lake Success 166
Lake Sutherland 61
Lake Tahoe
   97, 100, 134, **136**
Lake Wohlford 61
Lakehead 52
Lakeport 53
Lakeshore Resort 52
Lakeview RV 69
Lakeview Terrace 149
Lamplighter 119
Largemouth Bass 25–50
  live bait 50
  lures
    crankbaits 39
    jig and pig 43
    jigging spoons 49
    worms, grubs, reapers 45
    spinner baits & buzz baits
      41
    surface plugs, poppers,
      chuggars, stickbaits 40
    tube baits (Gitzits), darter
      jigs, p-heads 48
    zara spook 42
  seasons
    match the hatch 28
    early fall 37
    late fall 37
    post-spawn 33
    pre-spawn 28
    pre-summer 33
    spawn 32
    summer 33
    winter 28
  techniques
    dragging 46
    flipping 44
    jerking 39
    pitching 44
    stitching 46
    stroking 39
    swimming 46
    twitching 39
Las Vegas 72
Lassen Park 151
Lassen View 152
Laughlin 72
Lava Creek 151
Lazy Double B 119
Le Trianon 53
Leadcore 65, 99, 142
Lee Vining 124

Lemon-Cove Sequoia 166
Levitt Meadows Pack Station
  125, 161
Lewiston 109, 116, 149
Lewiston Lake 123, 149
Lewiston Valley Motel 149
Lighthouse Resort 168
Lincoln 167
Little Bear 154
Little Grass Res. 157
Little Grass Valley Lake 157
Little Shasta River 148
Little Truckee River 158
Little Walker River 125, 161
Live Oak 58, 119
Livermore 155
Lloyd's 68
Loafer Creek 157
Lobdell Lake 124, 125, **161**
Logger 158
London Bridge 73
Lone Pine 132, 146
Lone Pine Best West 132
Long Beach 167
Long Lake 132, 154
Los Angeles 167
Los Coches 59
Los Molinos 96, 107, 116
Lost Lakes 133
Lovey's 67
Lower Desolation Lake 133
Lower Twin Lake 125, 161
Lowerlake 53
Lucerne 53
Lundy Lake 124, 125, 161
Lundy Lake Resort 125, 161

M

M&M 53
MWD RV 168
MacDoel 148
Mad River 116
Madera 166
Magic Mtn. 58
Makinaw Trout 134–135
Mammonth Lakes 163
Mammoth Creek 163
Mammoth Lakes 124
Mammoth Mountain RV 163
Mammoth Mountain Ski Area
  163
Mammoth Pack Station 163
Manchester State 119
Manteca 56, 159
Marble Quarry 56, 159
Marina 150
Mariposa 56, 159
Markleeville 160
Markley Cove 54
Martinez 122
Martins Marina 68
Martis Creek Lake 158
Marysville 101, 106, 157
Mattole Resort 119
Mayflower 81
McArthur 151
McArthur Burney 151
McCloud Lake 148
McCloud River 52, 148
McClure Pt. 56

McClure Reservoir
  56, 123, 159
McGee 164
McGee Creek 88, 164
McGee Creek RV 164
McGee RV 88, 164
McSwain Lake 123
Meadows 69
Mecca 84
Meeks Bay Resort 100, 136
Mendocino 119
Merced 56, 159
Merced River 56, 159
Mesa 70
Middle River 7, 68
Mildred Island 68
Mill Creek 124, 125
Millerton Lake 25, 51, **166**
Mineral King Pack Station 166
Miner Slough 7, 68
Miner's 56
Mirabel 119
Miramar Lake 59
Mittry Lake 81
Moabi Regional 73
Moccasin Pt. 56
Modesto 56, 159
Mojave River Forks 70,168
Mokelumne River 56, 68, 159
Mono Creek 133
Mono Hot Springs 166
Mono Village 125, 161
Moons Bend 67
Morena Lake 60
Morena Village 60
Morgan Hill 156
Mountain Meadow 152
Mt. Whitney 132
Mtn View 119
Mtn. Mesa 58
Mtn. View 152
Muir Lake 132

N

Nacimiento 75
Napa 53, 54, 68, 119
Narrows 53
Navarro River 116
Negro Bar 55
Nelson Creek 154
Nevada
  E. Walker River 161
  Lake Mead 72
  Lake Mojave 72
  Pyramid Lake 130
  Topez Lake 130, **160**
  Truckee River 158
  Walker Lake 130
New Hogan 56, **69**, 159
New Melones 56, 159
New River 84
Newport Beach 167
Nice 53
Niland 84
Nimbus Dam 102
North Fork Feather 152
North Grove 56, 159
North Lake 133, 165
North Shore 53
Northshore 152
Noyo River 116

O

Oak Bottom 148
Oak Del 156
Oak Hollow 56, 159
Oak Knoll 69
Oakland 155
Oakvale 169
O'Banion's Sugarloff 52
O'Brian 52
Oceanside 61
Oh! Ridge 162
Ojai 167
Old Dairy 68
Old Lewiston Bridge RV 149
Old Lewiston Inn 149
Old Orchard 107
Old River 68
O'Neill Forebay 69
O'Neill Park 167
O'Nite Park 96, 107
Orleans 102, 116
Oroville 89, 157
Otay Reservoir **60**, 76
Owens River
  128, 162, 164, 165

P

Pack Stations:
  Agnew Meadows 163
  Bishop 165
  Cedar Grove, Kings Canyon
    166
  Levitt Meadows 161
  McGee Creek 164
  Mineral King 166
  Pine Creek 165
  Rainbow 165
  Red's Meadow 163
  Rock Creek 164
  Virginia Lakes 161
  Wolverton, Sequoia 166
Packsaddle Lake 133
Paha 125, 161
Paine Lake 133
Palm Tract 68
Palo Verde 79, 81
Palo Verde Dam 81
Paradise 157
Paradise Pt. 68
Paradise Cove 58
Paradise Shores 125, 161
Parcher's 165
Pardee 56, 97, 159
Parker 73
Parker Creek 124, 162
Parker Dam 73
Parkway Lake 156
Parkway Lakes RV 156
Paso Pacacho 169
Paso Robles 75
Pelhams 119
Peninsula 55
Pilot Knob 81
Pine Cliff 162
Pine Cove 149
Pine Creek Pack Station
  133,165
Pine Flat Reservoir 25
Pine Knot 168
Pine Trees 68

Pine Valley 60, 169
Pinewood Cove 149
Piru Creek 167
Piru Lake 167
Pit River 52, 148, 151
Pittsburg 122
Placerville 56, 159
Pleasant Valley Creek 160
Pleasant Valley Reservoir 88, 126, 128, **165**
Pleasanton 155
Pleasure Cove 54
Plumas Pines 152
Plumas-Eureka State 154
Poker Bar 149
Poker Flat, Tullock Lake 56, 159
Poker Flat, Trinity River 119
Pomo 119
Pomona 168
Poore Lake 124, 125, 161
Porterville 166
Porterville-Yokut KOA 166
Portola 154
Potato Slough 68
Prattville 152
Princeton 120
Prisoners Point 68
Project City 52
Prosser Creek Res. 158
Puddingstone Lake 168
Puppet Lake 133
Putah Creek Park 54
Pyramid Lake **70**, 129, 130, 167

Q

Queen Lily 152
Quigley's 119
Quincy 124, 154

R

Raging Waters Theme Park 168
Rainbow Pack Station 165
Rainbow Trout 137–144
   lakes, cool months 137
   lakes, cool weather 137
   lakes, warm months 140
   streams 142
Railroad Park 148
Ramona 61, 78
Ranchito 154
Rancho Los Coches 169
Rancho Marina 68
Rancho Montecello Resort 54
Red Bluff 96, 107, 116
Red Bluff Diversion Dam 102
Red Hill 84
Redding 52, 116, 148, 149, 150
Redlands 168
Reds Meadow 163
Reds Meadow Pack Station 163
Redwood Rest 94
Green Creek 124
Reno 100, 130, 136, 158
Requa 94
Reversed Creek 162
Richardson Grove 119

Richmond 155
Ricks 151
Rio Vista 68, 122
River Bend 119
River Oaks RV 149
River Pines Resort 154
River's Edge 154
Riverside 168
Riverside RV 94
Riverview 73
Riverwoods 94
Riviera 81
Robinson Creek 125, 128, 161
Rock Creek 88, 164
Rock Creek Lake 164
Rock Creek Lake Resort 164
Rock Pack Station 164
Rollins Lake 157
Rosachi Ranch, E. Walker R. 161
Roseville 157
Royce Lakes 133
Rubicon River 136, 147
Rush Creek 162
Russian River 93, 102, 116
Russos 68
Ruth Lake 9
RV Parks are listed on area maps
RV Rentals 6

S

Sac KOA 95, 105
Sacramento 55, 95, 105, 116, 157, 159
Sacramento Delta 68, 76, 122
   forage "hatch" 28
Sacramento R. 7, 76, 95–96, 102, 105–106, 116, 120, 122, 148
Sacramento RV 96, 150
Saddlebag Lake 124
Salmon 89–93
   back bouncing 92
   backtrolling 92
   plunking 92
Salmon Harbor 119
Salmon Lakes 154
Salmon River 116
Salt Creek 52
Salton City 84
Salton Sea 82, 84
Salton Sea State Park 84
San Andreas 56, 69, 159
San Andreas Shoal 68
San Antonio Lake 75
San Bernardino 168
San Diego 59, 60, 169
San Diego Animal Park 61, 169
San Gabriel River 168
San Joaquin River 68, 122, 163
San Jose 156
San Leandro 155
San Luis Obispo 75
San Luis Reservoir 69
San Pablo Res. 155
San Vicente Reservoir **59**, 76

Sandman 73
Sevenmile Slough 68
Sandpiper 53
Sandpoint Marina 73
Sandy Beach
   Lake Tahoe 136
   Rio Vista 68, 122
Sans End 81
Santa Ana 167
Santa Ana River 168
Santa Ana R. Lakes 76, **78**, 167
Santa Barbara 57, 167
Santa Clara Shoal 68
Santa Clara Valley 156
Santa Margarita Lake 66
Santa Maria 57
Santa Monica 167
Santa Rosa 53, 54, 116
Sante Fe Dam 168
Santee Lakes 59, 169
Sardine Lakes 154
Schober Pack Station 133, 165
Schoolhouse 101
Sea World 59
Seneca Resort 152
Serrano 168
Sequoia Park 166
Sespe Creek 167
Shad 62, 102–104
Shanghai Bend 13
Shasta Lake 148
Shasta Lake Trailer 52
Shastina Lake 148
Shaver 97
Shaver Lake 166
Shaver Lake Lodge 166
Shaw's Shady 53
Sherman Island 68
Sherman Lake 68
Ship Ashore 119
Shovel Creek 148
Sierra Brownbaggers 126
Sierra Springs 154
Silver Creek 160
Silver Lake 128, 162
Silver Lake Resort 162
Skinner Lake 62, 71, 168
Slaughterhouse Island 52
Sloat 154
Smallmouth bass 25, 26
Smith River **93**, 108, 116
Smokeshop 130
Snow Summit Ski Area 168
Solas 52
Solvang 57, 167
Somes Bar 102, 116
Somes Bar Resort 119
Sonora 159
Sonora Bridge 125, 161
Sorenson's 160
South Fork Lakes 132
South Lake 165
South Lake Tahoe 100, 136
Spanish Flat Resort 54
Spaulding 153
Sportsman Paradise 72
Spotted Bass 26
Spring Creek 151
Squaw Creek 52
Stampede Reservoir 97, 158

Stanislaus River 56, 159
Star Bend 13
Steamboat Slough 7, 68
Steele Park 54
Steelhead 108–115
Steelhead Lake 133
Steelhead Lodge 94
Steelhead RV 119
Stockton 56, 68, 122, 159
Stone Lagoon 9, 10
Stuarts Fork 149
Sturgeon 120–121
Sugar Pine State 136
Sugarloaf 52
Suisun Bay 122
Sunnyslope 166
Susan River 153
Susanville 153
Sutcliffe 130
Sycamore Slough 68

T

TW Express 164
Tahoe City 100, 136
Tahoe State 136
Tahoe Valley 136
Tamarack 163
Tannery Gulch 149
Taylor Slough 68
Temecula 71, 78, 168
Tenant 148
Terwer Park 94
The Hole 68
The Pines 119
The Trap 68
thermocline 34, 97, 98
Thermolito Afterbay 12
Thousand Springs 151
tide 63, 89
Tiki Lagun 68
Tillie Creek 58
Timber House 152
TJ Lake 163
Toms Place 164
Topaz Lake 130, 160
Topaz RV 160
Topaz Lodge 160
Tower Park 68
Tracy Oasis 68
Trail In RV 52
Travelers 167
Three Mile Slough 68
Trinity Alps Wilderness 149
Trinity Canyon 119
Trinity Center 149
Trinity Fly Shop 149
Trinity Lake 25, 51, 97, 123, 149
Trinity River 93, 102, 109, 110, 116, 149
Trout
   brook 124
   brown 126
   cutthroat 129
   general tactics 123
   golden 131
   mackinaw 134
   rainbow 137
Trout Creek 158
Truckee 100, 136, 158
Truckee Best West 136, 158

Truckee River 136, 158
Trumbull Lake 125, 161
Tulare 166
Tule River 151
Tullock 56, 159
Tuolumne River 56, 159
Turlock Lake 159
Turner Cut 68
Turnover 123
Twin Lakes
    Bridgeport 97, 124, 128, 161
    Mammoth Lakes 163
Twin Lakes Resort 125, 161

U

U-Save Auto Rental 164
Uvas County 156
Uvas Reservoir 85, 156

V

Vallejo 122
Van Arsdale Dam 109, 116
Van Damme 119
Vee Lake 133
Vegas Wash 72
Ventura 57, 167
Vermillion Resort 133
Vermillion 133, 166
Vermillion Valley Resort 166
Verona 13, 102
Verona Marina 106
Vierras 68, 122
Villa 157
Virginia Lakes 125, 161
Virginia Lakes Pack Station
    125, 161
Visalia 166

W

Wadsworth 130
Waliaka 148
Walker Creek 124, 162
Walker Lake 129, 130
Walker River 125, 161
Walker River Lodge 161
Walters Camp 81
Wards 67
Weaverville 116, 149
Webb Lake 166
Webb Tract 68
Weist Lake 84
Weitchpec 116
West Lake 125, 161
West Walker River 125, 161
Westlake Inn 58
Westmorland 84
Westwood 152
Wheel-er In 73
Whiskeytown Lake 148
White Bass 74
White Catfish 76–77
White Slough 68
Whiskey Slough 68
Whitney Pack Station 132
Wiest Lake 84
Wild Rivers Theme Park 167
Wildyrie 163
Will-O-Point 53
William Heise 61

Williams 53, 54
Willow Beach 72
Willow Creek 102, 119
Willow Springs 125, 161
Wishon Res. 166
Wohlford Lake 85, **169**
Woldfords Inn 160
Wolf Creek 160
Wolverton Pack Station 166
Woodfords 160
Woods 163
Woods Valley 61
Woodside 119
Woodson Bridge State 107
Wyntoon 149

Y

Yellow Creek 152
Yellow perch 8
Yosemite 56
Young's Ranch 116
Yreka 148
Yuba City 101, 106, 157
Yuba River
    101, 102, 106, 116
Yuma 79, 81